The First Quarter Century

Other books by Emil Lengyel:

The Danube
Turkey
Siberia
Dakar: Outpost of Two Hemispheres
America's Role in World Affairs
Americans from Hungary

Other books by Heinz Mackensen:

Great Britain
Germany

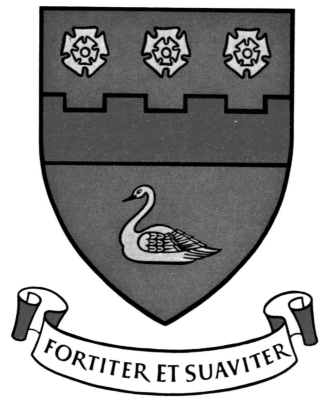

The coat of arms of Fairleigh Dickinson University.

The coat of arms of Wroxton College.

The
First Quarter Century

A History of Fairleigh Dickinson University,
1942-1967

Emil Lengyel and Heinz F. Mackensen

SOUTH BRUNSWICK AND NEW YORK:
A. S. BARNES AND COMPANY
LONDON: THOMAS YOSELOFF LTD

© 1974 by A. S. Barnes and Co., Inc.

A. S. Barnes and Co., Inc.
Cranbury, New Jersey 08512

Thomas Yoseloff Ltd
108 New Bond Street
London W1Y OQX, England

Library of Congress Cataloging in Publication Data
Lengyel, Emil, 1895–
    The first quarter century; a history of Fairleigh Dickinson
University, 1942–1967.

    Includes bibliographical references.
    1. Fairleigh Dickinson University—History.
I. Mackensen, Heinz, joint author. II. Title.
LD1771.F26L46   378.749'21   73-132
ISBN 0-498-01347-2

Contents

Foreword

The writing of a history of Fairleigh Dickinson University, even though it is for only the first twenty-five years of its existence, is a complicated and arduous task. It is fortunate that two persons who were closely involved in the development of the institution have enthusiastically assumed this labor. There are a great many phases to be considered: student development, curriculum construction, building expansion, faculty organization, and community responsibilities, each area capable of many interpretations and approaches. The important aspect, however, and one which the authors have constantly kept in mind, is the relation of the University to the total picture of higher education and especially to the situation in New Jersey.

They have brought out not only the myriad daily challenges that lead to growth, but the problems and heartaches of bringing up an ever-expanding faculty family. While Fairleigh Dickinson University bears many resemblances to other institutions, fundamentally it has had a development of its own, different from any other American institution of the twentieth century. But its fundamental inspiration by New College of Teachers' College of Columbia University has lived through a quarter-century and has nourished the very roots of the experimental Edward Williams College. The New College philosophy, nurtured by dedicated teachers in spite of the eroding influence of vested interests that inevitably arise in any college or university, was evident in every curriculum.

Leaving aside the few institutions that have a very high endowment per student, private colleges have to depend mainly on tuition income, good management of their meager resources, and the doleful handouts of charitable friends. Curiously, they cannot charge the higher tuitions of older and more prestigious institutions. It is a daily struggle for existence made more difficult by state planning bodies that proceed on the assumption that only they must provide a place within the state for every young man or woman who wants to go to college, completely disregarding the fact that private institutions had been founded to solve this very problem. The result is that today there are more empty places in both public and private institutions than at any time in the history of education in this country. We are showering the students with ever-more-luxurious buildings when they cry out for love; and in an attempt to decry this lifeless monumentalization of education, they desecrate in every fashion the luxuries that are being provided.

We never had luxuries at Fairleigh Dickinson. We used every cubic foot of space day and night. But as far as I know, there was never a lack of space, never a lack of books we really needed, and after the war period, never a lack of laboratories. Most important, there was never a lack of love for any student who needed help. And we never shirked the responsibilities of meeting community needs, whether they were in the health arts, or in continuing education for women, or in seeking out disadvantaged students who needed financial help to go to college, day or night. Foreign visitors who came to observe us were amazed at our panoply of services.

In a popular sense, people think of a university in terms of buildings, of numbers of students, of complexity of curricula. And yet it was in terms of our service to students and the simplicity of our approach that we found the greatest meaning to our lives. This service, we felt, was by far the most important aspect of Fairleigh Dickinson. This was the magic web that held us together and gave us the élan that was the spirit of the institution.

But through it all, we were humble, thankful that we had an opportunity to serve our fellow men. I firmly believe that it was this spirit exemplified by the two authors that was mainly responsible for the growth of Fairleigh Dickinson.

> Peter Sammartino
> Chancellor

October 15, 1972

Preface

The building of Fairleigh Dickinson University from small beginnings as a junior college into a large, multi-campus international university within the quarter century from 1942 to 1967 is a saga of higher education that should be told. In this day of large-scale development of state colleges and universities through plentiful public funding, our tale of how private individuals and groups, in the best American frontier tradition of self-help, joined together and sallied forth from a castle in northern New Jersey to meet the local needs for higher education, is both unusual and today no longer possible.

We have sought to present an accurate record of how this impossible dream was realized through the concrete steps of organization, building, and development.

But besides depicting the construction of the *Gesellschaft* that is Fairleigh Dickinson University, we have also tried to show how the *Gemeinschaft* that gives an organization its motivation and direction, its soul, came alive and flourished within the corporate structure. This spirit of community is basic to the long term effectiveness of any institution, whatever its tasks. It is above all essential, given its nature, for a university. We have therefore linked with our account of the growth of the University's outward structure an effort to depict the growth of the institution's inward *esprit* and the continued projection of its *élan vital*.

The preparation of this work has been a labor of love for the authors, both of whom have long been associated with the University. Chapters 1 and 2 consist of contributions by both Dr.

Emil Lengyel and Dr. Heinz Mackensen. Chapter 3 in its entirety was written by Dr. Lengyel. Chapters 4 through 11 were in their entirety written by Dr. Mackensen.

The authors wish to express their appreciation to the many trustees, administrators, faculty members, and others associated with the University who have supplied information, research materials, and other help for the preparation of this work. Particularly the assistance given by Chancellor Sammartino is acknowledged and appreciated.

Dr. Mackensen also wishes to express his appreciation to President Fuller and the Board of Trustees for granting an administrative sabbatical leave to him during most of 1971. This helped greatly by supplying the time needed to do the research and to begin writing this book.

E.L.   H. M.

Acknowledgments

Dr. Mackensen would like to express his acknowledgment to the archives and libraries of Fairleigh Dickinson University for use of their research materials in the preparation of this work.

He would further wish to acknowledge the following. They gave interviews in 1963 for Dr. Mackensen's historical introduction to the Report of the Committee on the Future or in connection with this work, or in some cases for both. Their help is greatly appreciated.

Henry P. Becton
Clair W. Black
Ara Boyan
Milton C. Cooper
Fairleigh Dickinson, Jr.
Nasrollah Fatemi
Harold Feldman
Olive Foster
Marinus C. Galanti
Joseph Green
Loyd Haberly
Kathleen Hillers
Forrest Irwin
Arthur A. Kron
Byron C. Lambert
Ray Lewin
Walter Mosmann
Robert Neiman
Samuel Pratt

Louis Rice
Amadeo Sferra
Peter Sammartino
Sylvia Sammartino
Harold Sprague
John E. Vaughan
Walter Wilson
and in remembrance of the help of
Clarence R. Decker and
Edward T. T. Williams

The First Quarter Century

1

The American Educational Background

This is the history of one American university out of many. It attempts also to be more: the picture of a microcosm within the macrocosm. This particular university could not have flourished in any other country, no matter how advanced. To place it in proper perspective it must be seen in retrospect, generations before its birth, within the larger context of American higher education, which is a unique phenomenon, without precedent in intellectual history. Not only is it unique, but paradoxical too, as will be seen.

The land of pragmatic pioneers, America's first settlers had to combat nature's resistance, as if they had started their labors on creation's first day. Their energies had to be expended in producing the "sweat of human brows" that irrigates the soil. Nevertheless, most of the Founding Fathers, and their sons too, were intellectuals. They belonged to the class of people the Russians used to call the *intelligentsia*, the seers, the thinkers. And doers, too! In their reading, the signers of the American Declaration of Independence required no translations from Latin or Greek. Some of them required no translators from the language of the ancient Israelites either, Aramaic and Hebrew. They knew foreign languages and the classics.

The higher education that they acquired was, naturally, that of their epoch, transmitted from the classics, detoured by the scholastics. Its pillars were the philosophies of their epoch, which centered around metaphysics. They had to master mathematics, including ancillary sciences such as astronomy. The broad curriculum embraced theology, rhetoric, grammar, and logic. In the first year of studies Latin was their instructional language. In the final years of studies it was also the classroom language of ethics, metaphysics, and natural philosophy. Nor was it enough to read and write the classics. Latin and Greek were used as living tongues. The New Testament, for instance, was read in Greek. When the Massachusetts Bay Psalm was printed in 1639, the colonists translated it from the Hebrew original.

A large number of signers of the Declaration of Independence were college-bred. Contrary to popular belief, it was not only the Bible these pioneers brought; they also carried with them sophisticated tomes from Britain. They were heirs to Britain's intellectual wealth. John Locke's philosophy was one of their treasures. They read George Berkeley and discussed David Hume. They may not have agreed with the concept of *Leviathan*, but they respected Thomas Hobbes. They employed his insights as the test of their dissents. The French Encyclopaedists, too, were among the founding fathers of American independence, the structural builders of intellectual concepts. The early American intellectuals devoured their writings. The basic material of the American Constitution was the content of *l'Esprit des Lois* by Montesquieu. The four ponderous volumes of Sir William Blackstone's *Commentaries on the Laws of England* were read in the colonies, discussed, analyzed, employed, and reemployed in the governments of the colonies, in the concept of government, and in jurisprudence. The classic reflection of the thinking of the nation's early leaders, the *Federalist*, is a proof not only of the profound political thinking of Jay, Hamilton, and Madison, but also of the learned spirit of the intellectual founders of a New World in North America.

John Hancock, the first signer of the Declaration of Independence, is a case in point. The Bachelor of Arts degree he received from Harvard was for the fulfillment of the requirements of that arduous intellectual discipline inherited from distant times when scholarship was a lifetime pursuit, the medieval *trivium* and *quadrivium*, the Seven Liberal Arts. Hancock, President of the Congress, and first governor of Massachusetts, was, at the same time, a full-time merchant. What about the Lieutenant Governor of that State, Samuel Adams, another signer of the Declaration? While not a successful businessman, he, like Hancock, was a distinguished Harvard graduate. So was John Adams; he was not "merely" an intellectual but a teacher of other intellectuals, the author of learned books.[1]

In those days, the nation's pacemakers pursued studies not merely in preparation for everyday life, but also in fulfillment of the other faculties of man, training and practicing their intellectual capacities for pleasure and leisure, for convivial occasions and the intellectual "fun" in conversation, for the matching of wits, for testing mental strength, and for transmitting the heritage to future generations. In the harsh environment of the frontier, beset by hostile forces of nature and its primitive native children who, justly, considered the pioneering of the newcomers an intrusion, one learned that man had to survive by his wits. Also social occasions on the frontier were few, the nights long. Reading, thinking, conversing became the necessities of life. Schools were vital, not only for the three R's but also for the countless problems to be solved. Thus America's virgin land presaged its uniqueness in higher education, the future profession of its colleges. The frontier itself was the progenitor of this unfolding trend. Fairleigh Dickinson University was and is one of the many products of the American past, part of its national heritage. There were many such products. This one was different because of its unparalleled growth in an unexpected place under uncommon circumstances.

A YOUNG FRENCHMAN COMES TO AMERICA

Before leaving this subject and a better understanding of the problem, let us round out a century and observe a young French aristocrat revealing the life of the United States. Incongruously he had come to study the prison system in the New World, and he produced a classic description of America. His name was Alexis Charles Henri Maurice Clerel de Tocqueville, and he was only twenty-six when he came, in the company of Gustave de Meaumont de la Bonninière. The name of the latter is barely recalled. That of Tocqueville will be remembered as long as there is paper for print and brain cells for thought. The two volumes he produced as a byproduct of his mission, *La Démocratie en Amérique*, is a description not only of what the United States was in 1840 but

---

1. James J. Walsh, *The Education of the Founding Fathers: Scholasticism in the Colonial Colleges* (New York: Fordham University Press, 1935), p. 41.

what it is today. That is so because the young man had the eyes
of the seer and the prophet's pen. His keen eyes fathomed the
core of American life. A new civilization, unmatched in history,
was in the making, and the young Frenchman was drawn to it.
His native land was troubled by a period of self-criticism; Europe
was teetering on a razor's edge. Discontent was flaring up in a
series of revolts. Meanwhile, the United States was carving out
its future through an underbrush of uncertainty. The young
Frenchman was optimistic about the prospects of the new civilization. A bold spirit was abroad in the New World, one ready for
skystorming experiments. Like all new beginnings, these too
were based on insights acquired in the learning process. This is
what the young Frenchman said:

> There is not a single district in the United States sunk in ignorance,
> and for a very simple reason. The nations of Europe started from
> the darkness of a barbarous condition, to advance toward the light
> of civilization; their progress has been unequal; some of them have
> improved rapidly; while others have loitered in their course, and some
> have stopped and are still sleeping upon the way.
>
> Such has not been the case in the United States. The Anglo-Ameri-
> can, already civilized, settled upon that territory which their de-
> scendants occupy; they did not have to begin to learn, and it was
> sufficient for them not to forget. Now the children of these Americans
> are the persons who year-by-year transport their dwellings into the
> Wilds, and with their dwellings their acquired information and their
> esteem for knowledge. Utility has taught them the utility of instruc-
> tion and has enabled them to transmit that instruction to their pos-
> terity. In the United States man has no infancy but is born to a
> man's estate.[2]

True, he pointed out, surrounded as they were by a challenging
new environment, most Americans could devote only the early
years of their lives to general education and much of the popular
instruction beyond age fifteen aimed toward a specialized and
profitable purpose. For that reason, one studied science, the
French observer noted, as one took up a business, and tackled
those applications whose prompt practicality was recognized.

Tocqueville was only fifty-four when he died, and thus he
failed to see the fulfillment of his prophecy. Education did become
the pivot of the life of the young in America. Soon the time came
when the high school, the privilege of the few in Europe, became
obligatory for all in America. That, too, was unique in public
instruction.

Books, 1945), 1:327.
2. Alexis de Tocqueville, *Democracy in America* (New York: Vintage

Many years went by as America experienced the throes of the Second Industrial Revolution. The insatiable machines of this revolution demanded completely new skills of the mind and hands. The mental skills claimed almost a new breed of man, trained in abstractions, Prometheuslike in defying the forces of nature. It was not the alchemist's almagest that the modern scientist sought to find. Nature had its order, he knew, different from man's clumsy handiwork. That order was immutable. Its rules must be known to subject them to man's will. The scientist learned that nature had placed secret codes within its armature. The ancients had sought it in the flame, water, and air. Was it the "eternal spirit," the ether, motion, or light? It was only in the twentieth century that the code was cracked and the limitless potentialities of the minute atom were revealed. Countless new disciplines sprang into life. High schools in the wake of this Promethean trend were not enough for the probing of new insights. There had to be schools of the highest learning, the best colleges and universities. They were the ones to fathom not only the material but also the spiritual secrets of the limitless universe. Matter could improve but could also destroy the world. Only the spirit could save it. Matter could perform its miraculous work only together with the spirit. The endless search for the essence of life went on. Knowledge was needed in immensely enlarged amounts. De Tocqueville's prophecy came true. The United States began to sweep onward with a speed that amazed the world. For every new university in the Old World, dozens were built in America. The United States acquired the material wealth with which it could acquire the additional intellectual wealth.

THE EARLY IVY LEAGUE

Now, still another look in retrospect. Already, in the early days up and down the coast, the newcomers had erected replicas of Oxford and Cambridge. No sooner were they settled than they founded their schools of higher learning. Young as they were, and scant in number, the duality of Oxbridge yielded to the multiplicity of the Ivy League. The College of New Jersey was among the first, in a territory where the number of the learned was particularly large. As Princeton, this early school was to acquire added fame. Across the Hudson King's College was to cast luster on Manhattan's rocky land. Farther up and down the continental ledge grew Harvard College, the College of William and Mary, the College of Philadelphia, which was to become the University of Pennsylvania, and the College of Rhode Island, later Brown University. Was it not an omen of American education that the first concern of the settlers was the school? And what schools they were!

Since we are tracing the roots of one illuminating instance of higher education in New Jersey, it is appropriate to single out the Princeton University of those early days. The state's varied topography, with its proximity to America's entry gate, its acceptable climate, and its natural attractions drew famous human beings into its orbit. In one single cemetery in Princetown, four signers of the Declaration of Independence are buried, joined by President Grover Cleveland and the ill-starred Aaron Burr.

The historic College of New Jersey, which sets us on the trail of higher education in the state, was at first located in Elizabethtown, the meeting place of the colonial assembly, the home of Alexander Hamilton and Aaron Burr. It did not retain the college, which was moved farther inland to a locality settled by the Quakers—Princeton, seat of the Continental Congress for a time.

Scholarly life in that part of the "wilderness" of America is well described by a note of a sophomore, preserved in the archives of the school. The young man wrote:

> At seven in the morning we recite to the President lessons in the works of *Xenophon* in Greek and Watt's Ontology. The rest of the morning until dinner time (11 A.M.) we have a recitation of Cicero's *De Oratore* and Hebrew grammar. The remaining part of the day we spend in the study of Xenophon and ontology in preparation for the recitation next morning and besides these things we dispute once a week after the syllogistic method and now-and-then we study geography.[3]

The students had to prepare *theses*, the ancestors of our term papers. Here is a *Thesis Ethica* of 1750, which certainly has "relevance" even today: "A ruler endowed with civil virtue though without military glory is much preferable to a prince who, though without civil virtue, is very illustrious for his courage in war."[4] This was the background of country and state of the school whose history we seek to trace.

---

3. James J. Walsh, *Education of the Founding Fathers of the Republic. Scholasticism in the Colonial Colleges. A Neglected Chapter in American Education* (New York: Fordham University Press, 1935), p. 154.
    4. *Ibid.*, pp. 143 ff.

A YOUNG MAN AND AN OLD CASTLE

The microcosm is Fairleigh Dickinson University, which, we believe, reflects the macrocosm, American higher education, and is instructive as part of the whole. Today it is a multicampus school, a private university of remarkably quick growth, and, therefore, endowed with unique features and not shaped in the standard mold. At one time it acquired the reputation of being America's fastest-growing school of higher learning. The tempo since then has become more sedate. Fast growth is possible under unusual conditions. To that extent the history of the university does not adhere to the standard record. It is a young university set in the oldest historical setting of a young country, exemplifying many contradictions and a paradox.

How does a school of higher learning get started? How does any institution begin? If it is to survive and flourish, there must be telling reasons. If it is to fail and fade away, that must have adequate reasons too. The basic causes feed the consequences through its roots. These are the "disposition," the ambience, and the surrounding circumstances. The disposition may sometimes abort and is insufficient by itself. It has to lead to a dynamic force for its success. Let us name it the "triggering effect," the "synthesis" of forces, the concurrence of the positive and negative poles, the closing of the electric circuit. Finally, the result of human work presupposes specific human effort, the personality of the creative human force.

To turn back for a moment to our list of pioneer colleges, the Ivy League; in each case there was the disposition, the triggering effect and the human personality. The disposition was the meeting of the most advanced civilization, from the British Isles, with raw nature. The triggering effect was the need of sophisticated individuals being forced to change their way of life, superabundant nature producing as yet scanty results, and the potentialities of the virgin forces of the uncorrupted environment, offering high rewards. Then there were the pacemakers, creative persons with the capacity to provide a better life and a higher potential of material, spiritual, and intellectual welfare.

Again to mention the pioneering Ivy League College of New Jersey (Princeton) closest to the location of the object of our study, the preconditions were available. There were the forces of nature waiting to be released with the aid of men employing their native ingenuity multiplied by their reaction to the challenge of nature. There was also the personality of the pacemaker, that notable Scotch Presbyterian minister, distinguished graduate of Edinburgh University, Dr. John Witherspoon, on whose work a student commented: "The piety, erudition, knowledge of the world and deep insight into human nature possessed by Witherspoon qualified him in an eminent degree for the presidency of the college."[5] His was the intellectual and spiritual strength that met the challenge of the "triggering effect." So it was on other parts of the coastal ledge too. The highly literate people of the "General Court" (legislature) of Massachusetts had England's Cambridge in mind when they appropriated in 1636 four hundred pounds toward "a schoale or colledge" in the New Towne, a six-year-old settlement of the Bay of Boston. (That "colledge" now has an endowment of more than a billion dollars.) John Harvard left his modest library to the "schoale" and thereby gained undying fame.

So it was with the other "schoales" too, responding to the equivalents of the "General Courts" or the Witherspoons: the men who captained the ship, along with their teams of men and women of good will, were ready to use their excess energy and to reveal their thankfulness to their community, the country, the divine force, for the improved condition of man.

It was this way with Fairleigh Dickinson University too. It was the product of a team effort. Obviously every team needs a coordinator. In this case his name was Peter Sammartino, whose uncommon personality and achievement may account for the fact that he became one of the best-known chief executives of a college in the country and abroad, the recipient of more public attention than many of his counterparts.

Even today, after years of *Sturm und Drang*, he has a youngish smile. His is not the cliché look of the scholarly Ph.D. His features are well-known from the public media: round-headed, with an impressive skull polished in front, fringed with the vestiges of darkish hair. The pictures cannot show the inner man or his ways. In this case the inner man is upward striving. He may have what the Quakers call the "inner flame." He is supremely effective, pragmatic. His voice does not strike one as that of the introverted philosopher but that of a man of action. He is an extrovert. When he gives of himself, he gives all he has. In his speech he concentrates on the point he makes with all his mental power, which he seems to propel upward and onward with his expressive

---

5. *Ibid.*, p. 161.

hands. His sentences come articulately and clearly in a resounding voice.

In his native New York—he is the son of Italian immigrant parents—Sammartino did his work at the College of the City of New York, one of the most scholastically competitive institutions in the land. At the uncommonly young age of twenty he had his first undergraduate degree, followed by continued concentrated work for impressive higher degrees. He took the Ph.D. hurdles with ease. New York University conferred the degree on him when he was twenty-seven, exceptionally young for the climactic degree. After his graduation in 1931, Peter Sammartino studied for a time at the Sorbonne. He had now collected an impressive array of credentials to teach. He taught French in New York at the Townsend Harris High School for highly gifted boys, and subsequently at his alma mater, City College. On December 5, 1933, he was married to Sylvia Scaramelli, a very pretty "egghead"—as attested by her college diplomas, bachelor's and master's degrees from Smith and Columbia. She was to play a role in college building.

Sammartino's "trade union card," his Ph.D. parchment, safely stuck in its frame, he could have settled down to a lifetime of teaching. Languages were his specialty. With his degree, effective personality, and self-confidence, he could have shifted among colleges, moving up the ladder of instructor, assistant professor, associate professor and, finally, the climax, professor. He might have become the chairman of a college department, perhaps a dean, if administrative work appealed to him, even the president of a college of someone else's making. For the time being, he followed the bright academician's way.

For a while, he was the publisher and educational editor of *La Voix de France,* a New York City periodical, promoted among the thousands of students of French in the metropolitan area. A former subscriber, then in high school, must attest to the solid help the paper afforded in turning the study of French into a pleasure. The periodical was an example of Sammartino's efforts to teach more students than individual classrooms could hold. An extremely ambitious young man, he wanted to make his mark.

Sammartino then produced two books for students of French: *Survey of French Literature* and *French in Action.*[6] He also wrote texts for students in French: *Grammaire Simple et Lectures Fa-*

---

6. Peter Sammartino, *Survey of French Literature* (New York: Longmans, 1937); *French in Action* (New York: Globe Book Co., 1933).

ciles; and for students in Italian: *Il Primo Libro, Il Secondo Libro, Letture Facili.*[7] Not for him were the "classic" exercises: *La plume de ma tante.* Aunts played no role in these books. Train conductors, hotel concierges, and everyday affairs played large roles. Pragmatism was in the blood of the ambitious young Ph.D. But there was more than that in his blood.

Avançons, his book for advanced students, showed him in another role.[8] To teach the language was not enough for him. Within that language was encapsulated the spirit of a people, *la mission civilisatrice* of the French, which he wanted to reveal to the reader. He knew that its language represented the spirit, the "soul" of the nation, particularly in the case of France. The Gallic tongue is the gateway to the Gallic spirit. One studied a language, Sammartino made it clear, not merely for talks with the concierge but also for fathoming the depths of a cultural heritage. Our young Ph.D. wanted to teach the language so as to back it up with a way of life, for which he had great esteem. He studded grammatical exercises with intellectual insights. His was the work of a cultural missionary. He also gave away the trail of direction toward which he was drawn. In *Avançons* he introduced ideas of the immortal Jean-Jacques Rousseau. In doing so in the first half of the twentieth century he anticipated a basic trend of the second. He may have foreseen the crisis of our contemporary civilization, the replacement of ablution by pollution. Man should go away from the contagion of large conglomerations of people, Jean Jacques had said, and should return to nature, uncomplicated and pure: to the air and the water, and to thoughts that were devoid of pretensions, mummery and play-acting as a way of life.

In the same book, *Avançons,* the young author showed a way to teach, again in the spirit of Jean Jacques. He referred to *Emile* of the great Frenchman, repeating the refrain: "Learn from nature . . . learning should be natural and spontaneous; training should begin with physical activities, the training of the senses, natural science and, finally, the social sciences."[9]

Yet author Sammartino was not a mere camp-follower of Rousseau. After all, the textures of civilizations are different in differ-

---

7. Peter Sammartino and Ray E. Mosher, *Grammaire Simple et Lectures Faciles* (New York: Harper, 1933); Peter Sammartino, *Il Primo Libro* (New York, Harper, 1936); *Il Secondo Libro* (New York: Harper, 1941); *Letture Facili* (New York: Crispen, 1937).
8. Peter Sammartino, *Avançons* (New York: Harper, 1940).
9. *Ibid.,* p. 311.

ent ages. The printed word in Rousseau's time was more preten-
tious, untrue to nature. He thought the world otherwise. Perhaps
as a result, books became more the keys to nature, if they were
worthy of the hallowed name—Book. Sammartino has always
displayed great reverence for books.

In all these volumes the young author had his reader in mind,
the young persons of different mental fibers, resistant or persistent, sometimes resistant to the influence of the outsider, the
teacher, or persistent in the pursuit of the true word, the comprehension. The student had a storehouse from which to choose.

NEW COLLEGE

To settle down for a lifetime of standard work was not for this
young man of novel ways. He was now ready for experiments. In
1932 Columbia University had launched an experiment. It was
undertaken in a branch of its Teachers' College, an undergraduate
sideline. It was called New College, new because it was meant to
be boldly experimental. Its opening Announcement sounded its
keynote: "Teaching must be a fine art." It was to be neither
pedantic nor dogmatic, but perceptively intuitive, and "experien-
tial." Dr. Sammartino joined the faculty of New College. He
became an "Associate."

To gain experience the students in that school had to spend
periods outside of classrooms—in industries, at work at a camp
run by the College in the Great Smoky Mountains of North Carolina, and in other ways. This was, indeed, "return to nature." The
students were to learn about real life, about agriculture and country life too. They were required to spend a period of study in a
foreign land. Other features of the bold program included seminars and independent studies.

Sammartino was profoundly influenced by his experience at
New College. His own impact there as an instructor was typical
of his methods and personality at any time.

In its edition of March 5, 1937, the student newspaper head-
lined an article on its first page with "Voulez-vous Me Passer Du
Sucre?" Reporter Rose Perlstein wrote that she had passed Room
446 in Emerson Hall on a Friday afternoon at three-thirty and
had been startled to hear this question coming from the room.

What was going on—a French class or a tea party? "Mais oui, 'twas both."[10]

Further checking revealed a class of eight girls and their professor having an actual tea party *in French*. A different girl acted as hostess each week. Every Saturday, all of the College's French majors met for lunch, in French, each in turn supplying sandwiches. "Dr. Sammartino, of course, makes his contribution of the long French bread—sandwiches *à la française*. After all, there is nothing like being realistic."[11]

This period of learning and teaching, along with glorious fun, came to an abrupt and disastrous end, and from it Sammartino learned a lesson he was never to forget.

New College had operated at a deficit each year, even though it had had the free use of available Teachers College classrooms, and had thus had no expense for physical plant. The deficits were not large, yet they were enough to persuade the administration of Teachers College to terminate the New College experiment, especially since the Depression seemed to be reviving during 1938. The faculty and student body of New College reacted strongly against the decision.[12] Protest meetings and various efforts to continue were launched. But the Teachers College Faculty voted its approval of the closing, 55 to 29.[13]

An experiment that had proven to be highly effective and rewarding as an educational experience and that had opened new vistas for higher education suddenly terminated because of financial reasons. Sammartino learned that hard work, devotion, and success in educational terms were not enough to guarantee the continuance of an institution if it failed in financial terms. This experience made him alert ever after to the financial implications of any situation or activity. The avoidance of deficits became a strong motivation.

It was typical of the man that he did not allow this blow to discourage him. On June 23, 1939, Sammartino wrote a letter to Dr. Thomas Alexander, the head of New College, which was

---

10. Rose Perlstein, "Voulez-vous Me Passer du Sucre?" *New College Outlook* 3, no. 14, New College, Columbia University, New York City (March 5, 1937) :1.

11. *Ibid.*

12. *Columbia Spectator*, November 11, 1938; *New York Times*, November 11, 1938.

13. Minutes of the Faculty of Teachers College, February, 1939.

scheduled to close its doors at the end of the current month.[14] Nothing came of his proposal to establish a junior college at Rutherford at the time.

THE CASTLE IN RUTHERFORD

From Morningside Heights in New York, headquarters of Columbia's New College, we have to move across the Hudson, to a pleasant metropolitan suburb, sitting on a small elevation created by the last glacier visiting this area tens of thousands of years ago. The name of the place is Rutherford. There a new educational experiment began, which led to a college "saga."

At the intersection of Fairview and Montross Avenues was the spacious house of the Scaramellis, parents-in-law of Dr. Sammartino. His wife, Sylvia (everyone called her Sally), was no less ambitious than her husband. Endowed with a keen and inventive mind, she had easily cleared the hurdles to two of the

---

14. *Sammartino to Alexander*, June 23, 1939.
Dear Dr. Alexander:
    In all probability, Dr. Snyder will take up this matter with you, but it will not be amiss to send you this letter.
    You will remember that some two years ago I discussed with you the project of establishing a practice secondary school and junior college in an unused castle home in Rutherford, New Jersey. I feel that at this time it might be advisable to look into the matter again. Briefly, some favorable points are:
1. The school would be considered an outgrowth of the New College philosophy.
2. The school could be started with a minimum of expense—perhaps about $10,000. I feel that if five or six of us looked around for financial supporters, we could find them.
3. The school would provide work for a limited number of New College instructors.
4. It could be used as a training ground for interne teachers.
5. The community (Rutherford and surroundings) is ripe for such a secondary school and junior college.
6. Roughly, since naturally the financial well-being of such an institution is a tough problem, I conceive the set-up to be as follows as far as the faculty is concerned:
    a. a skeleton staff of 4 or 5 (one for each major field) living in the building but who would have to depend for remuneration on the financial success of the enterprise.
    b. part time instructors coming in for dramatics, music, etc., who would also gamble on their financial remuneration.
    c. a larger number of internes helping out and working under strict supervision.
    I hope you will look into the matter. I have talked to Dr. Snyder, Dr. Camp and Miss Bornman. Your school and community in North Carolina is a success. With the same type of co-operation and hard work we can set up another center near New York. All we need is your moral support and educational leadership.
                                        Sincerely,
                                        Peter Sammartino

"Seven Sister" colleges. Her undergraduate degree, we have seen, was from Smith, while her graduate degree was from Columbia. Across Montross Avenue, on a slight rise of the land, stood—and still stands—The Castle, and there the Fairleigh Dickinson University story began.

It was a typically "authentic" French chateau in a typically late-Victorian style. Its model was claimed to be the Chateau of Amboise in the entrancing Loire castle country of France. Amboise had been the residence of French kings, while the Rutherford chateau was built in the eighteen-eighties for David Ivison, founder of the firm that became the American Book Company. (Much later it became a part of a conglomerate that sold not only books but also lawn-mowers and insecticides.) The castle was built on the site of an older house previously owned by the family Tomkins. Two unmarried sisters conducted a school for a while in that building in the seventies.

This "new old" chateau was quite impressive, with a skyward-pointing spire and gables, small towers, and wooden beams set in the walls. It did have (and still has) a medieval look, and was then surrounded by lush and neglected shrubbery. Its name was Iviswold.

It passed into other hands later, and became the Union Club in the nineteen-twenties. The depression finished off the Club and the Rutherford National Bank took it into receivership.

So there was the Castle and there were the Sammartinos, looking at it. Both husband and wife were school-minded, and ambitious. Peter was saturated with the bold idea of Columbia University's New College, which was no more, bankrupt. How would it be if the unused old castle in Rutherford were to be transformed into a practicum junior college? Had he had time to reflect on historical contrasts, he might have recalled that while the original Amboise was the site of a historic death—Leonardo da Vinci's—the imitation should become a place of birth, of a notable new life.

Occasionally on these visits to his parents-in-law Sammartino had commented that the building across the street could easily be used for a practicum junior college. He had even held a meeting at the Scaramelli home with three of his fellow-Associates at New College who shared his enthusiasm for a practicum school: John Taylor, then Dr. Alexander's assistant and later president of the University of Louisville; Paul Limbert, later president of Springfield College; and Winifred Bain, later president of Wheelock

College. But the termination of New College put an end to such conversation among the four future presidents.

It was not until 1941 that the sequence of events began that led to the incorporation of the college.

In the interim, since the cost of refurbishing Iviswold seemed prohibitive, Sammartino made another effort to start the college without spending any capital funds for construction. He approached a real estate development firm, Mott Brothers, with a proposal that the firm construct a classroom building in the then practically vacant western end of Rutherford and rent it to the college yet to be founded. But war was approaching and when the arrangements seemed on the verge of acceptance, new building restrictions were issued by the government and the venture came to an end.

Still not discouraged, Sammartino now proceeded, during the spring of 1941 and with the cooperation of the Rutherford Planning Board, to survey an area including ten neighboring communities regarding their needs for a local junior college. This project was carried out with the cooperation of the local high school principals and the conclusion was reached that there were at least 500 prospective students in the area for the kind of institution being planned.

Sammartino was determined that the new college should grow naturally out of the high schools of the area and be closely linked with them. At Scaramelli's suggestion he conferred with Guy Hilleboe, the Superintendent of Schools at Rutherford. Hilleboe gave his enthusiastic support to the project and drew up a list of high school principals whose support should be obtained.

During the summer of 1941 the Sammartinos visited junior colleges throughout the country and attended a workshop in Los Angeles at which the curriculum for such institutions was intensively studied.

Since the failure of the effort to have the real estate firm construct a building, Sammartino's thoughts had again reverted to the old Ivison castle. He approached his father-in-law and gained his enthusiastic support for the effort to give the old building new life by making it the site for the college.

As a director of the bank that was holding the building, Scaramelli had easy access to the bank's president, Colonel Fairleigh S. Dickinson. He arranged a meeting between Dickinson and Sammartino, which was also attended by Edward T. T. Williams.

After the meeting the Colonel asked Williams to look into the possibilities. At this point in the gestation period, Williams played the crucial role. Everything hinged on the nature of his report to the Colonel. After conferring with Sammartino and Scaramelli, the future chairman of its Board of Trustees showed his faith in the projected institution and submitted a favorable report.

Sammartino and Scaramelli felt that the sum of $30,000 would be needed to start operations. Scaramelli approached Dickinson, who told him, "Louis, whatever you give, I'll match." On the basis of his report Williams felt that at least $60,000 would be needed to begin, but this suggestion almost halted the whole project. Scaramelli felt that he could not increase his share proportionately if the sum were doubled. At this point Sammartino made the decisive move. He pledged practically all the cash he had to Scaramelli's share. Inspired by this act, Scaramelli hesitated no longer and asked Williams to report to the Colonel that he went along with the doubled estimate.

The encounter during these negotiations of Sammartino and Williams, of the future president and the future board chairman, was of basic importance to the institution. Out of it grew close cooperation and mutual trust. The personalities and abilities of the two men complemented each other to a great degree. They became a smoothly working team whose combined abilities proved capable of surmounting, one way or the other, the various difficulties that arose during the institution's first quarter of a century. They were also constantly alert to possibilities of many kinds that presented themselves and they stimulated each other to discover new ones.

A LOOK AT A SKYLINE AND AT NORTHERN NEW JERSEY

At the end of a tree-flanked alley in Rutherford, Orient Way, the traveler sees one of the most unusual sights of the world, the twilight sky aglitter with myriads of lights; those are the lights of New York. No other major city has anything like that, not even the capitals with historic landmarks like the Eiffel Tower, the Vatican, or St. Paul's. The sight from the glacier-made rise in the Jersey town is a panorama forcing admiration on even the most blasé mind. Behind the façade of skyscraping lights is a collection of some of the most notable schools of higher learning in the country: former King's College, Columbia University, with its worldwide fame; New York University, with it dozen different schools, embracing all phases of the human fate and with the largest student registration of any private school. Besides, there is the larger complex of city colleges, in Manhattan, the Bronx, Brooklyn, and Queens, "prestige" institutions because of the quality of their selected students, many of them to become leaders of men. There are the other schools of higher learning, scattered behind the façade of light. Was there any need for a new college on the west side of the Hudson, on a piece of land within sight of the artificial stars? To answer this question we have to take a look at the background of the proposed new college sited on the ancient debris of a glacial end-moraine in Rutherford.

The town is situated in New Jersey, which, while it is the most densely settled state of the country, is also one of the smallest. Northern New Jersey has the largest concentration of suburban population, living in strings of communities spreading in all directions, a maze of suburbia. Almost from the outset of American history, New Jersey was the most highly industrialized state. The reasons are obvious. It has one of the great natural harbors, the Port of New York, the major entrance gate of immigrants. America was their land. In that harbor the "New Colossus," the Statue of Liberty—"Goddess of Liberty"—greeted millions:

> Give me your tired, your poor
> Your huddled masses yearning to breathe free
> The wretched refuse of your teeming shore.
> Send these, the homeless, the tempest-tost to me,
> I lift my lamp beside the golden door.

Adjacent to the Golden Door was northern New Jersey, on the mainland, with space for people and their work—almost unlimited space—where industries began to sprout at a furious speed. Unlike nearby Manhattan, it had space for expansion, and had the largest concentration of rails, main arteries of commerce then, of feverish economic life, of prosperity. The silk output of this piece of land at the turn of the century was nearly one-half that of the entire continent. A few miles from Rutherford lay the first American industrial center, founded as an experiment by Alexander Hamilton and William Paterson. The City of Paterson came to be called the Silk City, the "Lyons of America." Nor was silk its only product. It turned out endless quantities of other textiles, machinery, and, later, planes and plastics.

Next door to Rutherford, the city of Passaic was also a textile

center, besides being the hub of other manufactured products:
dyes, rubber goods, mill machinery, steel cabinets, and springs,
among others. The area became the home of some of the country's
notable chemical, pharmaceutical, and surgical instrument companies, some of them linked with overseas plants. In endless
string of thunderous railway cars, heavy freight pounded by, also
on trucks and on the historic Morris Canal. One could take a trip
around the world in Jersey, meeting people from all parts of
Europe, especially from its east and south, ranging from the
steppes of Russia to the Mediterranean lands. In one single year
before the outbreak of the Great War more than a million immigrants touched land. America was the international magnet, the
miraculous land, where people made enough money not only to
fill their physical needs, but also to pay the tuition fees for the
higher education of their children. It was their Promised Land.

A WORD ABOUT A PARADOX

The folklore maintained that one made his way in America by
starting out as a newsboy then becoming a millionaire. The lowly
immigrant became the mighty chairman of the giant corporation
board. This was the American dream, mostly a fable, recounted
in countless books. But that was not so for long. Life in America
had become too complex and intensive, and merely selling newspapers for pennies was no longer the preparation for the board
room. Increasingly other factors came into play. One of these
was a piece of parchment.

Letters like A.B., B.S., M.B.A., and Ph.D. were mysteries to
most of the immigrants swarming ashore. Their route was "from
ship to shop." America was still different, as Germany's Goethe
had said: "America thou art better; thou hast no ruined castles."[15]
It had countless schools.

In the shop the immigrant beheld the new land. It is true that
he had to work ten hours a day in the mill, and seven days a week,
but he made big money. Some newcomers made as much as fifteen
dollars a week. They were *for* the American way of life. Besides
money they had human status. "The President of the United States
is called Mister," they wrote home boastfully, "and I am Mister,
too." At home, "in the old country," the literate people were snob-

---

15. Johann Wolfgang von Goethe, "Den Vereinigten Staaten," *Goethes
Werke* (Berlin, Leipzig, Vienna, Stuttgart: Deutsches Verlagshaus Bong
u. Co., 1940) 2:284.

The Castle as it was when acquired by Fairleigh Dickinson Junior College.

Colonel Fairleigh S. Dickinson.

During the summer of 1941 Dr. and Mrs. Sammartino traveled to California to study the junior college movement in that state in preparation for starting Fairleigh Dickinson Junior College. While there they also visited Hollywood and met two of the stars— Humphrey Bogart to the left and Peter Lorre to the right of the Sammartinos.

The Day of Dedication, September 12, 1942. Edward T. T. Williams, Chairman of the Board, is addressing the audience. The proceedings are being broadcast over WPAT.

bish, speaking a language the common people hardly understood, going to schools of higher learning, and holding all kinds of titles. The newcomers to New Jersey and elsewhere liked the thought that the President was Mister and they were Mister, too. But those letters, B.A. and all the others, still made no sense to them. The terms undgraduate and graduate meant just as little. After ten hours' work serving the flames of the open hearth furnace they were too tired to read. But they had money enough to buy meat and blessed America where life was that easy. Then they went to sleep to be in time to face the flames again for another spell of ten hours. Some of them were illiterate, others could read only in the language of the old country. The vernacular press catered to them. The learned man was not their kind. He was different and not democratic; they were anti-intellectual. Here was the paradox. No country could have anywhere near the number of schools of higher learning of America. Yet the people as a whole conveyed the impression of being anti-intellectual. This was so because of the historic memories of the immigrants. "Americans all, immigrants all," as the famed spokesman for immigrants, Luis Adamic, used to say. In a democracy all people had the same height and weight, intellectual height and intellectual weight, too. To be higher and weightier was undemocratic. The general attitude prevailed: "I am as good as you are." This was a defiant thought, reflected in defiant attitudes.

Then gradually a change began to take place. The anti-intellectuals began to ponder about the future, their children's fate. The working hours were lowered; the working week was shortened. Wages were raised. America was about to become the working man's Utopia, where the material rewards for work were distributed more evenhandedly. The "sanitary engineer" (garbage collector in a previous age) received the same pay as the college instructor with a Ph.D. degree. What sense did it make to send the children of the industrial ghettos to college? It did make sense, the father thought. The college gave diplomas, which enabled their holders to wear white collars. That, in turn, meant status in a society that had become increasingly conscious of status. The chairman of the board now had a row of diplomas and honorary doctorates. The qualification for high posts, selling newspapers, was replaced by the diploma parchment. The factory "hands" wanted their children to have academic "brains." The factory workers began to send their children to college.

THE CROWD AND A VACUUM

That skyline we observed from the ridge of the elevation on which Rutherford is situated explains another phenomenon. We have seen that a large concentration of schools was just a few miles away, in the shadow of the buildings with the blinking lights. At the same time, on the Jersey side of the river, there was a near-vacuum. There were a few schools there, too, several of them teachers' colleges. Rutgers was the exception, gathering patina and ivy. On the other hand, Paterson State Teachers' College was little more than a small cluster of classrooms in an old elementary school. Bergen Junior College, which was to play a role in our history, was a group of frame houses along the Hackensack. Seton Hall College was a Catholic school, approaching the century mark. St. Peter's in Jersey City and Upsala in East Orange were denominational and small. Montclair State and Jersey City State were teachers' colleges with limited class capacities.

There was now an additional reason why the Castle on the hill should be turned into the first classroom building of a new college: to save the creative thought of Columbia's bankrupt New College (bankrupt not because of its educational quality). There was now that large number of industrial families ready to send their children to college. And because of the "vacuum" in this corner of the state there was reason for the Sammartinos to eye the Castle with such interest from father-in-law Scaramelli's house across Montross Avenue at the beginning of the nineteen forties.

Could they foresee what was to happen in higher education after the Second World War? What did happen was one of the boldest educational experiments, the G.I. Bill of Rights. Ex-servicemen were to study at the expense of the government while the number of available colleges was woefully small to accommodate them all. Class enrollments in existing schools were to grow to enormous proportions.

One could not foresee then that America was to embark upon a policy that made the preparation and conduct of war into a permanent institution, a perpetual condition of what the Germans called *Wehrwirtschaft*, "defense economy," requiring not only a stockpile of weapons, but also the clinical skills for war. Nor could one foresee that the United States would have compulsory military service and that college students would be exempt from it while in school. Could one foresee the enormous increase of college populations? Expanded American higher education was one product of an American foreign policy that required more diversified skills. These potentialities, however, were still the secrets of the future when the two ambitious young people had that hopeful glint in their eyes while looking at the Castle across Rutherford's Montross Avenue.

OPERATION BOOTSTRAP

Every idealistic impulse needs a materialistic lever to realize it in fact. Money is needed even though the impulse results in an "Operation Bootstrap." This time the ideal motive was that of New College of Columbia University bent on creating the "holistic man" by drawing upon all his energies, intellectual and physical.

An institution is indeed greatly dependent on the economic and social factors of the site in which it is established. Yet the most fruitful field will lie fallow until men come along who know how to farm it, who have or can acquire the necessary tools and, most important, who determine to work that particular field. An act of will is the indispensable first step for every type of creative action.

On May 14, 1942, the State of New Jersey approved letters of incorporation for a college to be known as "Fairleigh Dickinson Junior College." Other names had been considered, among them "Boiling Springs," the original name of Rutherford, but this name was, fortunately, already in use for another institution.[16]

In alphabetical order the incorporators, who became the new institution's Board of Trustees, were: Maxwell W. Becton, Guy L. Hilleboe, Peter Sammartino, Louis J. Scaramelli, and Edward T. T. Williams.

Who were these men who founded Fairleigh Dickinson College, and what motivated them to take this step? A look at them will help answer the question.

Maxwell W. Becton was born in 1868, one of five sons, to a family in Kinston, North Carolina, and attended college in that state. After a fling at selling real estate in Montana he founded an instrument-making firm in Boston. While in Syracuse, N. Y., on his travels to sell his product, Becton encountered a fellow salesman, and this chance meeting proved to be the decisive turning point in his life.

---

16. Peter Sammartino, "How Does a College Get Started?", typewritten MS, p. 11.

> One day, the story goes, young Becton was travelling with a tiny
> sample case of clinical thermometers when he encountered a fellow
> North Carolinian, Fairleigh Dickinson, salesman for a paper concern,
> who was burdened down with weighty rolls. In no time at all the
> latter was persuaded to join Mr. Becton in his love for lightweight
> merchandise.[17]

Dickinson first bought out Becton's partner and then they established Becton, Dickinson & Company in 1897 for the manufacture of surgical instruments. Becton served as treasurer and secretary of the firm for many years. The company grew quickly and in 1907 moved to Rutherford, New Jersey.

Becton became very active in Rutherford affairs and was greatly respected in the community. He exercised his considerable influence in the company and the town quietly from the background and in close collaboration with his business partner.

Fairleigh S. Dickinson was not among the original incorporators of the college, nor was he ever a member of the Board of Trustees. Yet he played an essential role in the founding of the institution. Dickinson was born in 1864 in Beaufort, North Carolina, not far from Becton's native town. At an early age he went to sea and served as a sailor on a square rigger for several years. He then moved to Elizabeth, N. J., where he worked for the Singer Sewing Machine Company and attended night high school.

After the stint as a paper salesman Dickinson became president of the newly founded Becton, Dickinson enterprise and held this position until his death in 1948. During the First World War he was inducted as a lieutenant colonel to work with the Army Medical Corps on the supply of surgical instruments. In 1926 he became a member of the War Department's business council with the rank of colonel. The following year he became president of the Rutherford National Bank. During the Second World War Dickinson was the chairman of the surgical and medical advisory committees of both the Army and the Navy.[18]

The colonel was a highly capable, level-headed man who put great emphasis on correct business practices and concrete results. The bank and surgical instrument firm flourished under his leadership. Although he had received little formal education himself, he valued it highly.

The next incorporator in our alphabetical list, Dr. Guy Leonard

---

17. "Maxwell W. Becton," *obituary*, *The New York Times*, January 3, 1951, p. 25.

18. "Col. Fairleigh S. Dickinson," *obituary*, *The New York Times*, June 24, 1948, p. 25.

Hilleboe, was born in Necedah, Minn., in 1897. After serving as a second lieutenant in the First World War, he taught school in the Middle West and the Philippines and received a Ph.D. from Columbia University. Years as an elementary and high school principal led him by 1938 to the position of Superintendent of Schools of Rutherford. His career was punctuated by service on educational survey and study commissions in the Panama Canal Zone, Scandinavia, and India.[19]

Hilleboe was an active, outspoken man who loved innovation and was a leader among the school superintendents and high school principals of Bergen County.

Louis J. Scaramelli was born in 1878 in Galeazza Pepoli, a small town near Bologna. He attended the University of Bologna and afterwards worked as a surveyor, making military maps for the Italian Army, in which he held the rank of lieutenant. Around the turn of the century Scaramelli emigrated to Boston, Mass., and joined a food-importing firm in which he became a vice-president. In 1911 he started his own food-importing business in New York City and six years later established the American Syringe Company in East Rutherford, N. J. This business was later bought out by Becton, Dickinson and Company and soon after this transaction Scaramelli became a director of the Rutherford National Bank. He was also elected by his fellow citizens to serve a term on the Rutherford Town Council.[20]

Scaramelli was a very disciplined but affable man who fought hard for the causes in which he as a firm Republican believed. During his political activities he met President Theodore Roosevelt and President William Howard Taft. As a food importer Scaramelli was particularly interested in the tariff question. In the proxy fight for Giannini's control of the Bank of America he played an active role. Being an immigrant, he never took America for granted. He had a deep interest in education and a strong belief in its values and had gone to the trouble of sending his daughter to Smith College and then to Columbia University, where she had earned a master's degree in history.

At the time of the college's incorporation, Colonel Dickinson was seventy-seven years old. In still heading, at this age, the surgical-instrument firm and the bank, the colonel had found the

---

19. "Guy L. Hilleboe," *obituary, The New York Times*, May 8, 1957, p. 37.
20. "Louis J. Scaramelli," *obituary, The New York Times*, February 2, 1957, p. 19.

services of an energetic and competent lieutenant ever more essential.

Edward Thomas Towson Williams, the last on the list of original incorporators, was born in 1896 in New York City. At the time the United States entered the First World War he was a student at Brown University. He enlisted and emerged from the conflict as a captain in the U. S. Army flying corps. He thus had the experience of flying the planes of that period, also of working as a stunt pilot for a brief period after the war. Ever afterward, risk and challenge in any form seemed only to stimulate his energetic nature and strong-willed personality to their utmost.

After the war Williams joined Becton, Dickinson's sales force and soon became a management consultant. By 1932 he had become chairman of the firm's executive committee and, through proven and varied abilities, the colonel's trusted aide. In later years Williams was to leave Becton, Dickinson to head the Lambert Pharmacal Company, but ultimately returned to Becton, Dickinson as chairman of the board of directors.[21]

Williams's competence at judging men and events, his high intelligence, unfailing determination and courage were, at first acquaintance, somewhat masked by a tall, distinguished appearance and dignified bearing. When acquaintance had ripened into friendship and trust, he revealed a personality of great geniality and charm and a character whose strongest points were unending devotion and never-ceasing thought and work for the ideals, institutions, and persons in whom he had come to believe. He was a capable public speaker and, in a melodious, well-modulated voice, presented his content in styles that he could vary as needed throughout the gamut, from folksy colloquial through logical and informative to persuasively eloquent.

The institution about to be born was to be fortunate enough to have, during the whole period covered by this history, Williams as chairman of its Board of Trustees.

---

21. "Edward T. T. Williams," *obituary, The New York Times,* January 8, 1968, p. 39.

2

The Opening

In the fall of 1941 conferences with local high school administrators for the formulation of syllabi were held. During this period the location of the new institution in Rutherford was also studied by the principals and they agreed to the site since the town was in a central area and was "dry." Moreover, the Castle was by now a definite possibility as the first building for the college.

At the invitation of Scaramelli, who was an Elk, a dinner meeting was held at the Rutherford Elks Club on Wednesday, December 3, 1941. At this affair the beginning of a formal organization to establish the college was made. Those in attendance included Dr. Robert H. Morrison, New Jersey Assistant Commissioner of Education; Dr. Walter Crosby Eells, Executive Secretary of the American Association of Junior Colleges and a national authority and author of many works on the junior college; Sammartino, Williams, and sixteen high school principals from the area: Edmund Burke, Lyndhurst; Maurice A. Coppens, Wood-Ridge; George L. Dierwechter, East Rutherford; Marinus C. Galanti, Lodi; Floyd Harshman, Nutley; George A. F. Hay, Ridgewood; Francis J. Hurley, North Arlington; Ollo Kennedy, Passaic; Hugh D. Kittle, Belleville; John W. MacDonald, Hasbrouck Heights; George G. Mankey, Kearny; Wilmot H. Moore, Rutherford; Harold A. Odell, Rutherford;[1] Frank Paparozzi, Garfield; Charles L. Steel, Teaneck; O. F. Thompson, Hackensack.

---

1. Director, Adult School, Rutherford.

This group constituted itself "The Committee for the Organization of a Junior College in Rutherford." Sammartino was the committee's secretary. The vote to establish a junior college was unanimous. Thus the preliminary negotiation and work had created an organized group strongly devoted to its goal.

The dinner meeting and vote were held on a Wednesday. On the following Sunday the Japanese attacked Pearl Harbor. On Monday Congress declared that a state of war existed with Japan and on the same day an emergency meeting of the Rutherford group was held. Should they proceed with the venture in view of the uncertainties and risks of war? The motion to continue with the plans for a college won by only one vote!

Iviswold was now bought by the Board of Trustees from the Rutherford National Bank for $21,500. On the day after the purchase, Colonel Dickinson sent the Trustees a check for $25,000 to pay for the building.[2] A plant had been acquired without any actual cost to the new college.

Now Iviswold had to be renovated and outfitted for its new destiny. This was achieved during the spring and summer of 1942. Sammartino, who was still teaching in New York City, asked for a morning schedule so that his wife, Sally, and he could be at the Castle in the afternoon and evening to supervise the work. At the end of the spring semester the Sammartinos moved from New York to Rutherford.

The first public announcement that a junior college would be established in Rutherford was made on March 11, 1942. The local press generally responded favorably.

The Passaic *Herald-News* editorialized:

> The resurrection of Iviswold, Rutherford's show place that for so long has been a mere ghost of its former self, as Fairleigh Dickinson Junior College, is an enterprise worthy of serious attention. . . . It seems a bit daring to launch such an institution at this time, but its founders have faith and courage, and the active support of fifteen high schools in surrounding communities.[3]

The Rutherford *Republican* reported:

> Announcement Tuesday evening that the Castle had been sold, a junior college established there and that its chief sponsor was to be Colonel Fairleigh S. Dickinson, Rutherford's widely known indus-

2. Peter Sammartino, "How Does a College Get Started?", typewritten MS, p. 11.
3. Passaic, N. J., *Herald-News*, April 13, 1942.

trialist and banker created a topic of utmost interest in business centers this morning.

Reactions were most favorable. The prospect of the seven and one-half acre tract in the very heart of the municipality with its Castle long standing idle and unused, again being put to useful service, brought forth comment which reflected pride.[4]

There was also some negative community reaction, as reported by columnist Max Imhoff of the Passaic *Herald-News:*

The prediction by some observers of the Rutherford scene that establishment of the new Fairleigh Dickinson Junior College would be met by strident opposition has not been borne out yet, although some few murmurs of disapproval indicate what form protests, if any, will take.

The fact that the school will be operated as a nonprofit institution —and, consequently, tax-free—is the one feeble gripe. This loss in ratables, however, is the only thing deplored thus far. And it has been countered by favorable comment on the prospect of rehabilitating a long-neglected property which, when refurbished, will hardly be considered a municipal liability. Already landscaping on the eight acre campus-to-be is reportedly scheduled to begin next month.[5]

The renovation of the Castle was an even bigger job than it had at first appeared. The accumulated belongings of two generations of inhabitants and of varied activities had to be removed. After the emptying and cleaning of the building a general renovation, including the roof, the heating system, and the wiring, was carried through. Then came the painters and plasterers.

The Colonel, after spending the morning at his plant and the early afternoon at the bank, frequently visited the structure and found the Sammartinos busily at work. He began to send men from his plant to assist with the remodeling. His first project was the erection of a flagpole right in front of the Castle. The shelves in the library, patterned on those in his own house, followed. Many other aspects of the building's renovation similarly benefited from his help.

Besides giving material assistance, the Colonel also helped to maintain the Sammartinos' morale during this hectic period. He frequently invited them to dinner in his home, where a drink involving his favorite Canadian Club began the evening's conversation and further planning, after which the Sammartinos would return to the Castle to work with renewed spirit into the night.

4. Rutherford, N. J., *Republican*, March 12, 1942.
5. Passaic, N. J., *Herald-News*, March 17, 1942.

THE FIRST CURRICULA, STUDENTS, FACULTY, AND LIBRARY

A college must have students, and a catalogue is among the most important tools for recruiting them. The planning of syllabi had brought results and a small catalogue, prepared by Sylvia Sammartino, appeared.

A prospective student who, in the spring of 1942, was debating whether or not to attend newly founded but still inactive Fairleigh Dickinson Junior College could study a catalogue of sixteen (unnumbered) pages. It bore on the cover, besides the institution's name and location, a photograph of the Castle and the words "Co-Educational. Day and Evening."[6]

The title page also included a "Special Announcement Regarding Summer Session." If there were enough demand the new college proposed to conduct a summer session in 1942 in order to help the student accelerate in accordance "with the request of government agencies."[7]

On a subsequent page the dual purpose of the institution's programs, which continued to guide curricular development during the whole first quarter of a century, was stated succinctly and in bold print:

AIMS

Fairleigh Dickinson Junior College proposes to do two things for the student: first, to give a cultural background that is vital and dynamic and that will help the student to live a full and successful life; second, to give training in some semi-professional field so that the student may achieve economic security within a reasonable length of time after graduation.[8]

The first aim, namely, "Cultural Background," would include five basic elements. The first was the writing and speaking of the English language. In order to achieve "adequate facility" the prospective student would be required, along with his regular courses in English, to take "Guidance in Reading" during his two years at the college. This course consisted of the guided reading of works of literature, current publications, and general and professional reviews. A "Fairleigh Dickinson Junior College Reading List of Masterpieces of Literature" was sent to twenty local libraries in the form of a poster for display.

6. *Fairleigh Dickinson Junior College. Co-Educational, Day and Evening.* Rutherford, N. J., 1942. Sixteen unnumbered pages.
7. *Ibid.*, p. 1 (numbering added).
8. *Ibid.*, p. 3.

The second element was "Knowledge of Contemporary Society." The worthy citizen needed to know more and go deeper than the happenings of the day in a rapidly changing world. During his years at the college the student would attend the Contemporary Society Conference, at which history, economics, geography, and the social sciences in general would be brought together to give him "a unified understanding of contemporary society."[9]

"The Ability to Solve the Persistent Problems of our Daily Living" was to be the third element in achieving the aim of an adequate cultural background. The means to teach this ability was to be a Central Conference, attendance at which would also be required of all students during their two years. At these meetings a wide range of subjects would be presented. Interaction with family, friends, and others; the best utilization of the natural environment; sensitivity to enduring values; and the fullest development of the student's own personality would be considered.

The fourth element was to be "Health and Physical Activity." A health test would be required and the student would be encouraged to participate in such sports as golf, tennis, bowling, swimming, and social and folk dancing. In later years this emphasis grew into a considerable concern with the students' (and faculty's) nutritional patterns.

The last element in achieving the aim of a rich cultural background would be "Art and Musical Activities," which did not necessarily mean courses. An active program in these areas would be presented by the college, and students would have the opportunity to participate in them as their individual interests might determine.

English, the contemporary world, the problems of daily life, health and participation sports, art and music were thus the basic elements in acquiring the necessary culture for fuller and richer living.

The other expressed goal of the college, besides cultural enrichment, was to equip the student to make a living. The catalogue devoted ten of its sixteen pages to this "Second Aim: Semiprofessional Education."[10]

Fifteen curricula were presented for the student's choice. Each had been prepared by an advisory committee consisting of leaders and educators in the field. "The training in each field includes the

9. *Ibid.*
10. *Ibid.*, pp. 5–14.

theoretical background but stresses the practical approach and makes ample provision for thorough preparation."[11]

One advisory committee, including faculty members from Teachers College, Columbia University, San Francisco Junior College, and one quite successful businessman, Edward T. T. Williams, had all helped to prepare the seven curricula in the field of business: Secretarial, Accounting, Sales Management, Junior Business Executive, Traffic Management, Finance and (an international note) Latin American Business Curriculum.

Each curriculum listed the courses required. Instead of content-centered descriptions of each course, a brief paragraph characterized the curricular training, the type of personality and background needed, and the opportunities offered by each particular career.[12]

Besides the business curricula there were others, for Medical and Dental Assistant, Restaurant Management, Journalism, Photography, and workshops in art, fashion, and entertainment. A curriculum for Drafting and Blue Print Reading would be announced later in the spring.[13]

The curricula were characterized by practical and common-sense approaches to their subject areas. The student was to learn by activity in his field. Thus the students in the Restaurant Management curriculum would receive "practice in running all phases of the College dining hall."[14]

Students who chose the Fashion Workshop were advised that they were entering "a field that offers a multiplicity of jobs all fairly well paid and offering unlimited creative possibilities."[15] The required courses would be arranged in accordance with the student's individual talents and plans.

The catalogue's next-to-last page described the college's admin-

11. *Ibid.*, p. 5.
12.   SECRETARIAL
The Secretarial Curriculum offers training that leads to splendid opportunities for both men and women. All business executives need efficient and clear-thinking secretaries who can carry through the details of a business. Many of our outstanding executives have made their own start by acting as secretaries to the creative minds in the company thus acquiring special knowledge of the field from the very source where it is created. Technical preparation alone is not enough. The secretary who hopes eventually to fill a really important position must possess a rich background of knowledge of modern business and modern society. Such a secretary must be an actively cultured person and possess outstanding qualities as a human being. *Ibid.*
13. "Work in this field will be offered with a view towards filling the needs of defense production in the area." *Ibid.*, p. 14.
14. *Ibid.*, p. 11.
15. *Ibid.*, p. 13.

istration through an advisory board of school executives, advisory committees for each curriculum, individual educational consultants drawn from various areas and institutions, a board of educational directors consisting of the high school principals and the board of trustees.[16]

Several paragraphs were devoted to social activities, the library and spiritual guidance.[17]

On the last page a tuition charge of $100 a semester was announced, as well as the willingness of several local banks to extend personal loans to help meet this expense. In order further to encourage deserving but impecunious students ten partial work scholarships of $100 a year and five work scholarships covering the full $200 annual tuition were announced for those students "who rank among the first quarter of their class and . . . are in financial need. . . ."[18]

No admission standards were set except for the brief statement that "Admissions is based upon the recommendation of the High School Principal and the judgment of the Admissions Committee."[19] But high school graduation was required.

A cutout reply form completed the last page. On this the applicant was to indicate, besides name and address and preferred curriculum, whether he or she chose to attend the regular two-year course, an accelerated course with summer session leading to graduation by September 1943, or the evening session.

Dr. Paul Baker was employed as coordinator and to recruit students in the area.[20] He would report back each day on his recruiting activities, which might include conversations with housewives hanging up their wash in the back yards or planting their Victory Gardens.[21]

From the beginning to the end of the first quarter century the admissions work, including the preparation and publication of the catalogue, was the domain of Sylvia Sammartino, née Scaramelli. She began her work in the spring of 1942 as an unpaid volunteer

---

16. *Ibid.*, p. 15.
17. "The College feels strongly that any person who seeks to live a full life must have a proper appreciation of spiritual values." *Ibid.*
18. *Ibid.*, p. 16.
19. *Ibid.*
20. Paul E. Baker had taught social science at a private school in Honolulu and was a graduate of Trinity College in Texas. He held a master's and doctor's degree from Columbia University and had formerly been financial agent at Fisk University. Hackensack, N. J., *Bergen Evening Record*, April 6, 1942.
21. Sylvia Sammartino, "Suggestions on Admissions," typewritten MS, p. 1.

in a cubicle built in a Castle passageway just outside the President's office. In later years she became Dean of Admissions.

Peter and Sally, as they inevitably became known to all who had any close association with the institution, formed a hardworking team bound together by identical ideals and compatibility of background and personality. They generated action all around them. Sally was a natural leader among the women and an excellent public speaker. She had command, like Williams, of a variety of styles suited to different occasions.

The high school principals gave much help in the recruitment of students in their schools. In order to introduce the new college to the appropriate persons, Sally led in arranging a luncheon for the principals, each of whom brought two students from his high school as well as their guidance counsellors to Founders' Day. The links with the local high schools were to prove especially helpful in recruiting students during the years to come.

To supplement the lunch of tuna-fish salad and other items from a local delicatessen, Sally cooked one hundred hard-boiled eggs. Then she started to peel them one by one. Luckily, before she had peeled very many and was wondering how long it would take to peel them all, a delivery man pointed out, "Lady, it'll go a lot easier if you'll just roll each egg first."[22]

But all difficulties were finally overcome and the lunch was held on May 19th in the Castle's recently furnished first-floor class rooms. It was a great success. Forty two "student founders" from 21 local high schools attended, accompanied by 15 high school principals. Guy Hilleboe introduced the college's new president. Sammartino told the group:

> The distinction of being student founders carries along with it definite responsibilities. At least 200,000 persons in this area are watching the progress of the new college.
> The students will, therefore, be an important element in interpreting the college to the community. The pattern of American education is going to be very different by the end of this war, and Fairleigh Dickinson will be a potent force in the change that is taking place.[23]

The chairman of the new college's board of trustees also spoke. Williams emphasized that executives and personnel officers of many concerns had cooperated in planning a curriculum "that would train successful workers and creative personalities."[24]

22. *Ibid.*, p. 2.
23. Passaic, N.J., *Herald-News*, May 20, 1942.
24. *Ibid.*

After lunch the student founders, each wearing a name card in the new school's colors, maroon and white, explored the campus grounds.

Principals, students, and student counsellors returned to their schools to report that there really was such a place as Fairleigh Dickinson Junior College, and that the old Castle with its pines and bushes looked inviting and romantic. Public and social functions of many kinds, prepared with effort and verve, became a characteristic note in the building of the institution.

As a result of the recruitment drive and luncheon, an entering freshman class of 59 girls and one boy was admitted. About 90 evening students, half boys and half girls, were also admitted.

The first full-time faculty appointment was announced on May 7, 1942. J. Frederick Doering was a Canadian who had received an A.B. from the University of Western Ontario and two Master's degrees, one from Toronto and the other from Duke. He was completing his Doctorate. Doering had taught at Louisiana Polytechnic Institute and Anderson College and had specialized in radio college programs. At Fairleigh Dickinson he was to direct the speech clinic, teach English, and set up radio work.[25]

In June the second full-time faculty member, John A. Weishampel, was appointed to teach engineering and science courses. Weishampel was a graduate of Pennsylvania State College and had received a degree in civil engineering from the United States Military Academy at West Point and a degree in mechanical engineering from New York University.[26]

The third full-time faculty appointment was announced in July. Ray Farmer had received the A.B. from the University of Montana and a Master's degree from Teachers' College, Columbia. He had been superintendent of schools in Montana, had been employed in business, including Montgomery Ward, and had taught secretarial subjects at Goddard College in Vermont. He was selected to direct the secretarial and business programs at the new college.[27]

With these three appointments the full-time faculty was complete. The part-time appointments included Dr. W. Allen Messler, founder and former principal of the State Teachers' College at Jersey City, and Juan de Lara, who was on the faculty of Colum-

25. Rutherford, N.J., *Republican*, May 7, 1942.
26. Paterson, N.J., *Morning Call*, June 27, 1942.
27. Rutherford, N.J., *Republican*, July 9, 1942.

bia University and was to teach Spanish.[28] Dr. Messler was given the title "associate" and was to serve as an advisor in the development of the new college. Edward T. T. Williams stated:

> We are very fortunate in having the services of Dr. Messler in view of the fact that he has gone through the experience of organizing a new institution and can help us on many of our problems.[29]

Considering the fact that they would constitute the first faculty of an entirely new, untried junior college, the quality of preparation and experience behind these first Fairleigh Dickinson appointees was quite good. However, whether a professor's performance at a new and different institution will live up to the promise of his credentials is always a guessing game for both professor and institution.

The first students to be taught in the Castle were not, however, to be regular matriculants. A Rutherfordian, Mr. Gerald Tamblyn, asked whether a group of young men, including his own son, who were planning to enter the Air Corps could take non-credit courses unofficially at the new college before leaving for the service. There had been a delay in their call-up and they wanted to put their waiting time to use by preparing for their future duties. Mr. Tamblyn formed a committee and the request was presented to the college's authorities.[30]

The answer was in the affirmative. While the men were awaiting their call to duty, the college, assisted by a group of unpaid volunteer instructors, unofficially gave them courses in navigation, aeronautical mechanics, morse code, and trigonometry. Twenty-eight young men signed up for the courses, which began on August 5, 1942.[31] Completion of the program on August 29 was noticed by The New York (Sunday) *Times*, which reported "the graduation" of this first unofficial class of Fairleigh Dickinson students.[32]

The presence in the Castle of these unofficial first students overlapped in time the presence of the institution's first officially admitted students. On a Monday evening in late August, the newly registered day and evening students who were to begin classes in September gathered in the Castle for an informal meeting. They

28. Jersey City, N.J., *Jersey Journal*, July 20, 1942; Carlstadt, N.J., *Free Press*, August 8, 1942.
29. Hoboken, N.J., *Jersey Observer*, July 20, 1942.
30. E. Rutherford, N.J., *Enterprise*, August 6, 1942.
31. Lyndhurst, N.J., *South Bergen News*, August 6, 1942.
32. New York, N.Y., *The Sunday Times*, August 30, 1942.

were welcomed by the college president and after the meeting gathered about the new Hammond organ that had been donated by Colonel Dickinson and Maxwell Becton. They sang popular songs and the new college song, "O Fairleigh Dickinson," composed by Ralph Wingert, instructor in popular music.[33]

The actual start of educational activities through the giving of courses for the Air Corps cadets even before the college had officially opened its doors and in response to community demand created an educational momentum that was to continue and to accelerate through the years. Aside from the practical help given the young men themselves in preparing for service, there was the added factor of the new college's willingness to help the nation and the local community, which made for good public relations.

The library, like many other aspects of the new institution, began with a piece of good luck. Dr. Eells wrote the new college president that the assets of Arlington Hall Junior College, including its library of 4,000 books, were being sold at auction. Sammartino authorized Eells to make a bid for what might be a proper amount, and, busy with many things, forgot the matter. He and the others in the Castle were greatly surprised when, a week before the beginning of classes, two huge trailer trucks delivered ninety cartons of books. At one stroke, a small but suitable library had been obtained.[34] The offer had been made by Sammartino without getting previous approval from the trustees. Like Disraeli when acquiring the Suez Canal shares without approval of Parliament, he trusted that they would back him. In fact, Colonel Dickinson quickly sent a check to pay for the purchase. This sort of freedom of action by the president and close rapport with the trustees was to be an important factor in the success of the institution.

THE DAY OF DEDICATION

Finally the hectic period of preparation of plant and curricula, development of organization, and recruitment of faculty and students, begun at the pre-Pearl Harbor meeting of December 3, 1941, came to an end on Saturday, September 12, 1942, with the Day of Dedication. On that day seats had been placed on the lawn between the front of the Castle's porte cochere and the Victory

33. Rutherford, N.J., *Republican*, August 27, 1942.
34. Sammartino, "How Does a College Get Started?", p. 19.

Gardens, which had been planted toward the rear of the lawn area.[35]

About 800 persons attended the ceremony, which was broadcast over radio station WPAT. The program was begun at 4 P.M. by Edward T. T. Williams as chairman of the board of trustees. An invocation was offered by the rector of Grace Episcopal Church, whose Gothic edifice adjoined the small campus and was graciously lent during the succeeding years for many of the college's ceremonies.

Williams introduced the various speakers.

Dr. Floyd Harshman, chairman of the Board of Educational Directors and principal of Nutley High School, set forth the institution's double goal: "to prepare students for jobs, for their place in the industries of New Jersey, and to give them a cultural, physical and spiritual background."[36]

Guy Hilleboe emphasized that "a terminal junior college fills a great need in this area."[37]

The musical numbers included the National Anthem, "America the Beautiful," and "O Fairleigh Dickinson."[38]

Judge Guy L. Fake of the United States District Court in Newark, who lived near the college, recalled that Iviswold had been built by David Ivison from money he had earned through the manufacture of school books, and that it was most fitting that the building now be used for a school.[39]

Dr. Robert H. Morrison, New Jersey State Commissioner of Education, felt that the new college could provide two years of general education equal to the best anywhere.[40]

The Reverend Doctor Lester H. Clee, pastor of the Second Presbyterian Church in Newark, was the principal speaker. He congratulated the founders of the new junior college for their vision and courage, and added:

> The graduates of this school will be able to go out to be of value— to earn a living in the world of business and industry besides receiving a vital and dynamic cultural background.
> Two things must be in the forefront of this school; first, out of this school shall go men and women who will have caught a spirit

35. *Ibid.*, p. 18.
36. Passaic, N. J., *Herald-News*, September 14, 1942.
37. *Ibid.*
38. The text and music of this first of all Fairleigh Dickinson songs appear in the printed program for the First Commencement (June 1, 1944).
39. Passaic, N. J., *Herald-News*, September 14, 1942.
40. *Ibid.*

to help evaluate life in its true sense and, second, a willingness to put into action in real service the meaning of life they have discovered and developed in their own souls.[41]

President Sammartino, speaking last, said that the institution would be dedicated

to a disciplined use of the students' time so that they could find satisfying life work, an ever-increasing desire for cultural and intellectual pursuits and a rational basis for family and social life.[42]

Referring to the Air Corps cadets, some of whom were present, he closed by saying, "Our first class is leaving us to fly for our country. They symbolize the spirit of service of this college."[43]

THE EPIC OF A COLLEGE

Some universities are born, others are made. The state legislature, or the board of estimate of the city, appropriates a certain amount for the operation. Civic pride then surfaces and tops the funds. Rich people come forward with their donations. They have made their way to the top and feel a moral obligation to participate in community work, rendered still easier by tax exemptions. Also, their role in the development of schools of higher learning indicates status. They serve on the board of trustees or board of governors. Who knows? Their funds may mean a better chance for future Nobel Prize winners. Thus, indirectly, they enter history. Practical people combine their idealism with pragmatism.

Fairleigh Dickinson was now more than a gleam in a few peoples' eyes. It was in full swing. And what a remarkable "swing" it was, typically New World with new, down-to-earth ideas. Built on solid foundations, the ambitious plans were about to take off.

A comparison with older university traditions became inevitable. In the beginning they had fostered abstract thought. In those days it was the concepts of "realism" and "nominalism" that set the scholarly world afire. What was reality? Was it real or a mere phantom of reality? To hear the answer, thousands of young people from all corners of Europe were sitting at the feet of Peter Abelard and of Champeaux as they were to do in Bologna, Oxford, and Cambridge.

But this was mid-twentieth-century America, and here was the

41. *Ibid.*
42. *Ibid.*
43. *Ibid.*

announcement of the Official Opening of the Fairleigh Dickinson College on September 16, 1942, a classic illustration of pragmatism, with the emphasis on the practical. This was not the Cathedral School of Notre Dame. It was the Castle in a new city in New Jersey and that old castle, in Old World terms, was still very new indeed.

That announcement appeared to be the work of ardent people in a hurry to get started and not wanting to get mired down in long-winded committee sessions. There were countless wrinkles in the printed plan that would be ironed out. Some of the traditional academic decorum would be restored in due time, and the hyperboles removed. The announcement proclaimed a "unique educational work"—does this sound refreshing? And the student selects a career in advance. Implied was the prospect of a good living, the higher status of the college graduate, the white collar, which most of the fathers did not wear.

"Career courses" filled the curriculum, alluring to young people of a practical age, to the children of the densely populated industrial and commercial areas of the state, many of them from the underprivileged portions of Europe. Their sons should wear the coveted white collars. Some of the careers were more dazzling: radio broadcasting, journalism, aviation, fashion, and art. There were also prospects for positions as junior business executive, medical and laboratory assistants, and in Latin-American business, engineering, accounting, popular music, and others. One could almost hear the insistent voice: "Come one! Come all! Here are glamorous jobs for all." The influence of Madison Avenue was pervasive.

Who would shepherd the new students into the new school that called attention to itself so insistently in the giant shadow of Columbia, New York University, the City Colleges? The good shepherds were the principals of Jersey schools, of course. The Board of Educational Directors consisted of them, representing their schools in well-tended suburban towns as well as in the industrial ghettos of the neighborhood. There was much that appealed to these educators in their work of guidance. New York City appeared to be a Moloch, "alien," an apocalyptic monster to members of their communities, full of pitfalls, noise, and air pollution. Rutherford, on the other hand, was wholesome, serene, "American." Those gigantic private schools across the Hudson were also costly. In the metropolitan municipal schools the competition was fierce. This new college was propelled by energetic young people, strongly motivated, full of creative ideas. There was also this vacuum to be filled: the absence of schools within driving distance.

The Career Course Advisors, as listed on the original announcement, established a link to the New College of Columbia,—"*L'université est morte, vive l'université!*" These were the builders of what hero-worshipers called the "New College Epic." They were not only standing by, but were also ready to help, carrying on some of the work, if need be. There was the former head of New College, Dr. Thomas Alexander, with his truly missionary spirit, and the others: John Wilkinson Taylor, to be the president of the University of Louisville later to play a leading role in UNESCO as its Acting Director-General, the recipient of many well-deserved high honors in his field; Paul Limbert, to become President of Springfield College; and Winifred Bain, President of Wheelock College. They had been the founders of the New College, and godfathers of Fairleigh Dickinson.

The Advisors included "names" from a variety of occupations: Fanny Hurst, the novelist; Benjamin Fine, Education Editor of *The New York Times,* who was credited with being able to make reputations in the field; and a potpourri of distinguished people from various walks of life.

The faculty included sixteen full- and part-time members in a variety of fields of competence, including "sports," "fashion," "vocal music," and also history, psychology, English, Spanish, secretarial work, and art.

The offerings were scant, to be sure, but it was a beginning; all the rest, it was hoped, would follow in due time.

THE NEW MEETS THE OLD

"I have the dubious distinction," Peter Sammartino was to write in his *Of Castles and Colleges: Notes toward an Autobiography,*[44] "of having turned more old estates into colleges than any other person in the history of education." Sammartino collected castles as others collected books. He turned them into schools. That seemed to be his passion. He was to collect them abroad, too, as we shall see in England, in the Virgin Islands and, briefly, in Italy.

For the moment, he acquired period Americana buildings in New Jersey for expansion. The authenticity of lineage and age in

---

44. Peter Sammartino, *Of Castles and Colleges: Notes toward an Autobiography* (South Brunswick and New York: A. S. Barnes & Co., 1972).

a new country is always subject to interpretation. What type of reconstruction turns the authentic old into the authentic new? But it is better not to quibble about such things, since a definition of man is: "The only creature thriving on illusions."

The buildings Sammartino collected for his school in Rutherford may actually have the patina of age. One of them was Kingsland House, now headquarters of the Peter Sammartino College of Education of Fairleigh Dickinson University. It may actually date back to 1670, which in a new country is almost prehistoric. Originally it seems to have been a single-room pioneer cabin on an Indian trail now bearing the prosaic name of Union Avenue. It had a sand-covered earthen floor, complete with traditional open fireplace, hooded and flued to divert smoke through the roof.

Still in a fever of acquisition the Sammartinos learned about a notable example of Dutch architecture in East Rutherford, which was to yield to "progress" by being demolished, and replaced by an industrial building. This was the Outwater Homestead. The founding fathers (and mothers) of the new college thought that by salvaging this antique they would save one of the few historic buildings in the county. It was therefore decided to move the stones of the old house to the site of the new school. Each stone of the Outwater Homestead was marked, and replaced next to Kingsland House. When all this was done, no easy job, an unobtrusive passageway linked the two historic sites. The Sammartinos were keen on retaining the historic atmosphere; history wandered into the classrooms, too. The teacher's desk was copied from an antique design from a book on art history. A sea-captain's chair of olden times served as the model of the students' removable chairs. To keep the ambience in style, even the wastebaskets were handmade, woven into shape by an old artisan of handicrafts. The spirit of olden times was to breathe freely; a grandfather's clock, a wooden cranberry rake, and the fireplace andirons were fashioned on historic models.

Old buildings with traditional furniture are lovely to look at. But these were also uncomfortable for the young people to sit in. The roof of the old castle was leaking and the playful winds blew through the cracked walls. Physical problems could play havoc with ideals, no matter how lofty.

Luckily, the founders, their faculty and the students entered into the mood of creation and repair. In every American worthy of his salt there is a potential nation-builder. If there is no nation to build, there is something else. In this instance there was the school, and what could reflect more the ambition of the nation than a school of higher learning?

During all this time the spirit of New College of Columbia stood watch. The new institution was after all the product of the thinking of that school. This was a place not merely for reading, writing, and thinking, but also doing things with the hands, building, and relishing the results of one's handiwork. That was no less stimulating than the curriculum. The results were visible for all the neighbors to see and to marvel.

At first, professional roofers tried their hand with the work of repair in the Castle. The real tile roof, leaking profusely, they decided, had to be replaced by new asphalt tile. They forgot only one thing: there was a war on, and the tile was not available.

For the solution of this problem and for many others there was only one way out: ingenuity exercised by the collective efforts of the administration, faculty, and students. St. Thomas More would have reveled in watching the realization of this *Utopia!* The coordinated effort was not for the sake of material rewards. Some of the plasterers had the highest academic degrees. They were doing this for an inner satisfaction, that feeling of warmth which pervades one when doing something worthwhile for a cause and as part of a chain reaction encircling man's fate.

There was plenty to do: patching up the roof and plastering the walls. In the process, the academic workers may have spoiled the fun of the whistling winds. But one could not please everybody or everything. This was a community in action, the ultimate in the "do-it-yourself" method of pedagogy, and definitely "Operation Bootstrap."

The college is, obviously, not merely a roof and walls. It is also books and food, avenues of access and exit, and many other things. A contingent of the academic community turned to the problem of books. Priorities were established, while available funds were scrutinized. Books are the lifeblood of teaching, and therefore there had to be money for them. Underneath the grand staircase in the Castle, a small bookstore was opened.

There was also the question of food. President Sammartino had a strong nutritional orientation. He did not go, perhaps, so far as Mark Twain: "Nothing helps scenery like ham and eggs." But he did believe that an intelligently nourished body helped to energize an intelligent mind. One of the authors of this book will not easily forget the day when he first set eyes on President Sammartino. It was graduation day at the Stuyvesant High School in New York,

and Sammartino was the commencement speaker. It was graduation day for the co-author's son. In his strong, convincing voice,
the speaker set forth how important it was for the well-nourished
mind to have a well-nourished body too. Apparently familiar with
some of the ways of youth, he spoke of the importance of a hearty
breakfast to start a hearty working day. How much more sensible
this commencement address was than the stale exhortations that
tradition seems to require. "Now, my boys, go out into life and
save the world! We have tried it and lost. You should try it and
win!" As a footnote, the proof of the breakfast was in the eating.
Until then the co-author's son was indeed one of those young
people who scorned the early-morning food. Regular and intelligent eating habits, encouraged by the president's address, turned
out to be of help.

To nourish the body, a cafeteria was needed and student contingents of the commune wasted no time in providing its equipment. They scoured lower New York, where prices were rock-
bottom, and bought cheaply full equipment for top efficiency.

There was also the question of access and exit to the school. To
have the castle was one thing and to reach it was another. The
grounds neglected, nature ran rampant. It was difficult sometimes,
well-nigh impossible at others, especially on days of heavy snow-
falls. Again one had to shop around for cheap solutions. Who could
do the job well and yet at a low cost? A farmer was found in
Clifton who had a horse and plow, with which he opened the
pathways to the castle—no easy task. He was a decent chap and
$5.00 was all he charged for all the hard work. Perhaps the
remission of the rest of his fee was his contribution to the higher
education of America.

One day, looking out of a window of the Castle, the Sammartinos noticed two lonely cars on the forsaken parking lot and they
had a dream: "How nice it would be to have a few more cars on
that lot some day." That "day" came and it was not too nice, since
there were now insufficient parking spaces. With a vengeance
that problem was to haunt the school for years to come. This
brings us to another "headache."

THE COLLEGE AND THE NEIGHBORS

When the parking lots were crowded, some student cars had to
be parked in the streets. Many neighbors were amenable to this
accommodation. Americans are neighborly and they are commit-

ted to education. Some of them protested. The argument of the school to them was this: We pay taxes and go to wars—sometimes it seems endlessly—and we call it patriotism. Is it not love of country, too, if we love also our countrymen, especially youth, the nation's future, the new country-builders? Some people, evidently, do not think so. They like to see the young people going off to war, but they protest when their cars are parked in the neighborhood of the college so that they may become more productive Americans, building up an even better America. The day may come when patriotism will have a broader definition to include parking-space for students.

Luckily, there were no such problems on the Teaneck campus, which grew at a more dizzying speed. Who would have thought that the successor of the bankrupt Bergen Junior College, the Teaneck campus of Fairleigh Dickinson, would become such a success? It was also luck, too, that plenty of space was available for the college without intruding on community land.

There was no problem for the students in finding places for their vehicles on the Madison-Florham campus, either. That campus, too, was out of the way of the community, on a hundred and fifty acres surrounding the magnificent Twombly estate, a survival of America's Gilded Age, when the super-wealthy did not care even if they were thought to be show-offs. The estate was so large that it swallowed up the vehicles of students and faculty, leaving no threat to the outside world. The Madison campus of Fairleigh Dickinson University was considered by people-who-ought-to-know to be one of the most attractive campuses in this broad land.

What were the basic essential steps in getting Fairleigh Dickinson Junior College off the ground?

A man got the idea. He succeeded in enlisting the support of key community leaders in education, business, and finance. A formal organization was started. A minimal plant was acquired and equipped. A program of studies closely related to the actual needs of the local high school graduate was outlined. A recruitment drive was launched. A small faculty was hired. A beginning was made in the creation of a reputation and of institutional loyalty through public relations and events.

All these moves carried out with energy and determination generated an *élan* that carried the new institution over the various obstacles it inevitably began to encounter.

(Fortiter et Suaviter) A Case History

"Bravely and pleasurably" was the motto of the fledgling college. A wise man of the East, and it may have been Lao-Tsu, is reported to have said in his old days: "Half of my life I slept away, and the other half I dawdled away." What part of his life left was marked for posterity? In the interstices of the two halves, he achieved immortality. Fairleigh Dickinson was not to dawdle away the time, and therefore the ambitious motto. Hard work can be supreme pleasure too—the fulfillment, the euphoria of achievement.

The old castle on the hill in Rutherford, years later the school buildings along the river in Teaneck and, still more years later, those in the bucolic setting of Florham-Madison, were filled with young spirit. It was the soaring spirit of Sammartino's educational hero Emile of Rousseau that commanded that the measure of education was not merely subject matter. The measure was the man, the woman, the student.

The spirit in this youthful college was inspired by the titans of education. The concrete approach, and not merely its shadow in a pale theory, had emanated from the school of Johann Heinrich Pestalozzi, who used practical objects and case studies to develop the individual's powers of observation.

Lodestar of the new school was also William James, philosophical sire of pragmatism, a new term for old ways of thinking. The bottles change but not their contents. The sun shines on few basic novelties. Only the labels change, at times. The practical result is the only test of human cognitions, the pragmatist maintained.

Absolute truth is a mere mirage and all truths change their nature in conformity with their contemporary utility. The variety of human dispositions was infinite, James reiterated, focusing his attention on the *Weltanschauung,* changing with ages, spaces, individualities, creating a "pluralistic universe."

The pacemaker of American education—indeed, of world education—was John Dewey. Will Durant said of him: "He sees man as an organism, remaking as well as made."[1] Dewey said:

> It is of the nature of science not so much to tolerate as to welcome diversity of opinion, while it insists that inquiry brings the evidence of observed facts to bear to effect a consensus of conclusions—and even then to hold the conclusion subject to what is ascertained and made public in further new inquiries.[2]

Democracy was not just politics, Dewey maintained, but a way of life in all its phases, dependent on the degree to which individuals are themselves imbued with its spirit.

Fortiter, "bravely," the school should be centered around the student, its motto stressed. The house of learning was not to be an isolated outpost of a quasi-monastic order, esoteric, and unrelated to the world beyond its walls. The kinship of the curriculum and real life, therefore, had to be close. Since the measure was the student, his mind, which was the real "he," ruled as the determining factor. The needs of that mind thus became the needs of the school. When authority was an inner force, inherent in truth and logic and serving the academic calling, with strong emphasis on the individual mind and on its link of truth and logic, education became *suaviter,* "pleasurable." It was nature's way to equate the pleasure principle with the principle of life.

Thus the answer was provided to the eternal question: was teaching a special gift, the quality of the born educator? Granted that art was the emanation of the most creative aspect of the spirit, was teaching art? Creativity was seen as predicated on knowledge. Teaching was thus science, too, for the employment of the teacher's knowledge for the purpose of the remaking of man, as Will Durant said. That was the real meaning of *Fortiter et Suaviter,* the university's motto.

1. "John Dewey Lauded at Ninety," *The New York Times,* October 21, 1949.
2. John Dewey, *Intelligence in the Modern World* (New York: Modern Library, 1939), p. 677.

AT THE BEGINNING...

There is the student, and not the discipline or course. The college in the Castle did not have to relearn, to readjust, or to shift its ground. It started with the student as the measure. The school was small as yet, and intimate; close personal contacts were not only easy, but hard to avoid. The faculty members knew their students, and the president knew them, too. The students' backgrounds were known, as well. There were the tests of this statement. Occasionally a student was not alert in class. No teacher likes to gaze into a yawning gorge. He is on stage and close attention is the "applause" he craves. The student's gullet, however, did not bring down his wrath, but evoked his sympathetic interest, since he found that seeming inattention might be the result of the young man's sleepless hours. The student may have been working nights, while he went to school during the day. This was the only way he could finance his education. The possibility of remedial help was explored by the teacher, who felt it was his duty. When faculty members visited student homes, they learned a good deal. They would always give advance notice that they would call. One of the faculty members had a particularly intriguing experience. He expected to find the student at home, and perhaps the parents, too. It was a lower middle-class section of the town and the house was small. The teacher entered and was quickly taken aback. Had he made a mistake? This could not possibly be the place. He looked around; there were faces everywhere. Actually, the living room was filled with people, some forty of them, he learned. He promptly apologized for breaking into what seemed to be a family party. "Oh, no," a man replied, the father of the boy. "Our son is the first member of our family to go to college. A professor's visit is a great honor to all of us. We all wanted to be here—to greet you." When the teacher told the story to his colleagues, there seemed to be tears in his eyes.

One day the president of the college visited a family. As the door opened it disclosed a woman who burst into tears. She was the student's mother, asking anxiously if her son was doing badly. In the course of the chat a family tragedy was revealed. The boy was indeed not doing well, but for ample reason. There was a serious problem with the father, who had run off with his pretty secretary. When the president informed the faculty members of the state of affairs in the family, they did their best to help the boy.

Cut-and-dried "programmed" education was scorned. In those

days the campuses were still small enough to provide individual attention, especially if the returns on the work promised to be rewarding. The extra-bright students were encouraged to work out some of their educational objectives, to engage in out-of-class activity and get credit for it. One of the students was engrossed in French literature. She got the books of all the classics of France, in the original, from the school. She was also given records of dramatic and poetry readings by leading French players. Outstanding records of French songs were hers for the asking, and she learned close to a hundred of them. Then she was encouraged to go to France, to attend the performances of the Comédie Francaise and the Odéon, after having read the plays to be performed. This young woman took courses at the Sorbonne, too. She may have been one of the few young people who visited all—or nearly all—the Paris museums. Other courses she took were also related to the field of her principal interest.

At the other end of the spectrum there was another student, also a girl, whose interest was business. She read its literature avidly. This aroused much enthusiasm in certain teachers, but not in others. Some of those others took an interest in directing some of her attention to the liberal arts. Business was fine, they agreed, and the more she knew, the more she might prosper. But man was not merely a business machine. Out of a person's sixteen waking hours, a half is normally available for nonoccupational pursuits, although often these hours too are related to one's vocation. Books, plays, music, and informative print in all forms not only enriched life but made a person live more intensively. Such a person was more "alive," more part of the world. This young woman, too, never had cause to regret the college motto, *fortiter*.

Some of the early faculty members taught that the ideal arrangement would be the one of classical Greece, the equivalent of the Academy of Plato or the Peripatetic School of Aristotle, where there was constant close contact between the teacher and the student. That, of course, became impossible in modern times. But close contact with the teacher was desirable to the highest degree. It was discovered that this had to be a two-way arrangement, the "disciple" wanting to be as eager to meet the "master" as the master the disciple.

In years to come, the two-year Edward Williams College became a particularly good testing ground for personal contacts. The setting itself encouraged communication. It was attractive, even elegant and comfortable. Discussions were encouraged after classes too, along with oral presentations and lectures by outsiders, the *ipse dixit* of celebrities. From Edward Williams College, too, adjacent to the Teaneck campus, the fantastic New York horizon was just within view. That horizon encompassed the largest assembly of cultural talent in all fields. The students could get the best theater, opera, symphony, and ballet at low cost right across the Hudson, as part of the cultured person's life.

To study intensively means to live intensively. *Elan vital* was meant to be, not quite in the Bergsonian sense but more pragmatically, the building up of the individual to draw upon his mental resources at an accelerated rate, reducing the usual amount of waste of mental energy. As in *L'Evolution Créatrice,* the chef d'oeuvre of Henri Bergson, the individual was to participate, in all his perceptions, actions, and responses, in the actual processes of evolution, which, in turn, were continually taking place by change and constant movement.[3] Through the intensity of knowledge of the self associated with feeling, the individual could direct the evolutionary energy of life into the channels of his choice. Thus he would rise higher, and achieve greater progress.

This approach led almost unavoidably to the Honors Program of the College in years to come. In that program the student was treated as his own teacher, too. Under faculty sponsorship, he was encouraged to break paths and to move ahead toward the goal set by himself, following his bent, feeling, and inspirations while working in the fields that refreshed him, immersing himself in streams in which he wanted to be cleansed. The work turned out to be hard, but so were the rewards. The study was concentrated, contained in libraries and archives, in laboratories, or *ateliers,* in the company of the great of all ages, represented in selected books and works of art. Collective action helped individual growth in periodical meetings in which experiences were exchanged, authorities were consulted, and insights were mutually revealed. The seminar topics were both specialized and general. The object was to make use of all potentialities of the scholarly person within the stream of life. Thus half of one's life was not dawdled away.

"TRAVEL TEACHES TOLERATION"

The Earl of Beaconsfield knew whereof he spoke when he uttered these words. Travel does teach toleration. There was Britain, of

3. Henri Bergson, *L'Évolution Créatrice* (Paris: Presses Universitaires de France, 1940).

which he was the prime minister. In his days much of the world was England's backyard. Traveling became particularly essential for young Americans after the Second World War. Now they were heirs of a new empire, which was more a trading than a political empire. Yet so many of them knew so little about the world, in spite of the fact that their fathers had come from all corners of the globe. Paradoxically, that may have been the reason for their isolationism. They looked down upon the old, while extolling the new. *Fortiter et suaviter* meant also to expand the students' horizon. Now a group of students of Fairleigh Dickinson University were expectantly sitting on the red plush chairs of the house on Teen Muri Marg, which had been the official residence of the commanders of the British armed forces in India. Those armed forces had still been there, a dozen years before this visit of the students from New Jersey. These students were on a tour around the world, encouraged and helped in that undertaking by the school they attended, the tri-campus school in New Jersey.

They were to have a briefing by a man who was, in everybody's eyes, a living legend, an architect of history. It was early morning, before the work of the man they were expecting began. Finally they saw him descending the stairs, in the way he was seen in countless representations, on the screen, in the press, and in the imagination of the people. He wore his white jodhpurs, loose as far as the knee and tight below. He had the pink rosebud in the lapel of his tunic, without which he was never seen. He wore his white cap, without which he was never seen. His face was remarkably fresh and smooth. Before the students stood "Mr. India" —the Brahman from Kashmir, Jawaharlal Nehru, the prime minister of the most populous democracy in the world.

This was a class session for the New Jersey students in New Delhi. In preparation for this visit they had studied the life of the man they were going to see. "Long years ago," the man standing before them had said, "we made a tryst with destiny, and now the time comes when we shall redeem our pledge. . . ." Now he was telling the students how that pledge was to be redeemed. It was to be redeemed in a matter-of-fact and yet heroic way. Large dams were to be built, some of the largest in Asia. Those dams contained the torrents of water that provided the electricity that ran industrial plants. These in turn provided—and the legendary man spoke about such earthy things as fertilizers and tractors. For India they meant life and, perhaps, prosperity.

In the American Embassy in New Delhi the students listened

to the Ambassador of the United States, who happened also to be one of the most noted economists of the country. It was on India's independence day, a national holiday, when business usually came to a standstill. But the Ambassador opened up his office and talked to the students about the problems of livelihood in a hungry country. He was John Kenneth Galbraith.

Princes and commoners briefed the students from New Jersey as they moved from country to country: ambassadors, premiers, and other high government officials, in Japan, Thailand, Hong Knog, and Singapore. They had briefings all along the route. This was a summer's experience and a summer's academic session. While this was the most ambitious one, there were others, too.

Other students spent summers in a venerable mansion in the Tuscan hills, in the house of one of the century's great historians, Guglielmo Ferrero, in his home near Florence. The great Italian historian was dead but his spirit was alive, as were his library and his archives, which breathed the spirit of the epochs about which he wrote: *Greatness and Decline of Rome: Ancient Rome and Modern America.*[4]

Years later the young New Jersey college acquired a historic old mansion in England, Wroxton Abbey, which became its overseas campus.

The upshot of these efforts was an attempt to instill world-mindedness into young heads, many of them very provincial, to make them aware not only of the rest of the world but also of their ancestral heritage and of their heritage as members of the human race.

THE SKYLINE AND A NEW DIMENSION

It was not only that New Jersey visited the world but also that the world got into the habit of visiting this part of New Jersey. It came from the United Nations headquarters, and from the "Embassy Rows" of the East Side of New York. The United Nations building was—and is—a landmark on the Manhattan side of the East River, so close to that glacial mound of Rutherford that one felt one could almost touch it on clear nights. President Sammartino thought that the proximity of the U.N. made New York, and not merely Washington, the political hub of the world.

4. Guglielmo Ferrero, *Greatness and Decline of Rome: Ancient Rome and Modern America* (London: Wm. Heinemann, 1909).

Peter Sammartino delivering the concluding speech on the Day of Dedication. Maxwell Becton, with hand to face, is in the first row. The Educational Directors in the second row include Marinus C. Galanti and Charles Steele, third and fourth from left.

Guy Hilleboe, Peter Sammartino, and Edward T. T. Williams at a conference during the period of the college's foundation.

Miss Fannie Hurst, the novelist, spoke to the students on the first day of classes, September 16, 1942.

He also thought that the ambassadors accredited to the world body were ideal teachers about the ways of their countries. That is why there was a long procession of U.N. ambassadors across the Jersey Meadows, up the incline to the glacial mound, down the lovely alley quaintly called Orient Way to the Rutherford campus. Teaneck was to have its share of foreign dignitaries too, and, to a somewhat lesser extent because of its greater distance, Florham-Madison as well.

The ambassadors came from many parts of the world. The largest number of them came from Africa and Asia. Politically and in world relations, these two continents that form the bulk of our globe were as much the New World as the Western hemisphere had been centuries before. An entirely new situation was to be studied in these countries. When the United Nations opened its gates on April 26, 1945, it had fifty members. A quarter of a century later the membership was almost tripled, nearly a hundred and forty. The procession of the ambassadors across the meadows brought with it the New World, which we have come to call the "Third World." We might have called it *Terra Incognita,* which the ambassadorial visits were to turn into *Terra Cognita* for the students in the old Castle, along the Hackensack River, and in Florham-Madison.

In the very creation of the school and its ancillary services, diplomats played important roles. Prominent among these was one of the highest officials of the Secretariat of the United Nations, Benjamin Cohen, former Ambassador from Chile and, later, Under-Secretary of the U.N. Several prominent diplomats, U.N. and otherwise, were to leaven the international composition of the college. They came not only from the Third World, but also from the Second and First Worlds, to coin new phrases—from the lesser developed nations of Europe and from the farthest West: Greece, Yugoslavia, Rumania, and Britain, too, in a series of lectures and seminars on the three campuses, and also from Iran, Afghanistan, and other countries. The wife of the Indian Ambassador was also on the faculty, teaching English until her death. So was James Roosevelt, the son of the New Deal President. He gave a special seminar for several semesters. Among other prominent Americans who taught were Secretary of Labor Arthur Goldberg, Assistant Secretary of State Harlan Cleveland, and many others.

In the history of the college some of the ex-diplomats were to play leading roles. One of them was the former Ambassador to

Washington, Dr. Najib Ullah, a scholar of distinction.[5] The roots of Nasrollah Saifpour Fatemi, another leading diplomat, were in Iran.[6] As the mayor of historic Shiraz, his foot was on the political ladder in his country. After having served the governor general of the province of Fars, he filled numerous assignments in the West—as the representative of his country at UNESCO, a delegate to the International Conference of Americanists, delegate of Iran to the U.N., member of the Iranian Mission presenting the case of Iran to the Security Council, then economic and political adviser of the permanent delegation to the world body. After a stint of teaching Oriental culture at Princeton, he joined Fairleigh Dickinson University, where he became Dean of the Graduate School and, subsequently, Director of the Graduate Institute of International Studies.

The breath of distant lands reached the school also by way of its foreign students. The college was always bent on having a fair representation of East and West, North and South. Many of the African students had their homes on the Bulge of Africa from Sierra Leone to Nigeria. Asian students came from India, Pakistan, Iran, Turkey, Thailand, the Philippines, Taiwan and, indeed, there was hardly any country in Asia unrepresented on the three campuses. International Relations clubs were formed, where the spirit of these far-off lands was re-created.

MENS SANA IN CORPORE SANO

"A university is a huge stadium," says the well-known quip, "with some classrooms attached." It would have been lovely to have had a vast stadium at Fairleigh Dickinson. Indeed, half-a-dozen stadia would have been even better, for the main campuses and the ancillary ones, too, including the one in Shakespeare country, Wroxton, England. But the choice was this: stadium or Shakespeare? The campuses were growing fast. They had many

5. Najib Ullah (Bachelor of Letters, University of Kabul; Docteur de l'Université, University of Lyons) was Professor of History at the Teaneck Campus from 1962 until his death in 1965. He was at one time Afghan Ambassador to the United States and a relative of the King of Afghanistan.
6. Nasrollah S. Fatemi (A.B., Stuart Memorial College; M.A., Columbia University; Ph.D., New School for Social Research) came to Fairleigh Dickinson in 1956 after teaching at The Asia Institute and Princeton University. He was Chairman of the Social Science Department at the Teaneck Campus, 1960-1965; dean of the Graduate School, 1965-1971; and thereafter became Director of the University's Graduate Institute of International Studies. In 1971 he was awarded the title of Distinguished Professor of International Affairs.

advantages; convenient location was one, while quality was taken for granted. The tuition fee was within the reach of lower-income groups. With all those stadia around, the tuition fees might not have been within lower-income reach. The president of the college set forth the problem on one occasion, and not in terms of dollars and cents. In the American economy, cents no longer played a role. He presented the problem in terms of hundreds of thousands of dollars.

He said, by way of an example, that he knew a college that had two thousand students. It had a stadium costing three million dollars, with operating cost and amortization about $600,000 a year—about twenty percent of the total cost. This meant an expense of $300 a student a year, and this did not include faculty expense in the sports arena. Then he continued:

> Now suppose we said to a student: look, your tuition is $1000 a year but for $300 you can have a gymnasium to play around in. For $100 you can have the use of an outside field. For another $50 you can use our tennis courts and for $200 our golf course. On that basis, how many of our students—or parents, who are in most cases paying the bills, would be ready to pay for the extra services? To go a step further, how many students would be willing to pay extra to subsidize intercollegiate sports for a relatively small group of athletes? A friend of mine used to play polo when he went to Yale. But each player bought and paid for his own horse. He did not expect Yale to subsidize the sport.

Gymnasia were built on the campuses, but not stadia. Suburbia was getting crowded and acres of ground represented "acres in diamonds." Public playfields, on the other hand, were not in short supply in parts of the metropolitan area, especially where land had been set aside before its value passed into the field of astronomy.

"AND GLADLY WOLDE HE LERNE AND GLADLY TECHE"

The class was over and for a moment the teacher stood alone. There was something empyreal about him. The students stood up; some of them left the room, others went to the teacher to talk. They asked questions, since their interest had been aroused. The teacher had touched on sensitive points. Was there an answer to the question or was it to remain a puzzle, a doubt, and at the same time an incentive to look around, to ask more questions, to fathom new depths. Then these students, too, left the room, followed by the teacher. He was still somewhat dazed, close to a condition of euphoria. It had been a successful class session.

To describe the teacher who leaves his classroom in that condition is far from easy. Descriptive words sometimes begin their careers aloft and then lose their capacity to soar. *Dedication* is one of these words, magnificent at first and now trivial; because of overusage, a mere cliché. What is worse, it has no synonym. Perhaps *consecration* comes closest to it. But that word is somewhat pompous and ostentatious. Yet, it is consecration the teacher feels at his task—if he is really a teacher. He is a guide, indeed, a missionary. He has lifted a veil of the celestial creation, maybe in mathematics, biology, other natural sciences, or history, philosophy, and the humanities. To call him a priest would be unctuous, yet he is that, irrespective of his creed. It may be no coincidence that orthodox Jews refer to the synagogue as the "school." It is because of the teacher's mission that every class hour is a divine service.

Schools of all types, on all levels, from the crèche to postgraduate institutions, are looking for these missionaries in layman's garb. How does one find them? The expert on faculties recognizes telltale signals. He may not know; but he feels the presence: *voilà un homme*. Mistakes are constantly made, of course.

Mistakes are less likely to occur in schools that do not attract the crowds dazzled by prestige. These schools are even less likely to attract the disingenuous if they offer hard work and low salaries. That work, in our case, included physical labor, too, apart from a heavy academic load. The remuneration had to be modest, too. In the academic world, as elsewhere, it is success that breeds additional success, money that breeds more money. Who does not want to help Harvard University? Its billion dollar endowment is an attraction few affluent benefactors can resist. Fairleigh Dickinson University's day was to come.

The "consecrated" people came to the three campuses scattered all over New Jersey: the Pulitzer Prize winning author, novelists, writers of scholarly books, the noted philosopher, and scientists of fame. Writing and research mix well with teaching, each supporting the other. There was no shortage of recognized skills.

"And gladly wolde he lerne and gladly teche," as the story in the Canterbury Tales tells. So it was also in the old Castle, the Twombly Mansion, and in the budding Atheneum along the Hackensack. Promising young people were working for their doctorates across the Hudson, and teaching helped them to sustain themselves and their work for the coveted degree. Here was the *chela,* to use the Hindu word for disciple, who was at the same time the *guru.* For him this combination to "lerne" and "teche" was ideal. Many of them came to be the pride of the school, occupying positions of prominence in the classrooms and also guiding the destinies of the school.

"The greatest need is for research and study mainly for doctoral goals," the president of the school stated on more than one occasion. And then he added: "The University will attempt to make as many financial grants as possible for that purpose." Sabbatical leaves for the *chela-guru* combination were part of the pattern. Inspiration and encouragement moved hand in hand.

Who could teach better about the ways of the world than those who saw it? The college arranged for teachers to see the globe that they were to introduce to students. They were enabled to go far afield, even to the farthest regions of Asia, and the "darkest" portions of Africa. They returned, their horizons expanded. More than before, they had that feeling of euphoria in their classes which springs from inside knowledge combined with insight, the ability to transmit intellectual acquisitions to students, the blessed moment of giving, the moment of creation.

ON THE OTHER HAND...

This may sound like Utopia. It was not quite that. In any large organization there are bound to be problems. Colleges have their share, too. A false impression would be created if one were to assume that all the members of the staff were "missionaries."

"Teaching does not need quiet, weak men who want to creep into some little niche." Gilbert Highet, who uttered these words, surely knew what he was talking about. For thirty years he observed the teaching profession from Morningside Heights, as professor of Latin Language and Literature, an Olympian figure in the teaching profession's Hall of Fame.

A colleague related the following incident about him at Columbia University: "I remember once when some faculty members were reviewing the record of a student who was doing poorly. Everyone was making excuses for the student, saying he had problems with his girl friends or his fiancée. Then one professor shouted: 'I have had enough; this student is just stupid, stupid, stupid.' That professor was Gilbert Highet."

The lesson of this story is this. In trying to understand, teachers sometimes misunderstand. They assume readiness to learn, industry, comprehension, ambition. Perhaps they are right—or wrong. Perhaps G. K. Chesterton uttered the right word: "A teacher who is not dogmatic is simply a teacher who is not teaching."

The criticism applies to teachers, too. Everybody is familiar with the Shavian *bon mot:* "He who can does. He who cannot teaches." Shaw was, of course, anticipated by the master of the paradox, Oscar Wilde: "Everybody who is incapable of learning has taken to teaching—that is really what our enthusiasm for education has come to."[7] Wilde, in turn, was anticipated by Pope, this time in rhyme: "The bookful blockhead, ignorantly read/With loads of learned lumber in his head."[8] One can trace this line all the way back to Ecclesiastes: "Much study is weariness of the flesh."[9]

Criticism of the profession is not *comme il faut.* Facing their faculty meetings, college presidents and deans usually address their assemblies of supermen—brilliant, scholarly, filled with the missionary spirit. The cliché is as old as the faculty assembly, and who would dare to question its eternal validity?

The teacher, of course, comes closest to the prophet. His word is to be merely for the hour. Read the autobiography of a notable figure—the statesman, the scholar, the successful stockbroker. The niche he has carved out for himself assures him the right to speak about himself, for the benefit of the reader, of humanity, of posterity. Who had the greatest early impression on him, launched him on his career, showed him the path and the goal, filled him with inspiration? The celebrity who rates the publication of an autobiography has read the literature, has viewed the works of art. Yet, it will not be a giant of creation he lifts up to his niche, but a Mr. or Mrs. Smith, a teacher of mathematics or humanities. The eulogies of the college administrators at faculty assemblies seem to be justified from that point of view.

Thus, all is serenity on the surface. But do not penetrate the gilded surface of the empyrean. The pure element of fire the ancients suspected within its reaches may spell destruction, too. It would be hypocritical to say that all was *fortiter et suaviter* in the collegiate paradise, as in any handicraft of men. Besides greatness, knowledge, consecration—yes, consecration—there were also hatred and greed. That angry word of Gilbert Highet would

---

7. Oscar Wilde, *Critical Heritage Series*, ed. Richard Ellmann (London, Routledge, 1954), p. 375.
8. *Bodley Head Bernard Shaw Edition*, ed., Dan H. Lawrence (Oxford: Bodley Head, 1960), 1:87.
9. Ecclesiastes 12:12 (King James Version).

not be misplaced in this presumed "paradise" either—stupidity and, perhaps, laziness. This is the failure of a minority, to be sure, but it is a reality.

In writing about higher education, distortions should be avoided. The same rule should apply to it as to any other professional field. In the United States a Ph.D. degree is hard to achieve, sometimes inhumanly hard. A long series of hurdles have been set up to test the stamina of the long-distance academic runner. In many cases these are artificial creations, without any practical use. "There is nothing new under the sun," the sage said thousands of years ago. Yet, the doctoral dissertation must be "original." Originality can be achieved mainly by plucking a trivial case out of the world of bagatelles, providing it with awesome footnotes, and garbing it in incomprehensible jargon. The harder to understand the simplest proposition, the more hurrahs for the apprentice scholar. If one fails to understand his meaning, it means he is a genius.

All the hurdles are finally cleared and the parchment is in hand. The long-distance academic runner is now exhausted, sometimes for the rest of his life. Yet, he now qualifies for the academic Pantheon. He has performed his act of creation that is "something new under the sun." Perhaps he will follow it up at intervals with editing selected readings, in hard cover, under his own name. Perhaps he will even write an "original" book. The harder it is to understand, the greater his glory, and the more fulsome the panegyrics. No Ariadne could lead Theseus out of *this* Minoan labyrinth. This unpalatable feature of academe is cited here to maintain the proper perspective. Higher education is no more free of humbugs than other professions. By leaving this unsaid one would be guilty of distortion and even deception. This book is meant to be a picture of a way of life in a profession, the microcosm in the macrocosm. In this part the *dramatis personae* are presented. Not all of them stand on towering heights.

One can say how much a person weighs and how tall he is. The amount of energy he displays is harder to say. As to his industry and mental capacity, the accuracy of the measurements is even harder to ascertain. Think of the learned professors' attempts to fathom the problems of the unfortunate student. And think of the Olympian Gilbert Highet's rapid-fire burst: "Stupid, stupid, stupid." Did he say, at least in thought: "Indolent, indolent, indolent." And this time not *à propos* of wretched students, but about "missionaries without consecration," the academic frauds.

The measurement of inner values is more difficult in certain disciplines than in others. The natural sciences have more objective yardsticks. That is not always true of the social sciences. Shall we agree with Lord Chesterfield that "history is only a confused heap of facts?" Leo Tolstoy was even more outspoken: "History is nothing but a collection of fables and useless trifles, cluttered up with a mass of unnecessary figures and proper names." And to top this all off, there is this word by Aldous Huxley: "Generalized history is a branch of speculation, connected (often rather arbitrarily and uneasily) with certain facts about the past." If these giants of the intellect are right, the larger the number of fables, the greater the historian. The question must be repeated: where are the objective standards?

THE SPIRITUS RECTOR

The *spiritus rector* of Fairleigh Dickinson University was its first President. "Peter the Great," some of the "Young Turks," new instructors, sometimes called him. The similarity with the original model, the great Czar, was of course, superficial. The Romanov Peter had a capital built in the swamps of the river Neva. Peter Sammartino had the largest segment of a university built in the swamps of the Hackensack River. Even his critics conceded that his achievement was on an epic scale. But the "New Jersey Peter" had neither the unlimited authority nor the taxing power of the gigantic Romanov.

All he wanted was the best school for the least. After all, this was "Operation Bootstrap," and one attraction of the school was its low cost. At the outset he knew every member of the faculty and many students, not only professionally, but also personally, intimately. This was the Age of Collective Action.

Contradicting modest expectations, the college grew at an accelerated rate, a veritable magnet to students in the state and adjacent areas. New faculty members had to be recruited. The construction of the new buildings was placed in highly professional hands. It became impossible for all teachers to know all their colleagues on all the sprawling campuses. Necessarily, the president, too, lost something of the intimate contact only a limited ambience could assure.

To insure quality, he was watching performance. Being a strong personality, he wanted his administrators to reflect his policies. Some of the new teachers he favored, and on them he lavished praise. At the same time, if the performance of others displeased him, he sought to divert them into different paths. Undisguised criticism was to upgrade performance. The aim was clear: the student's interest was the gauge.

The question of student evaluation of instructors caused heart-searching. Was it a valid move? Is it ever a productive measure? In deciding the issue, the students' maturity was the dominant fact. A freshman student may be mature, while a senior may not be mature enough. How could the disciple judge the master's standing, especially in fields removed from his "major?" Of course, the student had instinctual reactions, telltale signs: the teacher's apparent self-confidence; the wiser and older students' grapevine; the teacher's ability to "communicate" on the student's level. Did the guru appear to deserve incense? Was his personality engaging? Then came the reservations.

Many students are pragmatists, for whom the college diploma is merely a certificate for the display of a white collar. These pragmatists judge the teacher by the "softness" or "hardness" of his tests. The ultimate criterion of his worth is his marking policy. Is the teacher an easy or hard marker? The easy marker is good, the hard marker is "below average." Thus the guru is reduced to the lowest-denominator *chela*. A trivial problem on the surface, all of this was important, even vital, because faculty status and teaching standards had to be assessed. Was the assumption correct? In this seemingly trivial matter the entire macrocosm of education was involved; more than that, its quality, perhaps even its value.

This phase of academic life is stressed because it was to play a role in events behind the scenes. Some of the new faculty members found themselves one day without a job with the dreaded terminal contract. Whispers of arbitrary actions were overheard. Chapters of the American Association of University Professors—a self-regulating professional endowment—entered the scene at this point in the early nineteen-sixties. Members of the chapters on the campuses asked pointed questions about faculty dismissals. What were the criteria? Student evaluations? Auditing reports? Other factors? And again the perplexing problem: How was one to judge merit in disciplines without positive yardsticks, especially if the art of instruction played the dominant role?

The AAUP engaged its interest in other areas of campus life, too. "The administration does not provide an adequate salary for full-time faculty positions . . . ," the charge resounded. To this the holders of the purse-strings reacted. This university had special problems to face—to establish itself, to create the proper instruments. Salaries were to be improved. The improvement was to begin where most needed, in the lowest ranks. First things first. The salaries of the instructors were the lowest and therefore were the first to rise. Then came the higher ranks. As the college grew, so did the staff remunerations.

"There was a tendency to talk down to the faculty, and an insufficient opportunity for faculty participation. Policies that affect the faculty are rarely determined by faculty action. . . ." Thus said some faculty members at AAUP meetings in those days. The Age of Innocence was over. Was this the beginning of the Age of Discord?

The economic condition of the teaching profession in those days was pitiful, lagging behind comparable professions. The Revolt of the Intellectuals was for higher living standards. Gradually, slowly at first, the condition of the academic profession began to improve throughout the land. Not long before, there was a time when noted professors at prestige schools made the lowest living. "Immodest," bitter critics might have corrected the adjective. That period was about to pass out of history. Fairleigh Dickinson University, too, overcame the travail of institution building. In a letter of September 8, 1961, President Sammartino, as the secretary of the Board of Trustees, invited prominent faculty members, who had played roles in the struggle for the teaching corps' "self-determination" to accept appointment as members of the University Council. "This is a historic event," the president wrote. "I hope you can join us on this historic occasion." Associate professors, professors, and, eventually, elected representatives of the other ranks formed the Council, which discussed pertinent issues as an advisory to the college's Board of Trustees.

LE STYLE C'EST L'HOMME

Throughout the ages these celebrated words of the great French naturalist, Comte Georges de Buffon, have resounded. It is exotic, indeed, that the director of the *"Jardin du Roi"* should deliver a *Discours sur le Style* when admitted to the company of "The Immortals," the members of the French Academy, two centuries before. Somewhat in the same manner Chesterfield wrote to his son: "Style is the dress of thought."

In analyzing the components of our microcosm, reflecting the macrocosm of American higher education, one has to say a word about the head of the central administration, the president, key to the University's failure and success.

The style of the *spiritus rector* of the college about which we write, Peter Sammartino, did indeed reflect the man: clear, outspoken, blunt, and pragmatic to a fault. The writings of men of action have to be accepted as self-analysis. He has written several books, in his own style, which is always the man himself. *The President of a Small College* by Sammartino is the perfect mirror of the man. (The college he founded ceased long ago to be small.) The reader who expects philosophical dissertations and theoretical psychology in multisyllabic words is baffled. He finds none of that. Instead he finds a practical presentation for daily use by other college leaders. That is the Sammartino style, in writing, thinking, and action. Abstractions do not entrap the pragmatic man. The writer is of the William James pragmatic school, as American as the Rocky Mountains. Existentialism is not his philosophy. As a practical man of driving force, he knows that life is riddled with complications, pitfalls, potholes, handicaps, problems to solve. The practical man exclaims: "Find the heart of the problem, these atoms that form its inner core. Break them down into their component parts. Then harness them in your service, which, in turn, is in the public weal." Then he goes on: "Do not make the obvious dim by wrapping it in murky verbiage to convey the impression of profundity. Clear thoughts are set forth in clear language. They are all practical thoughts." Speaking about fundraising, an unpalatable but unavoidable occupation for a college president, he advises how it should and should not be done. The orientation must be toward the donor and not the beneficiary. One must place oneself in his place, become a different personality.

How should the parents and the student be treated? He provides the answer. Seeming trivia may be grave. What should be the student's choice of food? He sets forth his views, and here we are back to that "good breakfast" again, the energy builder, the brain stimulant. The library is, of course, one of the most important components of the school, and he treats it with reverence. Indeed, he is a worshiper of books. The custodial service is not forgotten by him. The teacher is dependent on those who can make his surroundings pleasant, inspiring good work.

Instead of philosophical dissertations, Sammartino also tells us how the president of the college should live so as to give the best he has. He should, of course, keep himself in proper trim. He needs physical vigor for his concentrated work. His vacation is to be of generous proportion, to make him ready for his arduous working days. His office, too, should stimulate him to better performance. Above all, we are told,

> he needs a sense of humor. He needs to realize that the college can go on without him, that people will be thoughtless at times, that matters which loom large at the moment, will be unimportant tomorrow and that other people are as imperfect as he is.[10]

In another book, *Of Castles and Colleges,* Sammartino illustrates that sense of humor, reflected in the chapter titles themselves: "Prank in Dental School," "Honorary Degree and Indian Chief," "Undersea Capers," "Passing the Tin Cup."[11] Good times and good work go hand in hand. The reader sees that in spite of his uncommon achievements he wears no stuffed shirt. Who else would begin the history of one of America's educational epics with the story of "Two Martinis" which, he claims, helped to transform the old castle on the hill into the pivotal point of a major school in American education?

What should be the relation of the president of a flourishing college to the rest of the world? One would expect in a democracy where "all men are created equal" that he would be able to approach his fellow men, even those of high standing, on legitimate business. One knows, however, how hard and well-nigh impossible it is to break through the "secretarial barrier," even in matters of interest to the protected Great Man. Although President Sammartino had more than his share of tasks, his door at the school was never closed. He wore no blinkers; he saw, heard, and knew what was to be seen, heard, and known. An article, a book, a lecture, other public services by members of the college community brought his prompt encomium, the deserved praise. The artificially cold, blasé attitude that seems to be the hallmark of the day was not his style.

As president and, later, chancellor of the university, he knew the importance of the exchange of ideas, the stimulation caused by the active principles of different minds; not vapid locution exercises, but the spark and sparkle, the electric current through the brain, were his fare. People were taken aback sometimes when they bumped into the "Sammartino way."

10. Peter Sammartino, *The President of a Small College* (Rutherford, N.J.; Fairleigh Dickinson College Press, 1954), p. 16.
11. Peter Sammartino, *Of Castles and Colleges: Notes toward an Autobiography* (South Brunswick, N.J.: A. S. Barnes and Company, 1972), chap. 13, pp. 97–100; chap. 12, pp. 91–96; chap 17, pp. 122–28; chap. 21, pp. 158–67.

There was a conference, for instance, with several speakers, at which he presided. Each of the participants had a segment of the whole to analyze, dissect, and explain. Some speakers did that with an economy of words that illuminated the subject. They did not bury it in floral verbiage. Others, however, became enamored of their own eloquence, their favorite words, the "purple phrase." It was at that point that the traumatic event occurred. Sammartino pulled a notebook out of his pocket and detached a page on which he scribbled a word in capital letters. It was a four-letter word: STOP. Was this rude? Some people thought so, until they learned that it was neither meant to be that, nor was it to their detriment. At the point of STOP, the law of diminishing returns had set in, and points previously presented were about to be engulfed in a tide of verbiage.

QUAND LE BATIMENT VA...

Gallic wisdom has coined the felicitous term: "When the building goes up . . ." *tout va.* The buildings were going up on the three campuses. The myriads of lights in the windows of the phalanxes of office buildings on the other side of the Hudson had their reflections on this side of the river, too. The Teaneck campus was ablaze with the light of work—in classrooms, in laboratories, in the expanded library with its specialized collections, in student buildings, and in halls for the lectures of celebrities. So it was on the other campuses of the university, too. The number of buildings was increasing. Who could count them any more? The parking lot along the Hackensack extended toward the distant horizon. To see those thousands of cars was an awesome and warming sight. The number of students on the three campuses and their annexes now amounted to twenty thousand. This was, indeed the fastest-growing university. Many of the students would have been halted in their progress toward the higher goals if it had not been for Fairleigh Dickinson.

The cost of education was rising, too, precipitously, particularly on the highest levels. The teaching profession had found its voice. Too long had it been left behind in remuneration among the professions. Now living salaries were the rule. The price of physical labor and of materials soared fantastically. The great American monetary inflation was in full swing. Then on October 4, 1957, a historic event occurred in American education. Strangely, that event took place thousands of miles away from the nearest American territory. It occurred in the arid interior of the Soviet Union. The first man-made satellite, Sputnik I, was launched by Russian scientists, a 184-pound sphere that circled the earth about every 1½ hours in an elliptical orbit at altitudes ranging from about 140 to 560 miles above the earth. The United States was stunned.

Russian education had been seen from this side of the sea as spending its time in an ideological wasteland. Now, suddenly and dramatically, the truth was revealed. Incredible as it sounded at first, in space science the Soviet Union was ahead of the mighty United States. An intensely competitive nation such as ours could not let the sun of its technical progress stand still. The government in Washington began to pour colossal amounts into education, particularly into the sciences building up the space program. But, because of the interlinked interests of diverse phases of knowledge, the other disciplines, too, got their share. This was the beginning of a new educational era, the American "Sputnik" revolution, that eventually, conveyed the Stars and Sripes to the moon.

A blue-ribbon Carnegie Commission of Higher Education explored the question of college expenses some years later. It found that three years after Sputnik the cost of American higher education was $7.8 billion, more than twice its cost a score of years before. A decade later, in turn, it reached the stratospheric figure of $25 billion a year, with the expectation, or apprehension, that in another ten years it would be $51 billion.

Government subsidies in the wake of Sputnik enabled the three campuses of Fairleigh Dickinson, too, to speed up their building programs. They were accompanied by modernization, which turned the school into a model in scholarly conveniences and attractive looks. Yet, the governmental funds were still not enough, because of the high costs induced by a relentless inflation.

Here we return again to a phase of the function of the president of the college. As the key man in the hierarchy with a strategic overview of its activities, he is in position to size up its financial needs. In other words, a college president must be a fund-raiser, too, a *Schnorrer,* whose "tin cup" craves millions of dollars.

Yet, "I never really worried too much about raising money . . . ," Peter Sammartino said in his *Of Castles and Colleges.* Precisely because he did not worry, but acted, he became an excellent fund-raiser, sometimes *malgré lui,* in spite of himself. His pragmatic mind instinctively knew where the potentiality for donation was greatest. As the president of the fast-growing college he had to cultivate, and did cultivate, the company of people of great wealth. There were many of them in the highly industrialized metropolitan region, the greatest concentration of wealth in the world.

In America wealth is often "outgoing" because it feels a deep social obligation. Few better places for donations can be found than in the schools of higher education, especially if they happen to be on their way up. *Sic itur ad astra.* As the school was reaching for the stars, the donor's prestige was also rising. Man does not live by making millions alone. He also wants the surplus of his wealth productively placed. His personal prestige is linked to that of his beneficiary. No matter how powerful a man, he still likes *kudos.* Seeing his name engraved on a bronze tablet or standing out boldly on the façade of an impressive building, carrying that name into history, gives his pulse an additional throb. He feels that he becomes part of history.

Thus money kept on being dropped into the "tin cup." By the mid-fifties Fairleigh Dickinson was one of the "Selected Colleges with Major Endowments" in reference books. Its endowment matched those of such prestige colleges as Barnard, Mt. Holyoke, and Brandeis and Colgate universities. Its endowment fund in 1964 amounted to $11,625,000, a sizable sum in those days.

Sammartino wrote of those days:

> I solved the problem of keeping contacts with donors, large or small in a way that blended with our living pattern, and which turned out to be pleasurable for us and, I feel, for the donors, too. One rule I had was that wives were always included in the invitations, and this for two reasons: first, the contribution comes from the family; second, there is no good reason for taking a man from the companionship of his wife to attend a meeting that does not involve state secrets.[12]

That was one of his minor *modus operandi.* He realized that there had to be a cause, a realistic and profitable social investment for the donation. Business people act in a businesslike way in charities, too. Sammartino had to ferret out the persons whose actions encompassed a large measure of socially oriented generosity. Then he had to find the auspicious moment for action. Here is an illustration: An ultramodern dental school was being erected on the other side of the Hackensack River by Fairleigh Dickinson University. There was genuine need for that, and the federal government provided the seed-money. But three million dollars more were still needed and the president had only one million pledged for the project. Quick action was imperative. The son of

12. *Ibid.,* p. 162.

the man whose name the school carries, Fairleigh Dickinson, Jr., received an urgent telephone call from Sammartino. He set forth the details. Was the moment auspicious? It happened to be just the right moment, and the donor made his decision promptly. "I'll give two million," he promised, and later he "stretched" it to $2,300,000. That is how the new building became a reality, not only a pride of the school and a monument to the donors, but also a credit and of real use to the State. It became a benefaction to the surrounding communities too. Even though the presidential approach in this case was low key, it was intense, convincing, overwhelming. If this is a typical case, the best fund raisers seem to be the dedicated persons who do not like to raise funds, or so they assert.

Some people have it, others have it not. What is that "it?" It is that intangible something which cannot be defined. If we say *personality, consecration, intensity,* we are using words that defy definition. Perhaps that is the description of the dynamic person. He cherishes something, perhaps an "inner light," that illumines his path, leading to his goal. It may be the mysterious unknown.

Ours is an "all-or-nothing civilization." Some people are overwhelmed with work and honor. Others, who lack that unknown something, the "mysterious Z," live out their lives in obscurity. So it was that the founder of Fairleigh Dickinson University was sought out by all and sundry to initiate, carry out, advise, and teach. From one end of the world to the other, governments sought his advice and aid. His advice was sought on the highest levels in his own country too, and abroad, including the President's Commission on Higher Education and, at the White House Conference on Education, in an advisory role on the Peace Corps. The shower of medals and decorations that descended upon him came from many countries of Europe, Asia, and Africa. The Third World was his particular interest. The developing world, he held, had to change into a developed world if there was to be a world at all. Thus the road led from the old Castle to the newest problems of the youngest world.

In the following chapters, the reader will find a more detailed account of this bold undertaking in modern American education— the steep road from the old Castle to the fuller unfolding of one of the country's most unusual universities.

4

The Wartime Junior College, 1942-1945

THE FIRST YEAR

The new institution functioned as a junior college for only six years. During the first half of this period the nation's energies and priorities were concentrated on war. The growth of the junior college was inevitably determined and restricted by this fact.

The 153 students who began classes in the fall of 1942 experienced a highly informal and experimental operation. At one point, due to wartime restrictions, only two cars encumbered the tiny parking lot. Students brought or made their own sandwiches for lunch during free periods, and ordered and bought their books from a closet under the staircase leading up to the second floor of the Castle.[1]

Yet, these difficulties did not prevent the students from continuing. A continuous round of intellectual, cultural, and social affairs supplemented their class work and made the small college a fascinating place.

On the first day of classes, Wednesday, September 16, 1942, Miss Fannie Hurst was brought by car to the Castle from New York City by a group of five students to open the reading guidance program. The famous novelist told her audience that a combina-

---

1. Peter Sammartino, "How Does a College Get Started?", typewritten MS, p. 21.

tion of reading, personal contact, and experience had prepared her to write such books as *Imitation of Life* and *Four Daughters*. She urged the students to fall in love with their college librarv and to make it a second home.[2]

On Thursday and Friday of that first week, tests in spelling, reading comprehension, vocabulary, accounting, and Spanish were given to discover the extent of the students' knowledge. Professor John Weishampel, who was to teach the subject, gave a special test for prospective engineering students.

The students were also informed that there would be a field trip to New York on September 26 to visit the city markets, a long hike using maps to teach geography on Sunday, October 4, and an afternoon of classical music at the Castle the Sunday thereafter, to which parents were invited.

A committee of fourteen students was formed to plan and put into operation a lunch room that would serve sandwiches, cocoa, milk, and desserts. A dietetics student headed the committee, assisted by a student in accounting to handle the finances and another to buy the food.[3]

On October 1 the students were informed that arrangements were available for exchange study in Mexico City. The exchanges would be made with Mexican families who had sons or daughters who would agree to study at Fairleigh Dickinson Junior College at the same time and who would give the American students room and board in Mexico City in return.[4] The concern for international studies at the college began early, although this first program seems to have had little success at the time.

A week later the college president announced a policy that was to remain in force for the next two decades. Dr. Sammartino informed the student body that the Trustees had decided against the formation of fraternities or sororities at the college. He stressed that he was not against such groups in principle, that he had himself been National Secretary and later president of a large social fraternity, and had been active in the National Interfraternity Council, of which Edward T. T. Williams had been president. But the system of student life at Fairleigh Dickinson would simply be an extension of the fraternity system to all students, and therefore there would be no need for separate societies.[5]

By mid-October a Student Council of seven members, with no

2. Passaic, N. J., *Herald-News*, September 17, 1942.
3. *Ibid.*, September 21, 1942.
4. Rutherford, N. J., *Republican*, October 1, 1942.
5. Lodi, N. J., *Independent*, October 8, 1942.

officers except a rotating chairman, had been elected. Student committees on canteen, campus activities, general maintenance, swimming, social affairs, and reception were formed. A special student committee, guided by the Business Department under Professor Ray Farmer, handled the purchasing, selling, and accounting of all textbooks. Several male students formed a squad for emergencies and to check the operation of the school's heating system.[6]

The first dance was held on October 16, 1942.[7] The occasion was utilized to begin a separate organization for the evening students. Plans were made for dances, a theater party, and a hayride.[8] At other coming events, such as a ballet party at the Metropolitan Opera House, the evening students would join the day students.[9]

The first musical event on campus was an organ recital by Westervelt Romaine, F.A.G.O., sponsored by "The Friends of Fairleigh Dickinson Junior College."[10] Selections from Johann Sebastian Bach, several chorales, and a part of Vierne's Sixth Symphony were performed.[11] Among the "Friends" was William Carlos Williams. The famous poet was a Rutherfordian and took an interest in the new college from the start.

In November a 15-piece college orchestra was formed by Ralph Wingert, instructor in popular music, who commented, "Several persons are still needed for the violin and string sections."[12]

Music in both an active, performing sense and for general appreciation began to assume an important role in the institution's life.

In December the first student publication, *Fairleigh Dickinson News,* made its appearance.[13] It reported among other items that in a poll for student preferences, Harry James had won first place in bands while Tommy Ryan had beaten Frank Sinatra for first place in the male vocalist division by four votes.[14]

The new college received the Christmas present it needed most

6. Passaic, N. J., *Herald-News,* October 15, 1942.
7. Newark, N.J., *Evening News,* October 16, 1942.
8. Paterson, N.J., *Totowa Union,* October 22, 1942.
9. East Rutherford, N.J., *Enterprise,* October 22, 1942.
10. Hackensack, N.J., *Bergen Evening Record,* October 26, 1942. The "Friends" included, among others, Judge and Mrs. Guy L. Fake, Mr. and Mrs. Edward T. T. Williams and Mr. and Mrs. Carlos Williams.
11. Program, "Organ Recital, Westervelt Romaine, F.A.G.O., October 25, 1942," one mimeographed sheet, F.D.U. Archives, Rutherford Campus Library.
12. Hoboken, N.J., *Jersey Observer,* November 25, 1942.
13. *Fairleigh Dickinson News,* Rutherford, N.J., vol. 1, no. 1 (December 28, 1942).
14. *Ibid.*

when Oscar W. Jeffery, president of the New Jersey State Board of Education, officially announced that Fairleigh Dickinson Junior College had been accredited by the state and commented that this was the first time accreditation had been granted within three months of the founding of a college.[15]

Edward T. T. Williams commented:

> The accreditation will be especially helpful in effecting the war program of the college. Technical training is the basis of victory, and the army and other services can deal only with accredited institutions in setting up their various programs.[16]

Accreditation by the Middle States Association, the all-important regional group, was to take six years longer. However, state accreditation was an essential first step.

The first calendar year of the new school's existence came to a close on December 19, 1942, with a Christmas formal held in the Castle's North Hall, decorated in blue and white for the festive occasion.[17] Little more than a year before, the original organizing meeting had been held at the Rutherford Elks Hall. Now, almost thirteen months later, a small but enthusiastic student body could celebrate Christmas at their one-building junior college and could look forward to beginning their second semester of studies in the coming new year. Events had moved rapidly and successfully from conception to realization.

In most colleges enrollments have a tendency to drop for the spring semester. News of the active programs at FDJC had been spreading among the young people of the area. The institution's second (spring 1943) semester saw an increase in enrollment for a total of 192 students (83 day, 109 evening).[18]

Where did these students come from and what were they like? Rutherfordians made up one-third of the evening but only one-eighth of the day enrollment. Clearly those Rutherford students who could afford to go away to college were doing so, while those who had to live at home and work during the day were finding evening classes at the new junior college in their home town a welcome innovation.

Passaic, just across the river of that name from Rutherford,

---

15. Generally the process took from two to six years. Rutherford, N.J., *Republican*, December 17, 1942.

16. *Ibid.*

17. *Ibid.*

18. The students are listed by name and town under "Students 1942–1943" in *Bulletin of Fairleigh Dickinson Junior College* 2, no. 1 (March 1943):unpaginated.

contributed one fifth of the first year's class. Clifton, East Rutherford, and Garfield, towns very close to the new institution, also sent large contingents. Few students came from the northern half of the county. Only one student came from outside the state (Ogdensburg, N.Y.). There were no foreign or dormitory students. The student body was drawn almost wholly from the immediate locality surrounding the college.

These students had met minimal entrance requirements and most of them were aiming for a two-year terminal diploma. Many were happy to have been admitted by any college.[19]

The class that began its studies in September 1943 was required to meet more extensive admissions requirements. Besides high school graduation, recommendation by their high school principal, and approval by an admissions committee of three high school principals chosen from the Board of Educational Directors, this second class had to present proof of ability to profit from junior college instruction.

These remained the four requirements for admission until 1946, when three more were added: 1) the student's high school transcript; 2) passing of an entrance examination prepared and given by the college; 3) the presentation of high school prerequisites as required for the student's chosen field in the college catalogue. Entering advanced students had to present proper transfer documents for advanced credit.[20] There were no further additions or changes in the admission requirements as long as the institution remained a junior college.

Under these admission standards, a large percentage of the students inevitably had a poor high school record. Yet many succeeded in graduating from the new institution and, after going on to senior colleges, did acceptable or good work. The small size of the student body permitted a faculty involvement with and concern for the individual student, which frequently helped raise the quality of his work and encouraged the flowering of latent talents if he had any.

The spring 1943 semester began with a reorganization of the student government. The Student Council, previously elected by vote of the assembled students would, under a new constitution

---

19. Interview, May 13, 1971, Dr. Ara Boyan, chemistry teacher, Fairleigh Dickinson Junior College, 1943–1948; Fairleigh Dickinson College, 1948–1950.
20. Dion Walter Hill, *Fairleigh Dickinson University: Some Aspects of Its Growth.* Master's thesis presented to the College of Business Administration, Fairleigh Dickinson University (June 1961), pp. 84f.

unanimously approved by the Central Conference of all students, be appointed by a judiciary committee of three students, which committee had itself been appointed by a faculty committee of four members.[21] After appointing the Student Council from a list of names nominated by the students, the judiciary committee would keep confidential files containing records of all students who took part in school service and would issue periodic reports on the efficiency of their work.[22]

The war affected everything, even the studies of the women students. In March 1943 the first meeting of the FDJC unit of the Women's Reserve Corps took place. In the event of war emergency at Rutherford, the unit was to take over the Castle as the base for its operations. To prepare for such a situation the members of the Corps studied automobile mechanics, first aid, community feeding, and child care.[23] A photograph of the period shows a group of the unit's members wearing neat uniform suits of Air Force blue, with peaked caps to match, and black leather belts and shoulder-strap pouches. Grouped around the raised hood of a pre-1941 vintage car, some look with obvious confusion at the car's machinery while others are busily studying diagrams.

Forty-two men, former day and evening students at FDJC, had entered the service by this time, and the college proudly unfurled a service flag with this number at the Castle.[24]

Since there could be no commencement at the end of the first academic year, the chief event was observance of the first anniversary of Founders Day on May 5, 1943. Spencer Miller, Jr., New Jersey State Highway Commissioner and a prominent figure in the state's educational world, was the principal speaker at a dinner meeting at the college, presided over by Edward T. T. Williams.[25]

THE FIRST SUMMER SESSION AND BEYOND

But the end of the first academic year was not permitted to slow the momentum of the institution's growth. As early as March, plans for a summer session to begin on June 2, 1943, had been approved by the Board of Educational Directors.[26] The sum-

21. Passaic, N.J., *Herald News*, February 13, 1943.
22. Newark, N.J., *Evening News*, February 15, 1943.
23. Hoboken, N.J., *Jersey Observer*, March 11, 1943.
24. Hackensack, N.J., *Bergen Evening Record*, March 12, 1943.
25. Passaic, N.J., *Herald News*, May 6, 1943.
26. Paterson, N.J., *Morning Call*, March 24, 1943.

mer session ran on into September in one unbroken sequence, and included a full semester's work. By attending it a student could reduce the time needed for his associate degree from two years to fifteen months.

All classes were held in the Castle, the institution's only building which, like most in those days, was not air-conditioned. The summer students understandably competed with each other to sign up for morning classes, when classrooms were cooler, leaving afternoon and evening classes to late registrants, evening students, and those who had lost out in the competition for morning classes.[27]

During the day the institution was principally a girls' school, yet, from the beginning, especially in the evening, the more exclusively masculine concerns of science and engineering began to grow in importance. A small chemistry and a larger physics laboratory were established on the Castle's third floor, as well as a laboratory for photography.[28] Colonel Dickinson and Maxwell Becton donated the physics laboratory. Becton announced:

> Colonel Dickinson and I feel that the study of physics is of such great importance to our war effort that we wish the college to have the laboratory as a Thanksgiving gift.[29]

At the same time Dr. Joseph R. Morrow, medical director of Bergen Pines Hospital, was appointed to teach a course in laboratory techniques.[30] An early link with the medical world was thus established.

The growth in courses in science and engineering reflected the fact that war production was greatly stimulating demands for these studies and that the college was situated in one of the most heavily industrialized and technologically developed areas in the United States. Since the first instructor in these fields, although capable and hard working, would leave at the end of the next year, a search was made during the summer of 1943 for an effective replacement.

A prospect was interviewed by Williams, Hilleboe, and Sammartino and, after the interview, he waited in the hall outside the office to learn their decision. While waiting, the applicant pondered the advisability of tying his future to such an unprom-

27. Interview with Dr. Ara Boyan, May 13, 1971.
28. Kathleen C. Hillers, "My Early Days at Fairleigh Dickinson," typewritten MS, p. 1.
29. Passaic, N.J., *Herald News*, November 12, 1942.
30. *Ibid.*

ising, one-building college. By chance he fell into conversation with an older man, who seemed to know something about the place. What did he think of the future possibilities of this institution, the young applicant asked. "Oh," was the enthusiastic reply in something of an Italian accent, "don't worry. This place one day is going to be bigger than Princeton." Clair W. Black, encouraged by Louis Scaramelli, decided to accept the position offered to him.[31]

Black began to develop the sciences and engineering with the solid common sense and hard work that became his hallmarks during the three decades he was to give to the institution. He combined profound loyalty to the institution with the ability to speak his best judgment with the necessary degree of frank independence when this was essential. The first new curriculum developed by him was a two-year program in electrical engineering. Black also initiated courses in industrial management, a new area at the time. Enrollment in these classes began to rise rapidly.[32]

The college also appointed its first dean during the summer of 1943. Arthur Morris Wood, Jr., who began his duties on July 1, had been associated with the public school system of Nutley, N. J., for the past thirteen years as psychological counselor, director of placement, and in administrative work.[33] The new dean, besides his other assignments, was to establish and be in charge of the college placement bureau and was also to supervise a new course in merchandising to be offered in cooperation with a number of local department stores.[34]

The institution's second academic year began on September 21, 1943, with a total of 177 students enrolled (92 day, 85 evening).[35] All but three of the previous year's male students had entered

31. Interview with Clair W. Black, March 12, 1971. Black subsequently held the following positions at Fairleigh Dickinson: chairman, Department of Science and Engineering, 1943–1956; dean, College of Science and Engineering, 1956–1958; dean, Rutherford Campus, 1958–1965; vice president for governmental affairs, 1965–1971. He also belonged through the years to various committees and was chairman of the Committee on Student Life and Welfare of the University Council from 1963 to 1965. Black holds A.B. and M.A. degrees from the University of Pittsburgh and the doctorate from Columbia University.

32. Interview with Clair W. Black, March 12, 1971.

33. Nutley, N.J., *Sun*, June 4, 1943. Wood had studied at the William Penn Charter School in Philadelphia, and held an A.B. from Lafayette College and an M.A. from Montclair State Teachers College. He had also studied at the New School for Social Research in New York City.

34. Rutherford, N.J., *Republican*, June 3, 1943.

35. Hill, p. 92.

military service.[36] On the other hand, enrollment of freshman girls was fifty percent higher than for the first year.[37]

This second entering class encountered the institution's first tuition increase. Tuition went up twenty-five percent in September 1943, from $200 to $250 for the academic year. Part-time students were required to pay $6.50 per semester hour.[38] There is no record of any student protest or objection to these new tuition rates.

What did the students get for their money?

The students of the first year encountered the curricula described in the previous chapter and a full-time faculty of three— one in secretarial studies, one in English, and one in science and engineering. The first two left at the end of the first year without regrets on their part or on that of the college. The departure of the third at the end of his and the institution's second year was regretted by all concerned.[39]

From the beginning a larger group of part-time faculty also taught at the college, chiefly in the evening. Some members of this group were to teach for many years, since they were already permanently rooted in the area through their day-time employment and their established families and homes. Association with a local college benefited these professional and scientific people in various ways, although the pay they received was quite moderate. They provided another close tie with the local communities and served as a recruiting ground for full-time faculty.

Yet another element among the part-time faculty was composed of graduate students studying for their doctorates at nearby universities. Teaching at a junior college gave them experience and some income. Some of these faculty, in later years, remained with the college after receiving their doctorates.

Weekly faculty meetings, close daily association in a small institution, frequent social affairs and public events, to which the faculty were always invited and at which generous refreshments were offered began to build a spirit of involvement for many. But, since enrollments remained small during the war years and the institution's future seemed so uncertain, some of the faculty re-

36. Hackensack, N.J., *Bergen Evening Record*, September 20, 1943.
37. New York, N.Y., *Sunday Herald-Tribune*, September 19, 1943.
38. *Bulletin of Fairleigh Dickinson Junior College* 2, no. 1 (March 1943): unpaginated.
39. Sylvia Sammartino, "So Here We Are in Our 25th Anniversary Year," typewritten MS, p. 5.

mained skeptical of ultimate success and some sought positions elsewhere.

A round of educational, cultural, and social events and programs similar to those of the first year continued throughout the second year. One high point was the performance of three one-act plays by the Drama Workshop led by Professor Jerome Collamore at the Barbizon Hotel in New York City.[40] The group made a second appearance there later during the academic year.[41] Such activities began to make the small, new junior college better known to some circles in the great world city on the other side of the Hudson River.

THE FIRST COMMENCEMENT

The fact that its course of studies required only two years afforded the college an early opportunity to present the living results of its work to the world in the form of its first graduating class.

The First Commencement was held on June 1, 1944, on the lawn in front of the Castle. A service flag with the number 92 hung from the porte-cochere and proudly informed the world of the number of FDJC students in military service.

Edward T. T. Williams as chairman and Guy Hilleboe as secretary of the Board of Trustees led the academic procession. After the singing of the national anthem and an invocation, President Sammartino reported on the work of the institution's first two years. He announced that war conditions were preventing the construction of a new building, for which funds had been contributed and which would include a gymnasium and laboratories. The building would be known as Becton Hall, and Sammartino thanked Colonel Dickinson and Maxwell Becton for their financial support.

In his survey of the second academic year just ended, Sammartino placed the regional guidance workshops high on the list of accomplishments and praised the consumer surveys in local towns conducted by the students.[42]

Honor awards were then bestowed on graduates for academic

---

40. *Court Circular. The Barbizon. Activities for the Week, October 31, 1943.*
41. *Ibid., February 20, 1944.*
42. Hackensack, N.J., *Bergen Record*, June 2, 1944.

excellence in general and for excellence in special fields.[43] After the winner of the Third Honor Award had presented the senior farewell, the graduates joined in singing "O Fairleigh Dickinson."[44]

A "Charge to the Freshmen" was followed by the presentation of resolutions honoring Colonel Dickinson, Dr. Joseph R. Morrow, Dr. William Allen Messler, and most of the high school principals who had helped in founding the college.

The commencement address was delivered by Dr. Paul D. Moody, president of Middlebury College from 1921 to 1942. Dr. Moody emphasized that man could be in for a bad time if he did not reverse his current striving for perfection of means while still confused in his aims.[45]

The names of six of the graduates were listed at the bottom of the printed program under the heading "Alumni Executive Committee."[46] The newly hatched alumni were given an organizational structure at birth. For years the alumni organization inevitably remained small and incapable of great assistance. Yet the very fact that there had been a commencement and that there were alumni gave those associated with the new college the feeling that all the work had not been in vain. This intangible psychological factor was more important than the scanty number of alumni involved or their limited financial potential as supporters of *alma mater*.

The first edition of the annual yearbook, *The Castlelight*, was published by the Class of 1944, the small volume being dedicated to Colonel Dickinson for his "aid and encouragement."[47] The student editors took a look twenty years into the future and saw helicopters replacing automobiles as the general means of transportation. But they were worried whether the students of the future would have the same enjoyable good times that they had experienced.[48]

---

43. Doris Jean Sacawa (first honor award), Louise C. Muller (second), Phyllis Selma Gold (third), Roberta M. Clark (secretarial studies), Jane Campbell Davis (journalism).

44. *The First Commencement of Fairleigh Dickinson Junior College,* Rutherford, N.J., June 1, 1944.

45. Hackensack, N.J., *Bergen Record,* June 2, 1944.

46. Betty Jane Bleh, Jane Campbell Davis, Phyllis Selma Gold, Roland Werner Macher, Ursula Anita Scheu, Ruth Elizabeth Toitterington.

47. *The Castlelight. Published by the Class of 1944* (Rutherford, N.J.: Fairleigh Dickinson Junior College, 1944), p. 4.

48. *Ibid.,* p. 3. The first edition also included a page "For Those Who Come After," written in the flowery style appropriate to commencements. It seems to capture the experience of the college's small student body of the first year quite honestly.

THE FIRST TRICKLE OF THE GI FLOOD

The consumer surveys mentioned by Sammartino in his commencement remarks had been carried on by the college in cooperation with the Bergen County Committee for Economic Development. The students had interviewed financial and business leaders and local merchants, had distributed questionnaires, and had collated and written up the results of their surveys. Sammartino reported on the usefulness of the findings in an article in *The School Executive.* He emphasized that the information from the surveys

> was a tremendous assistance to the Veteran's Educational and Guidance Bureau established at the college by the guidance counselors. Approximately ten per cent of the men in the armed forces from this area have already received discharges. Many of them wish to study new fields, but relatively few have definite ideas of the subjects they desire to study. They require guidance, and such guidance must have a realistic and statistical basis.[49]

This sort of study and consideration of the practical needs of industry and commerce in the area served by the college opened new possibilities for growth after the end of the war.

As the summer approached, Dean Wood announced that the summer session of 1944 would extend from June 21 to September 8 and would have three aspects: 1) pre-induction courses in mathematics, physics, drafting and chemistry for men shortly to enter the service; 2) pre-nursing instruction for girls lacking credits needed to meet hospital entrance requirements and, 3)

The candle of the present senior class, with its flame small and flickering when the college welcomed us in September 1942, is now a serene, shining castle light. We, the first class to cross its threshold, have gained in experience and responsibility.

As autumn sunlight weaved through the foliage of birch and pine and highlighted the towers of the castle, our campus took on a friendly air. Students sat in gay groups on the lawn. They formed lasting friendships as they prepared for life. The flame grew brighter.

With winter's snows covering the grounds and crowning the peaks of the castle roof, its warm halls held a definite charm. Classes looked down the road of knowledge to see their goals ahead. The flame grew stronger.

Spring touched her magic fingers to the lilacs and trees, once more decked them in newness. We strolled over the grounds in wonder at this miracle we could always know in an uncertain world. We realized nothing could change nature's course, not even war. The flame leaped higher.

We hope our candle flame has cast an enduring silhouette upon our stately building. May our memories glow for the future in "The Castlelight," pointing the way for those who come after us.

49. Peter Sammartino, "School and Business Plan Together," *The School Executive* (May 1944), pp. 44–45.

courses in English, public speaking, contemporary society and psychology for those wishing to accelerate.[50]

The summer passed quietly in accordance with this schedule. Its most important achievement was the preparation by a special Committee on Veterans Education, consisting of Dean Wood, Clair Black (engineering), Harold Wertheimer (business), and Ollie Gardner (English), of a series of six recommendations, as follows: 1) admission of ex-service men to include consideration of the tests of general educational development they had taken while in service; 2) the wife of a veteran taking a full curriculum at FDJC to be permitted to take one course tuition-free; 3) engineering studies to be correlated with courses in personnel management, estimating and contracting; 4) a special curriculum to train prospective owners of small businesses to be established; 5) work-study programs to be set up by the college in cooperation with nearby industries, and 6) whenever possible special classes to be established to meet veterans' particular needs.[51]

The small college was beginning to prepare for the wave of returning veterans but these plans were ultimately changed by the actual course of events.

The junior college's third academic year, that of 1944–1945, was the last during which the nation was at war. A total of 250 students enrolled (105 day; 145 evening).[52] Thus the student body increased by an average of 20 percent during the three years of wartime operation and Fairleigh Dickinson had become, even before the arrival of peace, the largest junior college in the state.[53]

At 10:00 A.M. on Monday, September 18, 1944, the entering freshman class, representing 27 New Jersey towns, convened in the Castle's North Hall to meet the faculty and to receive instructions regarding their orientation examinations.[54] Several days before, President and Mrs. Sammartino had entertained the faculty at a tea.[55] The best known among the new faculty, who were just beginning their work, was Ellsworth Tompkins. He had been a radio announcer and station manager on important stations. Tompkins had served as announcer for Calvin Coolidge, Herbert Hoover, and other prominent men of the pre-New Deal era. With degrees from Princeton and Harvard, he was to teach public

---

50. Passaic, N.J., *Herald News*, June 14, 1944.
51. East Rutherford, N.J., *Enterprise*, September 7, 1944.
52. Hill, p. 92.
53. Hackensack, N.J., *Bergen Record*, November 27, 1944.
54. East Rutherford, N.J., *Enterprise*, September 14, 1944.
55. Hackensack, N.J., *Bergen Record*, September 15, 1944.

speaking at Fairleigh Dickinson Junior College.[56] A man like Tompkins added considerably to the lustre of a small, unknown school, particularly at a time when radio announcers loomed larger than they do in an age of television.

In October the Board of Educational Directors gave its support to a plan prepared by Guy L. Hilleboe in his capacity as head of the Rutherford school system for the creation of an evening high school for returning veterans. The school would admit ex-service men from any town in Bergen or Passaic counties. The Rutherford Board of Education approved the plan as well, and it was put into operation.[57]

The evening high school gave many veterans the chance to acquire the high school diploma without which they could not enter FDJC. Without any cost to the college, an evening preparatory school came into being, which accustomed the ex-service men from the two counties to come to Rutherford in the evening for classes after work and made it possible for them to enter the Rutherford junior college after graduation.

A service man who had attended Fairleigh Dickinson Junior College but who was never to return to continue his studies was Edward J. Rembisz of Clifton. Private Rembisz was killed in action in November 1944 while serving in the United States Army in Belgium.[58]

FIRST LINKS WITH INDUSTRY

Just before the beginning of the spring semester of 1945, an important step was taken to place the institution's growing links with local industry and commerce upon a more formal organizational basis. A Board of Industrial Advisers, consisting of industrial and business leaders, was formed.[59] These men were to advise

---

56. Rutherford, N.J., *Republican*, September 21, 1944.
57. *Ibid.*, October 28, 1944.
58. Clifton, N.J., *Leader*, November 16, 1944.
59. Its members were: Joseph Brunetti, president, Columbia Protektosite, Carlstadt; Lansing Chapman, publisher, Medical Economics, East Rutherford; Marinus C. Galanti, personnel manager, United Piece Dye Works, Lodi; George P. Heppes, vice-president, The Flintkote Co., East Rutherford; Karl Helfrich, assistant to president, Forstmann Woolen Co., Garfield; Col. Charles F. H. Johnson, president, Botany Worsted Mills, Passaic; Frank Kozick, manager, Alexander Hamilton Hotel, Paterson; John S. Leslie, vice-president, Leslie Co., Lyndhurst; Clifford F. Lindholm, president, Falstrom Co., Passaic; A. F. Metz, treasurer, The Okonite Co., Passaic; E. E. Poor, Jr., managing owner, Standard Bleachery, Carlton Hill; A. J. Royce, president, Royce Chemical Co., Carlton Hill; Paul Troast, president, Mahoney-Troast Construction Co., Passaic; Edward T. T. Williams, Becton, Dickinson and Co., Rutherford.

and assist in the development of the college's placement services and to clarify the needs of area industries for trained personnel. A special evening course was established for leaders in industry. The course stressed the psychology of human relations and the general and specific education needed to manage an industrial or commercial enterprise.[60]

The Board of Educational Directors had supplied invaluable ties with local secondary education before the establishment and during the first three years of the college's life. The new Board of Industrial Advisers did the same for industry in the new era of peace that was just about to begin. Students, new curricula and courses, and the development of a corps of financial sponsors resulted from the formation of the group.

In further response to the new vista of possibilities as the war drew to its close, four new courses, especially designed to meet veterans' needs in the fields of small business management, plastics, refrigeration, and electronics were introduced with the spring semester of 1945.[61]

The Second Commencement, on June 1, 1945, was held in Grace Episcopal Church. Twenty-eight graduates received two-year curriculum diplomas.[62] As a symbol of graduation, each graduate received a hood.

In his commencement remarks President Sammartino stressed the general friendliness and cooperation of all concerned, which had helped the institution's progress. He brought out the successes with which Fairleigh Dickinson graduates were meeting in business, and described the plans under way to serve the returning veterans. He stressed that the organization of the Board of Industrial Advisers had been the past year's most important development.[63]

Guy L. Hilleboe presented resolutions of appreciation to Maxwell W. Becton; William L. Chapman, publisher of works in medical economics; George J. Geier, principal of Hawthorne High School and a member of the Board of Educational Directors; and Ellsworth Tompkins.

---

60. Hackensack, N.J., *Bergen Record*, February 1, 1945.
61. Hoboken, N.J., *Jersey Observer*, February 10, 1945.
62. No academic degrees were awarded at the first two commencements. The State Board of Education did not adopt a policy permitting approved New Jersey colleges to grant two-year associate degrees until March 1, 1946, although Princeton University had been doing so for several years before that date. Princeton could do this because its charter antedated the legal existence of the state and it therefore did not need state approval.
63. Hackensack, N.J., *Bergen Record*, June 4, 1945.

Dean Wood distributed scholastic awards to three graduates and four departmental awards.[64]

The commencement address was delivered by Thomas Roy Jones, president of the American Type Founders, Inc., in Elizabeth, New Jersey, and chairman of the state-wide Committee on Economic Development. The industrial leader told the graduates that half a human being's success in life depended upon luck, but the other half would depend on his being prepared for the opportunity when it came.[65]

The summer session of 1945 constituted the first step in the actual transition from war to peacetime operation. Two important aspects of the institution's later growth—its multi-campus nature and its international concerns—were briefly foreshadowed by proposals publicized in connection with the first peacetime summer session.

The impending end of the war also caused the leaders of the junior college to begin planning the development of international educational aspects, something that had also been emphasized at New College and that had been introduced at Fairleigh Dickinson in its first catalogue in the form of a curriculum for business management in Latin America.

In August Sammartino announced that, as soon as the war was officially over (September 2, 1945), the junior college would begin planning student group travel led by faculty members to Europe, Mexico, and Canada. Later, he stated, air trips to South America, Asia, and the Pacific islands would be organized. In order to begin immediately to acquire the necessary experience, a group of Fairleigh Dickinson faculty and students would make a literary pilgrimage in the early autumn to New England, including the Wayside Inn at Sudbury, Massachusetts. There the literature students would read Longfellow's poems around the hearth of the old-fashioned kitchen, Sammartino said. Other excursions would be made to Boston and Williamsburg, Virginia.[66] As soon as the wartime restrictions were finally lifted, Fairleigh Dickinson group travel to foreign countries would begin.

In a way, the fact that the institution had been founded and first developed during the difficult war years actually proved to be

---

64. Arthur Van Schott (first), Shirley Stapleton (second), Frieda Suyers (third), Gertrude Zalewski (secretarial), Shirley Stapleton (journalism), Bernice De Lucia (merchandising), Gloria A. Malatesta (medical arts).
65. Hackensack, N.J., *Bergen Record*, June 4, 1945.
66. The trip to Sudbury took place in the spring of 1946 and was featured in the Sunday supplement, *Parade*, March 10, 1946, pp. 4-6.

The first Christmas Dance in the Castle, December 19, 1942.

The new college's sign being placed at the Rutherford Railroad Station.

A social affair during the early days of the junior college.

Singing of the National Anthem at the First Commencement, June 1, 1944. Sylvia Sammartino is on the extreme left of the platform, Peter Sammartino and Edward Williams to either side of the singer. Dean Wood and Clair Black are to left and right of the podium. The graduating class occupies one whole row.

a blessing in disguise. Since enrollments remained small, a simple basic plant could be brought into operation at relatively low expense. A small faculty had the chance to attach itself to the institution and to become well acquainted with each other. A minimal administrative and service staff acquired the necessary experience to deal with operations on a small scale before being inundated by the titan wave of veterans that was about to descend upon American higher education. The effort to establish the institution *ex nihilo* in the midst of the G.I. flood would have been much more difficult and, perhaps, impossible.

Moreover, the impersonality that so often pervades institutions that are founded and begin operations on a large scale was avoided by Fairleigh Dickinson's small beginnings. The school was able to grow organically. The small wartime college had generated a sense of community and a common spirit of enterprise and adventure that could be transmitted to, and was successfully kept alive in, the much larger peacetime institution that was about to appear.

5

The Postwar Junior College, 1945-1948

GROWTH IN STUDENTS, FACULTY, AND CURRICULA

On Friday, September 14, 1945, 120 entering freshmen took part in the academic procession and ceremony in the Castle at which they matriculated as students at Fairleigh Dickinson Junior College.[1] The whole student body had not been much larger three years earlier when the college had first opened its doors.

The enrollment for the academic year 1945–1946, the first in peacetime, revealed what the future would bring. Day enrollment increased to 165, a growth of fifty percent over the preceding year. Evening enrollment went up sharply from 145 in September 1944 to 483 in September 1945, a growth of 230 percent. The average increase of the total enrollment from September 1944 to September 1945 amounted to about 160 percent.[2]

The very large increase in evening students for the first peacetime year was most significant. It reflected the beginning of the return of millions of young men from military service. Some of these had postponed their college educations due to the war. Still others, probably the majority of those entering college at this

1. Hoboken, N.J., *Jersey Observer*, September 15, 1945.
2. Walter Hill, *Fairleigh Dickinson University: Some Aspects of Its Growth* (Rutherford, 1961), p. 92.

time, had not thought of going to college before the war. Upon discharge they found that industry and the professions were eager for men with college educations. Moreover, the G.I. Bill of Rights had been passed by a grateful Congress and public money was available on a large scale to finance the veterans' studies. Millions were to take advantage of this arrangement and in doing so changed the nature of American higher education.

These young men were eager to complete their studies and to begin building a family as quickly as possible. Many got married, took daytime jobs, and looked around for a college to attend in the evening. Others decided to go to college full time during the day and thus also swelled enrollments.

Toward the end of the war Sammartino had led the Board of Educational Directors in a survey of 400 industries in the area and had personally visited many plants to confer with their managers regarding the types of graduates they needed. The survey was the beginning of close contacts with the industrial leaders of the area, which were to have important results at the time and later. The organization of the Board of Industrial Advisers had resulted from the survey.

The effects of the new peacetime pressures and of the survey of industry upon the college's curricula become apparent when the catalogue issued at the end of the war is compared with the one for 1947–1948, the last year of operation as a junior college.[3]

By war's end, of the curricula originally projected in the first catalogue in 1942 only the secretarial, accounting, journalism, and medical assistant curricula remained unchanged. In the catalogue for 1945–1946 the others had either been dropped or placed under new headings and changed substantially.

New two-year curricula had been created in engineering, laboratory techniques, supervisory management, liberal arts, pre-law, premedical, and pre-dental studies, as well as a one-year pre-nursing program. The war years had led to a shift in emphasis away from such areas as art, fashion, and entertainment, as originally projected, and toward the sciences, engineering, business administration and pre-professional preparation. Significantly, along with these highly specialized and vocational programs a curriculum in liberal arts had also become into existence.

---

3. *Bulletin of Fairleigh Dickinson Junior College, 1944–1945.* (Rutherford, N.J.: Fairleigh Dickinson Junior College, 1945). *Bulletin of Fairleigh Dickinson Junior College, 1947–1948* (Rutherford, N.J.: Fairleigh Dickinson Junior College, 1947).

The catalogue for 1947–1948, the last issued by the institution as a junior college, revealed the continued growth of the above-named areas since the end of the war. A new factor was represented by the "Transfer Programs for Rutgers University."[4] The Fairleigh Dickinson student was given detailed instructions about the courses he would need to enter the various colleges and schools of Rutgers University as a third-year student.

Although some students ended their college careers after two years at Fairleigh Dickinson Junior College, larger and larger numbers decided to continue their studies for a four-year degree. Many of these students strongly regretted that they could not earn the bachelor's degree at the institution at which they had spent the first two years.

The catalogue for 1947–1948 also revealed a marked growth of the college's faculty, both in number and in qualifications. Forty full-time faculty members were listed, nine of whom (almost 25%) held doctorates.[5] Except for four bachelors (in the academic sense), all the remainder of the faculty had achieved the master's degree.

FIRST STEPS IN CONSTRUCTION

The greatly increased student body required more space. In order to meet the immediate need, classes were held in Grace Episcopal Church and in rented rooms over Woolworth's Five and Ten Cent Store on Rutherford's Park Avenue.[6]

At the 1945 commencement Sammartino had announced that Colonel Dickinson and Maxwell Becton had donated funds for the construction of a new classroom building, to be known as Becton Hall. In November of that year the college made known that construction would begin in the coming spring.[7]

It was hoped that the building would be ready for use by the fall semester of 1946. When it became apparent during the spring of that year that Becton Hall might not be available for use until a year later than originally planned, the college sought further temporary means to alleviate the space situation.

A former Army barracks was acquired from Camp Shanks in New York State and moved to the campus. It was erected on

4. *Bulletin of Fairleigh Dickinson Junior College, 1947–1948* (Rutherford, N.J.: Fairleigh Dickinson Junior College, 1947), pp. 15f.
5. *Ibid.*, pp. 3f. The distribution was as follows: Ph.D.–5; J.S.D.–1; Ed.D.–2; M.D.–1.
6. Hill, p. 15.
7. Hackensack, N.J., *Bergen Record*, November 17, 1945.

lower-lying ground to the northeast of the Castle. East Hall, as it was named, was partitioned into four classrooms, a utilities section, a dental hygiene clinic, an X-ray laboratory and student commons. The temporary building gave adequate, much-needed service until it was razed in 1957 to make way for the new Student Union Building on the same site.[8]

On the fourth anniversary of Founders' Day, May 1, 1946, Sammartino broke ground for Becton Hall with a gold-tinted spade. Others who took turns at the spade included Guy Hilleboe; Mae Lanzara, chairman of the student social committee; Madeleine Dunne, president of the student council; Peggy Reid of the class of 1947; and Dean Wood.[9]

Due to delays in the delivery of building materials, Becton Hall was still not ready for occupancy by September 1947. It was not until late in the fall semester, more than a year later than originally planned, that the building could be used. But when taken into use Becton Hall proved a delight, especially for the science instructors and students.[10] On three floors the building housed five physics and chemistry laboratories, ten classrooms, offices, and a cafeteria and auditorium in the basement.[11] And these laboratories were outfitted with the latest equipment of the time. It was a contrast to the Castle.

Becton Hall was built close to the southwest corner of the Castle on land lying on a somewhat lower level. As a result, the status of the Castle as the dominant architectural feature of the small campus was preserved. The new building, named after Maxwell W. Becton, was built in red-brick Georgian style. It did not set a trend for the more than thirty buildings subsequently erected by the institution during its first quarter of a century, but remained, to this writing, the only building in Georgian style built by the institution itself.

The ground-breaking for Becton Hall on the Fifth Founders' Day seems to have been the first occasion at which the Fairleigh Dickinson Alma Mater was sung, although the words of this first version differed somewhat from the version that has become well known and traditional since then.[12]

---

8. Hill, p. 50.

9. Hackensack, N.J., *Bergen Record*, May 2, 1946.

10. Kathleen C. Hillers, "My Early Days at Fairleigh Dickinson," typewritten MS, pp. 1-2.

11. Hill, p. 51.

12. The following text is reproduced as found on the back of a one-page, mimeographed program sheet entitled "Fifth Founders Day, May 1, 1946" in the FDU Archives at the Rutherford Campus Library:

Indications that the college would ultimately be compelled to move toward the creation of dormitories began to appear at this time. Shortly after the end of the war a number of students from the more distant towns of the area began to rent rooms from Rutherford townspeople in order to stay in town during the school week rather than commute.[13]

When the tide of newly married veterans began, many sought to rent or acquire housing in Rutherford, but had difficulty in finding suitable accommodations. In order to alleviate the situation the college, in January 1946, acquired free of charge thirty-two surplus housing units from the Federal Public Housing Authority. But efforts to erect them as a housing development near the college were opposed by many townspeople and came to a halt as a result. At a large public meeting held at Rutherford High School to discuss the matter, Louis J. Scaramelli warned that "youth was being driven out of Rutherford."[14] All was to no avail and the plan had to be given up, but the units were later built in an outlying district.

As private housing projects were rapidly built in the more outlying towns, the young men who had led the building drive, many of whom had been born or brought up in Rutherford, bought homes in the new developments.

This appears to have been the first instance in which a segment of the Rutherford populace successfully prevented the development in the town of a project sponsored by the college.

FOREIGN STUDENTS AND VETERANS

Among the first students living in private homes in Rutherford were some of the institution's first foreign students. Hector and Hugo de Bedout were brothers from the city of Medellin in Co-

---

Praise to thee, O Alma Mater, pridefully we sing
Hymns to laud thy wond'rous beauty, Fairleigh Dickinson!
Loyalty we pledge thee ever, loud our voices ring;
We salute the flying colors at the setting sun!
Alma Mater, we will cherish each day of the years
We are privileged to spend here as our parting nears.

Praise to thee, O Alma Mater, faithfully we sing;
Thru your portals now we're passing; farewell, Dickinson!
Castle halls will oft recall us, memories will bring;
Castle lights will ever cheer us, when the day is done.
Alma Mater, we will cherish each day of the years
We were privileged to spend here, tho' our parting nears.
　　　　　Music by Luther W. Goodhart
　　　　　Words by Jane Davis, '45

13. Interview with Dr. Ara Boyan, May 13, 1971.
14. Rutherford, N.J., *Republican*, February 23, 1946.

lombia, South America. Hector majored in engineering and Hugo in business administration. Miss Claude Hugo from Lille, France, followed the liberal arts curriculum and Miss Marie Scaramelli from Bologna, Italy, prepared to become a medical assistant. All entered fully into campus life and seem to have benefited from their study at a small new college in a foreign land.[15]

The major new element in the student body was the veterans. An immediate effect was the transformation of the student government of the junior college. In the elections held during the spring 1946 semester a predominantly male veterans' slate overwhelmingly defeated the largely female slate, representing continuance of the formerly typical student governments.[16]

Special help was extended to veterans who entered the college beginning with that semester. The Board of Educational Directors approved a policy that provided that veterans who had completed most of their high school work would be admitted on a provisional basis. As soon as they had completed high school through concurrent attendance at Rutherford Evening High School, they would be admitted permanently to the college.[17]

At the same meeting the Educational Directors also decided that six fields of study that afforded above-average placement opportunities would be stressed for veterans: salesmanship, real estate, hotel management, estimating for general contracting, and civil service. New classes in these areas began in February 1946.[18]

About 40 new students, 36 of them veterans, registered for spring semester. The greatest enrollment of the new students was in the field of engineering.[19] Increase in enrollment, even for spring semesters, became an expected phenomenon for many years.

But newly hatched high school graduates were not forgotten amid the flood of veterans. In April 1946 the Admissions Committee awarded scholarships of $200 or $100 to 25 June high school graduates with merit credentials who had been admitted to Fairleigh Dickinson.[20]

STATE APPROVAL FOR THE FIRST DEGREE

The granting of approval by the New Jersey State Board of Education for Fairleigh Dickinson Junior College to award the

15. *Ibid.*, April 4, 1946.
16. Passaic, N.J., *Herald News*, May 17, 1946.
17. North Arlington, N.J., *Leader*, December 6, 1945.
18. *Ibid.*
19. Lyndhurst, N.J., *South Bergen Eagle*, February 14, 1946.
20. Passaic, N.J., *Herald News*, April 22, 1946.

associate in arts degree for two years of work was the most significant event of the spring semester of 1946. The granting of such degrees had not previously been permitted in New Jersey.

Upon approval by the state of the principle of granting the two-year degree, Fairleigh Dickinson had immediately applied and was the first junior college in the state to be granted the right to award the new degree. Dr. Sammartino commented that the action was important for veterans who could spend no more than two years in college and could now show a terminal degree for the work they had accomplished.[21]

Somewhat later during the semester the college established an integrated program for engineering students who expected to transfer to the Newark College of Engineering. The program had been worked out by William Hazell, Jr., of NCE and Clair Black. At the end of one year's study the Fairleigh Dickinson student would have the exact equivalent in semester hours of what he would have earned by attending the Newark institution.[22]

The semester ended with the announcement on May 20, 1946, that Dean Wood was resigning effective June 30th. The first Fairleigh Dickinson dean, who had served three years, stated that he was going into rural retirement on a dairy farm he had recently bought in Sussex County.[23]

The Third Commencement was held on May 31, 1946, at the Union School, a public grammar school about six blocks from the campus. The academic procession, led by Williams and Hilleboe, formed on the campus and walked through the Rutherford streets to the school. After the customary opening ceremonies the college president presented his report and Dean Wood presented the various honor awards.[24] The commencement address was delivered by William Bradford Huie, who had been the official historian of the "Seabees" or Construction Battalions during the war.[25]

The newly approved degree of associate in arts was then conferred upon 45 candidates. Thirty-three of these were members of the current graduating class. Twelve others were alumni of 1944 and 1945 who had completed the necessary requirements for the new academic degree, which had not been in existence in New

21. Hackensack, N.J., *Bergen Evening Record*, March 2, 1946.
22. Hackensack, N.J., *Bergen Record*, May 17, 1946.
23. *Ibid.*, May 20, 1946.
24. Blanche Herman (first), Ruth Egerton (second), Barbara Bussing (third), Ruth Meyers (secretarial), Ann Powers (journalism), Roberta Voorhis (merchandising), Margaret Reid (medical arts).
25. Hackensack, N.J., *Bergen Record*, June 1, 1946.

Jersey when they had finished their studies at the junior college.[26] Thus, although no academic degrees had been conferred at the first two commencements, those graduates of the classes of 1944 and 1945 who went to the trouble to meet the requirements did become, in 1946, recipients of valid degrees.

VETERANS' VARIED NEEDS

The summer session of 1946 began on June 4 with about 500 students in attendance. Classes were held, both day and evening, and by the end of the session on September 16, the students had completed a whole semester's work. Dean Wood stated that the session was particularly designed to provide veterans with the courses they were seeking.[27]

Guy Hilleboe issued a joint statement announcing that the Rutherford Evening High School would be in synchronized session throughout the summer and that veterans who wished could take a split program at both schools, thus speeding the acquisition of their high school diplomas and also earning college credits at the same time.[28]

That Fairleigh Dickinson was quite successful in attracting veterans to its first postwar summer session was borne out in a report by Charles W. Hamilton, director of the Division of Higher Education in the State Department of Education under date of July 17, 1946. Among all New Jersey institutions only Rutgers University with 1,100 veterans exceeded the 314 enrolled at Fairleigh Dickinson that summer.[29]

The demand by the veterans for engineering courses was so strong that it became necessary to establish priorities. During the summer Dr. Sammartino made known that engineering students who wished to enter Fairleigh Dickinson for the fall would be organized into three groups. Only those would be admitted to morning classes who could present the required 16 high school units in fulfillment of the specific pre-engineering requirements. Afternoon classes would be limited to those who lacked the specific engineering prerequisites but had the 16 units. Evening classes would be open to those students who still lacked some high school units but gave evidence of the necessary mental maturity.[30]

26. Rutherford, N.J., *Republican*, May 29, 1946.
27. Lyndhurst, N.J., *South Bergen Eagle*, April 11, 1946.
28. Hoboken, N.J., *Jersey Observer*, June 12, 1946.
29. Elizabeth, N.J., *Journal*, July 18, 1946.
30. Hackensack, N.J., *Bergen Record*, July 29, 1946.

During that summer an effort was launched by a group of institutions to meet the veterans' housing needs. Fairleigh Dickinson cooperated in this project and also sought to link it with the development of a second campus in Bergen County. The project assigned the approximately 2,000 housing units that were being created at Camp Shanks from former army barracks to a consortium consisting of Columbia University, the College of Physicians and Surgeons, Teachers College, Manhattan College, Bergen Junior College, and Fairleigh Dickinson Junior College. The veterans' community thus created would have a library, churches, stores, parking areas, and other amenities. Fairleigh Dickinson was to be allotted 200 of the dwelling units.[31]

In connection with these housing units the junior college announced plans to utilize the facilities of the Nathan Hale High School for its evening classes for the veterans living at Camp Shanks Village, as the transformed army base was to be known. The high school was located in Northvale, New Jersey, very close to Camp Shanks. The town's board of education had approved evening use of the high school for the college classes. The principal of Nathan Hale High School, Fred Zimmerman, was to serve as administrator of the junior college extension.

The town of Northvale is situated in the northeasternmost corner of New Jersey's Bergen County, only two miles from Camp Shanks, just across the state line in New York State.[32] Thus, if the project succeeded, the junior college would gain an extension in close proximity to the new veterans' village and its prospective evening students. Yet the extension would still be located in the state in which Fairleigh Dickinson was accredited to hold classes.

By mid-September the Pulitzer Prize-winning columnist of the Hackensack *Bergen Record*, William A. Caldwell, noted that the effort to convert Camp Shanks to civilian use had failed. At the beginning of that month the junior college had learned that only 100 of the original 2,000 units would be ready for distribution among the six institutions in the consortium.[33]

Despite the failure to complete the housing effort, the attempt to begin the extension in Northvale was not abandoned by Fairleigh Dickinson. By late September extension classes at Nathan Hale High School did begin. Director Zimmerman stated that classes would be held on Monday, Wednesday, and Friday nights

31. Passaic, N.J., *Herald News*, August 7, 1946.
32. Hoboken, N.J., *Jersey Observer*, August 7, 1946.
33. Hackensack, N.J., *Bergen Record*, September 9, 1946.

in business administration, accounting, mathematics, and English. The extension would be open to all veterans, whether they lived at Camp Shanks Village or not.[34] Classes remained small, however, and the extension effort at Northvale was soon abandoned.

PARKING IN RUTHERFORD

Back at the Castle in Rutherford the academic year 1946–1947 began on September 16 with a central conference attended by close to 500 day students. President Sammartino told the group, more than half of whom were veterans studying under the G.I. Bill, that they needed professional training so that they would be prepared for a profession upon graduation. But he stressed that that would not be enough. They would need to learn flexibility in adjusting themselves to a rapidly changing world and hence a broader education than professional training would be needed. The new student government, now for the first time principally composed of men, was also presented to the day students at the conference.[35]

Day enrollment had more than doubled from 165 in September 1945 to 498 for September 1946. Evening enrollment had almost doubled from 483 in 1945 to 800 in 1946. The institution's total enrollment now passed the thousand mark and stood at 1,298 at the beginning of the new academic year.[36]

Bergen Junior College in Teaneck was growing even more rapidly during this period. It enrolled more than 1,400 students for its 1946–1947 academic year.[37] Bergen Junior had the advantages of being longer established (since 1933) and of being in the more centrally located Bergen town of Teaneck, just across the Hackensack River from the county seat named after the river. At this time it seemed as if Bergen Junior was well on the way to becoming the major junior college in the county.

But word that a new junior college was operating in Rutherford, New Jersey, had begun to spread. At this time it even reached the outposts of the then farflung British Empire. A letter postmarked "July 12, 1946," was received from an inhabitant of Lafiaji, Lagos, in Nigeria requesting enrollment.[38] The letter was

34. *Ibid.*, September 21, 1946.
35. *Ibid.*, September 18, 1946.
36. Hill, p. 92.
37. Hackensack, N.J., *Bergen Record*, September 20, 1946.
38. C. Akintunde Oke to Fairleigh Dickinson Junior College, July 12, 1946. The original letter of application is preserved in vol. 5 of the F.D.U. Archives, Rutherford Campus Library.

an early harbinger of the institution's many later contacts with and interest in the emerging nations of Africa.

The very great increase in enrollment in September 1946 brought with it problems with some inhabitants of Rutherford. The high school was being used for some of the college's evening classes. Every night hundreds of student cars descended upon the town streets surrounding the high school and were parked in crowded fashion everywhere. The homeowners along these streets found no place for their visitors and friends to park and were inconvenienced in a variety of ways. One difficulty that resulted from the parking problem was a claim by the chairman of the finance committee of the Rutherford Board of Education that the town was paying the cost of maintaining the high school while the college was making a profit from its evening use.[39]

At a meeting of the board the finance committee chairman stated that the high school was being used in the evening by 350 students, of whom only 70 or 80 lived in Rutherford. They were using 47 classrooms a week, he stated, and the college was paying a basic fee of fifty cents a room per night, or about $100 a month. He felt that a larger share of the maintenance cost should be borne by the college.[40]

Guy Hilleboe defended the existing arrangement by pointing out that the board two years earlier had sought to provide an evening high school for returning veterans but that so few had returned at that time that regional schools, such as that at Rutherford, had been established. Moreover, Fairleigh Dickinson was a nonprofit institution and the fee paid more than covered the board's out-of-pocket expenses.[41] Hilleboe further brought out that the rates charged by Rutherford to Fairleigh Dickinson were the same as those charged by the town of Englewood to Rutgers University for a similar arrangement.[42]

The parking problem around the high school at night was also brought up at the meeting and Hilleboe pointed to the new regulations just issued. As a result of this meeting the matter was referred by the board to its finance committee, which was charged with conducting an investigation and making a report.[43]

The upshot of the matter was that the rental fee was increased

39. Passaic, N.J., *Herald News*, November 26, 1946.
40. *Ibid.*
41. *Ibid.*
42. Rutherford, N.J., *Republican*, November 26, 1946.
43. *Ibid.*

200% to $2.00 per classroom per night retroactive to December 1.[44]

In the spring when the matter had been settled Sammartino used the occasion of a speech to the Rutherford Chamber of Commerce to present the college's case to the townspeople. He pointed out that the junior college was a nonprofit institution without an endowment and received no federal or state aid. The college president declared that Fairleigh Dickinson was an asset to business in Rutherford and helped further good public relations, since students came to it from eighty surrounding towns in the northern part of the state.[45]

This episode, which in retrospect seems like a tempest in a teapot, was nevertheless to have long-range results for the college. It was the first appearance of concern at the growth of the college by some townspeople, and it was expressed in official form. This concern led later to efforts to limit the institution's growth to dimensions some Rutherfordians believed should not be exceeded if the town were to remain what they felt it should remain—a small, quiet, residential settlement.

Some years later, in an effort to show the townspeople the economic benefits of having the college within their borders, resort was had to an unusual expedient. The seventy-four college employees of all kinds living in Rutherford received their salaries for December 1954 in the form of silver dollars.[46] Soon the town's stores, banks, and offices were flooded with the heavy solid coins. Like the burghers of old Hamelin, the Rutherfordians, wherever they turned, saw not a rat but a silver dollar. A man making a dollar purchase with a ten-dollar bill might receive nine of the large metal discs in change. Trouser pockets had holes worn in them. Women's handbags became very heavy. Bus drivers had no slots for them. Faculty children were given their weekly allowances in this form and promptly flooded local candy store proprietors with the coins. No one in those days seems to have realized that the silver coins, due to inflation of the paper currency, would some day be worth considerably more than their face value. At any rate, whatever the reaction of individual Rutherfordians, the flood of silver had made its point.

By focusing on the college's key outward necessities for growth —classrooms and parking facilities—this early controversy set the stage for permanent limitations on the growth of its Ruther-

44. Passaic, N.J., *Herald News*, December 10, 1946.
45. Rutherford, N.J., *Republican*, March 27, 1947.
46. Rutherford, N.J., *South Bergen News*, December 2, 1954.

ford site and compelled the college to give more definite thought to acquiring more facilities for such use elsewhere. Thus the single most important factor for the institution's future development, physically and also academically—its multi-campus nature —was partly predetermined by the problems at Rutherford.

ENTER ATHLETICS AND RECOGNITION OF ACHIEVEMENT

A new field entered by the junior college during the academic year 1946–1947 was that of intercollegiate athletic competition. During the fall semester A. Charles Ingraham was appointed to hold the post of director of athletics along with his position as director of the evening session. Ingraham had earned four letters as an athlete at Rutherford High School before going on to Tufts, where he played on the basketball team. After earning the degree of master of education at Tufts he served in the army. Ingraham planned to play teams from the other junior colleges in the area.

At the same time George Melankovich was appointed coach of the newly formed FDJC basketball team. Melankovich, or "Mel," had played on Notre Dame's basketball team and had coached for three years at St. Michael's High School in Newark.[47]

Athletic Director Ingraham also proceeded to the formation of a baseball team. Forty-two men, most of them with high school experience, answered the call. The first game away was scheduled with Jersey City Junior College for April 12, 1947.[48]

For the spring semester of 1947 the college registered increases of 100 new day and 170 new evening students over the number enrolled for the previous semester. The pattern of continuing increases, even for the spring semesters, that had first appeared in 1946, continued for the next year.[49]

At the Fourth Commencement, on the evening of May 29, 1947, 106 students received the associate-in-arts degree in ceremonies at the college. The Class of 1947 was the first to be about equally divided between the sexes.

The commencement address was delivered by Glenn Gardiner, president of the New Jersey State Chamber of Commerce, who stressed the interrelationships between the community, the college, and industry.

47. Rutherford, N.J., *Republican*, October 31, 1946.
48. *Ibid.*, April 3, 1947.
49. Hackensack, N.J., *Bergen Evening Record*, February 6, 1947.

But the prevalent mood at this commencement was one of recognition for students, faculty, and others who had been closely associated with the college.

Clair Black announced the customary academic awards for the outstanding graduates. The number of curricular awards had been increased from four to six, reflecting the growth of various new curricula.[50]

In his commencement remarks President Sammartino pointed out that the college, established four days before Pearl Harbor, had weathered the war and immediate postwar years and was graduating its first class with the normal proportion of men and women.

In recognition of the help that they had given during the emergency of coping with rapidly expanding enrollments, resolutions of appreciation were presented to 28 of the college faculty.[51]

The mood of recognition continued with the presentation of a testimonial scroll to the chairman of the Board of Trustees. Edward Williams had just accepted the presidency of the Lambert Pharmacal Company of St. Louis, Missouri. Williams had announced that he would remain on the college board and would spend a part of each month in the New York-New Jersey area, since he would also remain a director of Becton, Dickinson and Company and of the Rutherford National Bank.[52] However, his absence for longer periods could be expected. Thus the frequent contact between the college president and the board chairman, which had been so useful in developing the college, might not be possible on the same scale.

Williams was further honored at a dinner at the Alexander Hamilton Hotel in Paterson a few days after commencement. On that occasion a resolution adopted by the Board of Educational

---

50. Audrey E. Greiman (first honors), Rose Anne Blondek (second honors), Victor W. Sytzke (third honors), Walter Annaheim (engineering), Thomas S. Leitch (business administration), Irene Bogle (secretarial), Sally Bergen (secretarial), Fred J. Gilbert (merchandising), Hazel J. Zimmerman (medical arts).

51. As noted above, the faculty numbered 40 full-time members at this time. The faculty members who received resolutions of appreciation at the Fourth Commencement were: Merritt W. Bidwell, Clair W. Black, Ara Boyan, Michael A. Costello, Arthur Drucker, Harold Feldman, Raphael Fenili, George J. Geier, Virginia R. Graver, Paul J. Hagar, William Higgins, Kathleen C. Hillers, Francis Hurley, Allen C. Ingraham, William T. Kirscher, Elbert M. Ludlam, Arthur D. Markle, Allan W. Messler, Catherine Milos, William A. Monprode, Jr., Joseph R. Morrow, M. K. M. Murphy, Ruth W. Ricci, Daniel Roselle, Irene Roth, Ellsworth Tompkins, Austin Travers, Harold R. Wertheimer.

52. Passaic, N.J., *Herald News*, May 28, 1947.

Directors and the faculty was presented to Williams. Luckily Williams finally, after a company merger, returned permanently to the New Jersey area.[53]

The summer session of 1947 was again conducted as a full semester of 16 weeks, from June 2 to September 19. This arrangement proved particularly useful for veterans who had begun their studies with the summer session of the previous year. By attending both summer sessions as well as the intervening academic year, these veterans were able to transfer to four-year colleges as juniors in September of 1947. They had completed two years of college work in fourteen months.

A year had passed since the retirement of Dean Wood and no replacement had as yet been appointed. In order to help with the increasing administrative work, George Bainbridge was appointed assistant to the president.[54]

FIRST PUBLIC FUND-RAISING

The institution's last academic year as a junior college began on September 15, 1947, with an enrollment of 1,102 (632 day and 470 evening students). Day enrollment had increased by 134 over the previous year, but there was a drop of 196 students in the total college enrollment because of a decrease of 330 students in the evening.[55] This was due to the fact that the first postwar rush of veterans began to abate in 1947. This decrease below the pre-

53. Rutherford, N.J., *Republican*, May 28, 1947. The resolution read as follows:

"The Board of Educational Directors and the Faculty of Fairleigh Dickinson Junior College extend to Edward T. T. Williams their deep appreciation and their thanks. For five years, through the difficulties of the war period and the still greater problems of sudden peace, Mr. Williams has given unstintingly of his time and energy to the college. The institution could not have achieved its present position without his thought and guidance. In a democracy, the excellence of an educational institution must rest primarily on the good judgment of its lay board. Fairleigh Dickinson Junior College has indeed been fortunate in having as the chairman of its Board of Trustees a man of such high calibre and sound principles." *Ibid.*

54. *Ibid.*, June 12, 1947. Bainbridge had held the post of Director of Instruction of the Rutherford school system. He earned masters' degrees at Teachers College, Columbia University, and New York University. Bainbridge held the post of administrative assistant to the president until 1950. In later years he taught English and education and served as director of the Reading and Study Institute in East Rutherford. When this program was moved to the Wayne Extension in 1965, Bainbridge went with it. That same year he was appointed director of the Division of Adult Education and in 1967 was named director of the Wayne Extension.

55. Hill, p. 92.

vious year's total enrollment remained unique during the remainder of the institution's first quarter of a century.

Among the new faculty appointed with this year were Dr. Leon Canfield as chairman of the social science department and William G. Robinson as instructor in the business administration department.[56] Ellsworth Tompkins, who had been appointed to the faculty the previous year, received a leave of absence to accept a post as an assistant in the United States Office of Education in Washington, D.C.[57]

At the beginning of the new academic year the trustees adopted a budget of $306,191. The estimated income was as follows: day session, $225,000; evening session, $85,000.[58]

Along with the budget Edward T. T. Williams announced that another $100,000 not included in the budget would be spent to build a gymnasium. In connection with this project a campaign would be launched to raise $350,000, the remaining quarter of a million to be applied to the college endowment fund. Construction of the new gymnasium would make unnecessary the renting of public school facilities in Rutherford, Williams stated, and added:

> The Board of Trustees feels that in its five years of existence the college has demonstrated the need and effectiveness of the type of education it offers. . . . The development we are undertaking is limited to the minimum needs of the institution. The modest gymnasium proposed is essential to an adequate program of health and physical education. Endowment is an imperative step toward assuring the security of the institution and the continued maintenance of high standards of work.[59]

Albert F. Metz of Rutherford, treasurer of the Okonite Company in Passaic, and a member of the Board of Industrial Advisers, was chosen as general chairman of the college's first public fund-raising campaign. Judge Guy L. Fake was named honorary chairman and Edward T. T. Williams associate chairman.[60]

The appeal was officially launched on November 25, 1947, with a dinner in Becton Hall attended by the committee's 125 campaign

56. Leon H. Canfield (A.B., Syracuse Univ.; Ph.D., Columbia Univ.) had written works and articles on American history and had taught at the College of the City of New York. He remained with Fairleigh Dickinson as chairman of the social science department until his retirement in 1956.

William G. Robinson (B.S., Rider College; M.A., Teachers College, Columbia Univ., C.P.A.) was assistant to the dean of the College of Business Administration until 1971, having been appointed as such in 1964. Thereafter he was associate dean of the college for the Rutherford Campus.

57. Paterson, N.J., *Call*, August 27, 1947.
58. Passaic, N.J., *Herald News*, September 5, 1947.
59. Hoboken, N.J., *Jersey Observer*, September 18, 1947.
60. Passaic, N.J., *Herald News*, September 26, 1947.

workers from 18 participating communities, each of which had a quota to raise. Fannie Hurst, the well-known novelist, spoke at the dinner. She expressed amazement at the incredible growth of the college in five years and said she first knew of it when it was "just a gleam" in the eyes of the Sammartinos. She continued:

> Education is most vitally needed to prepare for the coming new world. When you can coordinate industry and education as is done at Fairleigh Dickinson, you are understanding the age in which you live.[61]

At the opening dinner the announcement was made that more than a third of the sum, $142,000, had already been received.[62]

When opening the local Rutherford drive, Judge Fake looked at the institution's impact and described it as

> one of the most important developments in this part of the state in my time. It is not difficult to foresee its development into a great four year college.[63]

The first fund-raising campaign revealed that the new college had won many friends and sponsors in government and industry during its brief life. The effort succeeded in mobilizing this good will for the purposes of institutional expansion and provided experience for further attempts at public fund-raising in the future.

Another means of winning good will and of relating the college faculty more closely to students and their home environment was the practice of faculty visits to students' homes. This policy, which encouraged the faculty to visit the parents and to discuss with them their offspring's work and personal development, continued until 1957. Through it the faculty became aware of the psychological and socioeconomic backgrounds of the students they were teaching in the classroom.

LINK WITH A SPECIFIC INDUSTRY — VARIETY OF ACTIVITIES

The spring semester of 1948 began with the added enrollment of 260 new students. The decline that had occurred in the preceding fall was, therefore, more than made good. The largest increase took place in the business administration programs.[64]

61. *Ibid.*, November 26, 1947.
62. *Ibid.*
63. Paterson, N.J., *Call*, November 7, 1947.
64. Rutherford, N.J., *Republican*, January 29, 1948.

Another link with local industry was now forged, in this case with a particular industry. At Sammartino's suggestion a committee of executives was formed, all of them active in the area's textile industry.[65] The committee chairman was Marinus C. Galanti who, as principal of Lodi High School, had been one of the original founding members of the Board of Educational Directors. After leaving his high school post Galanti had become assistant to the president of the United Piece Dye Works in Lodi, one of the major textile processing plants in the county.[66] Under Galanti's energetic leadership the committee proceeded to the formation of a syllabus that included studies in raw materials, textile chemistry, printing and dyeing, finishing, and personnel management.[67]

In order to bring this new opportunity of preparing for a specific industry to the attention of high school and college students, a conference on opportunities in the textile industry was held at the college in April. It was attended by 250 students, and the new textile syllabus, which had just received approval from the New Jersey State Department of Education, was presented to the group by Galanti; by M. M. Boring, manager of the technical personnel division of the General Electric Company; and by Herbert R. Mauersberger, president of the Textile Book Publishers Company in New York City.[68]

Galanti, reflecting his open, active style and optimistic emphasis in matters of both life and education, told the conference:

> Opportunity in industry is greater than in many professions. It is important that the person going to college be guided into an area in which he can breathe with ease and freedom.[69]

This effort to work closely with one specific industry in the area was later repeated with others. The involvement with the

---

65. Its members were as follows: Marinus C. Galanti, assistant to the president, United Piece Dye Works, Lodi, chairman; Dr. Werner von Bergen, head of research, Forstmann Woolen Co., Passaic; Charles Minoff, chief technician, Martex Print and Dye Works, Clifton; Nathan C. Caress, The Waldrich Co., Delawanna; Richard M. Poor, Standard Bleachery and Printing Co., Carlton Hill; Ludwig Schulze, Botany Mills, Passaic; and F. S. Richardson, The Waldrich Co.

66. At Fairleigh Dickinson Galanti (Ph.B., Brown Univ.; M.A., Columbia Univ.; LL.D., Fairleigh Dickinson Univ.) later held the following positions: Director, 1958–1960, and Dean, 1960–1961, of the Evening Session; Dean of the Teaneck Campus, 1961–1969; and, after 1969, Director of Wroxton College and Dean Emeritus of the Teaneck Campus.

67. Passaic, N.J., *Herald News*, March 4, 1948.

68. Lodi, N.J., *Messenger*, April 29, 1948.

69. *Ibid.*

local textile industry was also to bring the college an unexpected benefit.

The tempo and variety of activities at Fairleigh Dickinson now began to reach dimensions that were maintained for many years. In an article in the local Rutherford newspaper Sammartino pointed out that during one week in April 1948 the following events took place at the college:

> 1) the textile conference attended by 250; 2) dinner conference led by an FDJC instructor, to launch an experimental program for improving freshman reading ability; 3) a Saturday night dance for 150 evening students; 4) the chief of laboratories at Bergen Pines Hospital at the weekly career conference spoke to 100 students interested in medical arts; 5) Robert Tristram Coffin, Maine poet, addressed the English classes; 6) the vice-president of Lord and Taylor in New York spoke to business students; 7) an exhibit of historical fabrics from the Scalamandre Museum of Textiles in New York City was being held at the college.[70]

The momentum generated by new programs and many activities, and by the increasing enrollments and the growth of the faculty and of the institution's facilities, had created a situation, by the spring of 1948, that made Judge Fake's prophecy of impending four-year status for the junior college seem overdue.

FOUR-YEAR STATUS AND TWO-YEAR ACCREDITATION

On March 19, 1948, the New Jersey State Board of Education informed Dr. Sammartino that the application of Fairleigh Dickinson Junior College to offer courses for and to grant the degrees of bachelor of arts and bachelor of science had been approved. The request to drop the word "Junior" from the institution's name had also been approved.[71]

A week-end conference of the faculty was immediately called at which the matter was debated and the necessary new curricula and extensions of current curricula into the third and fourth years were worked out. As at every stage in the growth of the institution, some faculty members were filled with doubt and apprehension. They thought that the nearby four-year state colleges would limit Fairleigh Dickinson enrollments, and that the lack of dormitories would do the same. Yet the majority were

---

70. Dr. Peter Sammartino, "Noted Authorities in Many Fields Speak at College Here During Week," Rutherford, N.J., *Republican*, April 29, 1948.
71. Passaic, N.J., *Herald News*, March 20, 1948.

intrigued with the idea of attending the birth of a four-year college and wanted it for the students, who had exerted much pressure, as well as for themselves.[72]

And so the faculty finally voted in favor of the step. Many of the elective courses required by the expansion of the curricula were already being given in the evening. In many cases all that was required was to add some others. By the next week the new study plans were complete and had been approved by the faculty.

In general, the transition to four-year status was facile. The students who would compose the first junior or third-year class were already in attendance, finishing their second year. Most of the faculty were already qualified to teach the two upper years. The administrative organization and physical plant were at hand and in operation.[73]

During its six years of existence the junior college had been accepted for membership by the Junior College Council of the Middle Atlantic States, the American Association of Junior Colleges, the New Jersey Association of Junior Colleges, and the New Jersey Association of Colleges and Universities.[74] But state accreditation and membership in associations of colleges and universities did not make up for the lack, as yet, of the supreme accolade of accreditation by the regional accrediting agency, the Middle States Association of Colleges and Secondary Schools. Failure to obtain such accreditation had effectively prevented the growth of many colleges and, for a large number, meant their ultimate demise. Obtaining Middle States accreditation was almost a matter of academic life or death.

Fairleigh Dickinson had actively pursued its candidacy for accreditation. In March 1948 the Middle States Association sent an evaluating committee to inspect the junior college.[75] Two months later, on May 5, 1948, Sammartino was informed by telephone that the association had accredited the first two years of college work at what was still officially Fairleigh Dickinson Junior College. Middle States accreditation of the two upper years, which

72. Kathleen Hillers, "My Early Days at Fairleigh Dickinson," typewritten MS, p. 2.

73. Interview with Dr. Peter Sammartino, March 19, 1971.

74. *Bulletin of Fairleigh Dickinson Junior College, 1947–1948* (Rutherford: Fairleigh Dickinson Junior College, 1947), p. 1.

75. The members of this committee were: Dr. Paul Shafer, president of Packard Collegiate Institute, Chairman; Prof. Robert Patrick, Pennsylvania State University; Emily Lambert, Barnard College; Dr. Walter Daniels, Harvard University; Dean Margaret Hight, Centenary Junior College; Howard Knag, Queens College.

had just been approved by the New Jersey State Board of Education, would require another visit by a Middle States team after the necessary number of additional years of successful operation as a four-year college had passed.[76]

On the day after receiving word of Middle States accreditation as a junior college, a special chapel service of thanksgiving was held in Grace Episcopal Church.[77] The ceremony was brief. After an invocation, the singing of the national anthem and college hymn, and a bible reading, President Sammartino spoke. He said, in part:

> News of this accreditation which is the most significant step in the professional maturation of the college, practically coincides with its Founders' Day of May 5, 1942. . . . While graduates of the college have been given full credit for their work at Fairleigh Dickinson in over 35 colleges and universities this accreditation facilitates the process of inter-college evaluation.[78]

There were to be many more Middle States inspections and accreditations as the institution expanded its curricula, and the number of its campuses.[79] Yet, in a way, the very first accreditation was the most crucial. Bergen Junior College in Teaneck had never succeeded in being accredited by the Middle States Association and this was a lack it could not overcome in attracting faculty and students. If Fairleigh Dickinson Junior College had failed to receive this first accreditation, its later growth would have been seriously hampered and the institution might possibly have come to an early end.

The simplicity and brevity of the thanksgiving ceremony underlined the moment's importance. The experiment of founding a junior college arising from and closely linked with the high schools of the local communities had succeeded and had now been recognized by accreditation by the key regional association. But the needs and pressures for rapid growth had become ever stronger during the first three postwar years. They were met successfully. There was a brief pause, as if taking breath, and the institution began to move forward into its next stage of development.

---

76. Passaic, N.J., *Herald News*, May 6, 1948.
77. *Chapel Program. To Give Thanks for Middle States Accreditation*, mimeographed program, University Archives, Rutherford Campus Library.
78. Hoboken, N.J., *Jersey Observer*, May 7, 1948.
79. The various accreditation reports are considered as a body in a later chapter.

The Fifth Commencement on Thursday evening, June 3, 1948, was inevitably held under the spell of these significant acts of recognition. In the Rutherford High School auditorium 335 graduates received degrees of associate-in-arts for two years of work. Clair W. Black presented the usual honor awards.[80]

The commencement speaker was Dr. Paul M. Limbert, president of Springfield College. Limbert was Sammartino's former fellow associate at New College who had met with Sammartino and two others in the Scaramelli home during the dark days of the spring of 1939, when New College was going out of existence, to plan a practicum college in then-vacant Iviswold. Now, nine years later, himself a college president, Limbert spoke at the college that had grown in the Castle under the leadership of his erstwhile colleague, whom he knew well.

Limbert told the audience:

> It is our duty as citizens in a democracy not to be overwhelmed by our circumstances but to take hold at some point with courage and faith.
>
> It is the genius of democracy that no one, however humble in talent or experience, is expected to be a follower only. Nor is anyone, no matter how capable, expected to be a leader always.[81]

Three weeks after commencement, during this period of institutional transition, Colonel Fairleigh S. Dickinson died at the age of eighty-four.[82] His personal interest in the new college and his continued support of it, both in moral and material terms, had helped to bring the institution into being. But, like Moses, although the colonel knew of the plans and approval for moving into the Promised Land of a four-year college, he did not live to see it himself.

Fairleigh S. Dickinson, Jr., now stepped into his inheritance and was strongly to maintain the tradition of personal concern

80. Sylvia Mitbick (first honors), Anthony P. Alessandrini (second honors), Kalman A. Epstein (third honors), David Heebner (engineering), John J. Doremus (business administration), Phyllis M. Blondin (merchandising), Jean J. Andrisani and Elaine R. Cohen (secretarial), Ruth M. Wiessner (medical arts), Raphael M. Fronzaglia (journalism), Rose M. Skerpac (liberal arts).

81. Hoboken, N.J., *Jersey Observer*, June 4, 1948.

82. "Col. Fairleigh S. Dickinson," *obituary, The New York Times,* June 24, 1948, p. 25.

and support for the institution that his father had helped so significantly to establish.[83]

The three war years had been a time of relatively quiet growth, mostly in intramural terms, for what was essentially a junior college for girls in one building. The first three postwar years saw the rapid expansion of the small junior college in many directions at once: faculty, student body, curricula, fund-raising, buildings, accreditation—a swift and, at times, potentially explosive development culminating with state approval for becoming a four-year college.

83. Fairleigh S. Dickinson, Jr., was born in Rutherford in 1919. He attended Williams College, receiving the A.B., and served in the United States Coast Guard during the Second World War, emerging as a lieutenant commander. In 1948 he became chairman of the board of Becton, Dickinson and Company and chairman of the board of directors of the National Community Bank (formerly Rutherford National Bank). He served on the Board of Trustees of Fairleigh Dickinson University since 1948, becoming its chairman in 1968. From 1967 until 1971 Dickinson was a member of the New Jersey Senate.

6

The College, 1948-1953

With the fall semester of 1948, the institution began to face the
test of growing into its new four-year role. Could it preserve the
pioneering spirit that had created and built the small wartime
junior college and then the rapidly expanding postwar junior
college? Would the impending further expansion of curricula and
upgrading of the faculty permit that spirit to continue? Could
the needed additional physical facilities be obtained swiftly enough
to house the growing numbers? Would the institution remain
financially viable? Could Middle States accreditation for the upper
two years be won without much delay and resulting harm to the
institution's academic reputation? Would the administration and
supporting services remain adequate in meeting these increasingly
demanding challenges as they arose?

The institution's first academic year as a four-year college began
on September 20, 1948, with classes for 710 day and 600 evening
students.[1] The total enrollment of 1,310 was the largest in the
brief history of the college. Evening enrollment was on the way to
recovery from the previous year's decline, but remained smaller
than day enrollment.

All of the new third-year class, numbering 110, had completed
their first two years of college at Fairleigh Dickinson. Forty-seven
of the June graduating class had decided to transfer to the Newark
College of Engineering, for which they had specifically prepared,

---

1. Walter Hill, *Fairleigh Dickinson University: Some Aspects of Its
Growth* (Rutherford, N.J.: Fairleigh Dickinson College, 1961), p. 92.

and several others had chosen various other colleges and universities to complete their last two years. But the majority of the June graduating class decided to finish at what had been, for them, Fairleigh Dickinson Junior College.[2]

To serve as an evaluating mechanism for effective transition, an Educational Policies Committee of outstanding educators was formed.[3] The committee's members were: Dr. Ralph Burns, Dartmouth College, Chairman; Prof. Kenneth J. Conant, Harvard University; Prof. Lennox Grey and Dr. Paul Mort, Teachers College, Columbia University; Dr. Paul J. Salvatore, Brooklyn College; Clifford Lindholm, President, Falstrom Company, Passaic; and Dr. Ellsworth Tompkins, U. S. Office of Education. Sammartino announced that after one year the committee would evaluate the results of the new upper-level program and propose needed changes. He stated:

> College programs should not be statistics or mere conglomerations of separate courses. Students should have a chance to develop the many different sides of their personality and should be trained to assume their various roles of workers, citizens and heads of families.[4]

In order to attain these goals, Sammartino stated, the new third-year students would be involved in a five-point program:

1. At least 300 hours of work experience in their field of major interest, the work experience to be evaluated by faculty and reports to be submitted by employers;

2. Travel experience to part of the United States or abroad;

3. Participation in civic and political life, with students of voting age expected to vote in primaries and regular elections;

4. At least one summer of farm work;

5. Some time contributed to social welfare or public health agencies.[5]

A notable new addition to the faculty was Arthur P. Coleman, who had recently resigned from the faculty of Columbia University in protest against the acceptance by that institution of a grant from the Communist government of Poland to establish a chair of Polish literature. Dr. Coleman was appointed to teach Polish at Fairleigh Dickinson.[6] There is a large Polish population in

---

2. Hackensack, N.J., *Bergen Record*, September 17, 1948.
3. Rutherford, N.J., *Republican*, July 29, 1948.
4. Paterson, N.J., *Call*, July 29, 1948.
5. *Ibid.*
6. New York, N.Y., *Sun*, July 22, 1948. Coleman had earned his Ph.D. at Columbia University and had risen to the rank of assistant professor on its faculty. He remained at Fairleigh Dickinson College for one year.

nearby Passaic. He announced plans for developing a center of Polish studies, but he did not remain at his new post long enough to achieve this goal on any larger scale, since he was chosen president of Alliance College in Illinois the next year.[7]

Another new addition to the faculty on a part-time basis was Eugene O'Neill, Jr., son of the famous playwright. He was appointed to teach courses in literature.[8]

These men brought a breath of the great world of international politics and classical literature into the faculty, which by now numbered forty-four full-time members, eight special lecturers, and a larger number of part-time members. The full-time faculty included fourteen doctors (Ph.D.—10; J.S.D.—1; Ed.D.—2; M.D.—1). All the others held master's degrees.[9]

Chairmen were listed for five departments: business administration, engineering, English, secretarial studies, and social sciences.[10] Growth in departmental structure was taking place. Yet, the other aspects of operations were still on a minimal level. The clerical office staff totaled five. There were four persons on the library staff and a total of eleven supplied services of various kinds.[11]

Weekly meetings of the faculty continued to be held and there was practically daily contact between the members of the small administrative staff and the still relatively small faculty. However, for purposes of integrating the various curricula and courses established by the Board of Educational Directors and the Board of Advisors, a more formal representative body, a Faculty Council

---

7. Rutherford, N.J., *Republican*, May 19, 1949.

8. New York, N.Y., *Post*, November 3, 1948. O'Neill had earned the Ph.D. at Yale and had taught at Yale, Princeton, and the New School. O'Neill remained with Fairleigh Dickinson for only a short time, until his tragic and sudden death the next year. Interview with Loyd Haberly, March 31, 1971.

9. *Bulletin of Fairleigh Dickinson College, 1948–1949* (Rutherford, N.J.: Fairleigh Dickinson College, 1948), pp. 3-4.

10. *Ibid.* The chairmen were, respectively: Harold Feldman (business administration); Clair W. Black (engineering); Irene S. Roth (English); Dorothy M. Reeves (secretarial); and Leon H. Canfield (social science).

Harold Feldman (B.S., Rider College; M.A., Teachers College, Columbia; Ed.D., New York University) began to teach at Fairleigh Dickinson in 1946 and held the following positions: Chairman, Dept. of Business Administration, 1948-1957; Acting Dean, School of Business Administration, 1957-1958; Dean, School of Business Administration, 1958-1960; Dean, College of Business Administration, 1960-1966; Vice-President for Financial Affairs, 1966-1970.

Irene Roth held the A.B. from Barnard College and the M.A. from New York University. She began to teach at Fairleigh Dickinson as an English instructor in 1946. She held the following positions: Chairman, English Dept., 1947-1950; Administrative Assistant to the President, 1950-1955.

11. *Ibid.*, p. 4.

consisting of eight members, including the President, began its work at this time. It consisted of George Bainbridge, Clair W. Black, Leon H. Canfield, Kathleen C. Hillers, Dorothy Reeves, Irene S. Roth, and Peter Sammartino. The formation of this first Faculty Council was an important early step in putting faculty participation in college governance on an official, structured basis. It helped to set the stage and to create experience for the much larger organs created at a later period when the faculty had greatly increased in numbers.[12]

The weekly faculty meetings were busy affairs, energetically led by the college president. Discussion ranged over many of the institution's operations but principally centered on the students and the courses that should be added and those which could be dispensed with as the college grew into its newly acquired four-year status.[13]

The ties with local industry, already formalized through the Board of Advisers and the Textile Institute, were constantly growing. It became clear that a special administrator for these matters was needed and on December 22, 1948, Warren L. Duncan was appointed industrial relations coordinator at Fairleigh Dickinson College.[14] Duncan had a long career in the area's industrial and commercial communities. He was well and favorably known to the leading men and knew them. In a steady and effective manner, Duncan began to develop the already existing ties for the benefit of the college, its students, and local industry. He was instrumental in launching a "Training for Supervisors" program, which consisted of a series of evening institutes for local industrial and business executives and supervisors. On successive Monday evenings, more than 100 of the executives attended special programs at the college featuring such subjects as "industrial psychology," "industrial economics," and public speaking.[15]

Duncan also expanded the institution's placement services begun by Dean Wood. Every year, placement conferences were held on campus at which the graduating seniors and the personnel representatives of a growing number of concerns met for interviews.[16] Many Fairleigh Dickinson graduates were employed by local

---

12. *Ibid.*, p. 8.
13. Kathleen Hillers, "My Early Days at Fairleigh Dickinson" (typewritten MS), p. 2.
14. Paterson, N.J.. *Call*, December 23, 1949.
15. New York, N.Y., *Trends*, October, 1949.
16. Duncan was named Director of Placement in 1951, in addition to his position as Industrial Coordinator. He held both positions until his death in 1963.

companies and some succeeded in attaining executive positions in later years.

Another aspect of the institution's rapid maturation process was the establishment of the Fairleigh Dickinson College Press in December of 1948. This enterprise, at first, remained limited in scope to the publication of textbooks, manuals, and monographs written by members of the faculty.[17] The work was contracted out to local printers. One of the first products of the FDC Press was a specialized manual to be used in connection with the Contemporary Society course.[18] The press continued to grow and, in later years, became the third largest university press in the country. It soon became a self-supporting operation and caused no expense for the college.

Another new relationship inaugurated during the institution's first year as a four-year college was participation in the well-known radio and television programs conducted by Dorothy Gordon. Her program was called "Youth Forum" at this time, its name being changed later to "Youth Wants to Know." On April 27, 1949, Dr. Sammartino and six students joined Miss Gordon in considering the question "Does Democracy Offer the Best Hope for Mankind?"[19] This and succeeding programs on radio and television during the next two decades brought the institution's name to much wider circles than had known it before. Miss Gordon's lively, alert, at times dramatic handling of her programs made them occasions not easily forgotten by participants or audiences.

On April Fool's Day of 1949, the college held its first debutante cotillion on the St. Regis Roof in New York City. The twenty-five co-eds, each accompanied by two escorts, made their debuts before guests of honor, trustees, administrators, faculty and relatives, and friends.[20] These affairs were designed to give young ladies of more modest means a chance, if they wished, to make their debuts in society in the manner of the daughters of the more affluent. The cotillions were repeated annually for more than a decade, generally in the Grand Ballroom of the Hotel Plaza in New York City, and they became the most formal social function held by the college. Generally about a dozen United Nations delegates attended and each girl had the chance to dance with one of the diplomats.

The growing student body made necessary the formation of

17. Hackensack, N.J., *Bergen Record*, December 27, 1948.
18. Leon Canfield and Daniel Roselle, *Contemporary Society* (Rutherford, N.J.: Fairleigh Dickinson College Press, 1949).
19. New York, N.Y., *Times*, April 28, 1949.
20. New York, N.Y., *World-Telegram*, March 12, 1949.

effective and representative ways of dealing with student offenses. The student council, in April 1949, established a weekly court consisting of three student judges that was to pass upon "antisocial acts." The council drew up a code of punishments for offenses ranging from smoking out-of-bounds, which carried loss of lounge privileges for one week, to cheating on examinations, which called for immediate expulsion. The student judges wore black robes and were advised by the college attorney on procedure.[21]

As the spring semester of 1949 drew to its close, Loyd Haberly made his first appearance on the campus.[22] Haberly, besides being an English scholar, also cultivated archaeology, glass blowing, and carpentry, and was an expert on the lore of the American Indian. He maintained a printing press in his home on which he printed more than twenty books. Haberly's first public appearance in Rutherford occurred as a speaker to the Rotary Club. In his speech, he characterized the American Indian as "the first Rotarian." In his understated, whimsical style, Haberly informed his Rotary audience that

> Indians were tall men with long heads and great gum chewers. They loved to make speeches. They loved to get together in large gatherings —and on such occasions they loved to eat . . . up to 12 pounds of meat at a single sitting.[23]

With Haberly a representative of the reflective, humanistic style of life and learning entered the faculty and the ranks of the department chairmen. His type of background—Rhodes scholar, Harvard, poetry (he was also a poet)—supplied a necessary emphasis if the institution was to grow in the humanities. Haberly's long tenure as Chairman of the English department and, later, Dean of the College of Liberal Arts, put him in key positions to foster these concerns. Yet he also had a practical bent as carpenter and printer, which helped him appreciate the more practical approaches to life and education.

21. Hackensack, N.J., *Bergen Record*, April 7, 1949.
22. Loyd Haberly had received his A.B. from Reed College and, as a Rhodes Scholar, had earned the M.A. at Oxford. He had subsequently taught English at Harvard, Washington University, and the University of Massachusetts. At Fairleigh Dickinson, he held the following posts: Chairman of the English department, 1949–1959; Dean, College of Arts and Science, 1959–1960; Dean, Maxwell Becton College of Liberal Arts, 1960–1966; Dean, Wroxton College, 1966–1969. Haberly received the LL.D. from Fairleigh Dickinson University in 1955 and was awarded the title "Dean Emeritus of the College of Liberal Arts" and "Distinguished Professor of English" in 1966.
23. Rutherford, N.J., *Republican*, May 12, 1949.

Haberly succeeded Irene Roth as Chairman of the English department. He found a small department, practically like a family, which ate its meals together; he taught its large classes with enthusiasm, stressing especially the writing of clear, effective English.[24]

The Sixth Commencement was held on Thursday evening, June 2, 1949, in the auditorium of Rutherford High School. The graduates, numbering 207, received the associate-in-arts degree. This was the last commencement at which the two-year degree only was awarded. The commencement address was delivered by the Reverend James Keller, the Catholic priest who had founded and led the Christopher Movement.[25]

Judge Guy L. Fake was given a special award because

his contribution to the College has been in his emphasis on the growth of American democratic institutions and ideals.[26]

The summer session of 1949 introduced, as a new feature, a condensed interim session in the social sciences from August 22 to September 16. By attending four evenings a week, the enterprising student could earn four credits in as many weeks.[27]

The summer format that had by now become customary was a first interim session of four weeks in late May and early June, followed by an eight-week session from mid-June to mid-August, and finishing with another interim four-week session from mid-August to mid-September.

With the summer session of 1950, a new format was introduced, which continued without change for the remainder of the institution's first quarter of a century. Two sessions of six weeks each were held, one from the beginning of June until mid-July and the other from mid-July until the end of August. Classes were conducted until noon and in the evening. This pattern best served the convenience and comfort of both faculty and students during the hot summer months. A student could take either session and

24. Interview with Loyd Haberly, March 31, 1971.
25. Rutherford, N.J., *Republican*, June 9, 1949.
26. *Ibid.*, June 2, 1949. Others receiving awards were: Joseph Brunetti, president, Columbia Protektosite Co.; Edward DeMiceli, principal, Wood-Ridge High School; Mrs. Fannie Hurst; Charles Mintzer, principal, Fairlawn High School; G. Willard Phillips, treasurer, Phillips Oil Co.; Joseph Sveda, principal, Hasbrouck Heights High School; Leo Pollak, president, Pollak Engineering and Manufacturing Co.; Oscar Schwidetsky, research director, Becton, Dickinson and Co., Newark, N.J. *Herald-News*, June 11, 1949.
27. Lyndhurst, N.J., *Commercial Leader and South Bergen Review*, August 18, 1949.

still have six weeks free or, if he was particularly ambitious, could attend both sessions. Enrollments at the summer sessions grew steadily throughout the whole period covered by this history.

The need for more buildings continued to exert its pressure. On September 21, 1949, Sammartino dug the first spadeful of earth for the new gymnasium, for which funds had been raised by the college's first public fund-raising campaign.[28] Hilleboe, Black, and John Bruno, the president of the student council, were among those who spoke to the crowd of about 100.

Final cost of the gymnasium was estimated at $301,065.[29] It was to be built in contemporary functional style, and to house two sections. On the lower level, the gymnasium had a cafeteria and the faculty dining room, designed by the famous showman Billy Rose. On the upper level was the gymnasium proper, which included a basketball court and a stage and property rooms. Using folding bleachers and portable chairs, the gymnasium could be transformed into an auditorium seating 2,000.[30] The building would give more space to meet many long-felt needs of the constantly increasing faculty and student bodies. The cornerstone was set on May 28, 1950, by Sandra Rothman, the seven-year-old daughter of Matthew Rothman, a Navy veteran attending FDC.[31] Twenty-three years later Sandra graduated from the Madison Campus of her father's *alma mater*. The gymnasium was the first of the many buildings built by the institution in the functional, contemporary style.

A notable new appointment was that of Dr. Bogdan Raditsa. With his secondary education from the Classical Gymnasium in his native Split (Spalato), and the Ph.D. from the University of Rome, and with many years experience in the Yugoslav diplomatic corps, and as a newspaperman in the Balkans and the United States, he was well prepared for his assignment of teaching European history with special reference to the Balkans.[32] During the next two decades, Raditsa became well known for the forthright manner in which he spoke up at faculty meetings and for his verve and scope as a lecturer. At many a crucial moment, Raditsa's remarks, delivered in an intonation and style that always retained the traces of his native Croatian, broke the tension by directness

28. Hoboken, N.J., *Jersey Observer*, September 22, 1949.
29. Hackensack, N.J., *Bergen Record*, September 22, 1949.
30. Hill, pp. 52–53.
31. Hackensack, N.J., *Bergen Record*, May 31, 1950.
32. Passaic, N.J., *Herald-News*, January 6, 1950. Raditsa rose through the ranks from instructor to professor and attained emeritus status in 1971.

The first graduating class, June 1, 1944.

Garry Galanti closes his eyes while picking a chance at a meeting of the Board of Educational Directors.

Dance of the debutantes with their escorts at 1957 Debutante Cotillion in the Grand Ballroom of the Hotel Plaza, New York City.

The Rutherford Campus as it appeared in 1967. The Round Building marks the southwest corner. The Castle is in the center.

or humor. He left his audiences aroused and alternately outraged at him or others, or dying of laughter with him. His wife, Nina, was the daughter of the famous Italian historian Guglielmo Ferrero. She later taught Italian and history at the college.

An eminent scholar from the Balkans thus introduced an international note into the faculty of an institution that from the beginning had had the strong intention of cultivating this emphasis.

Two incidents during the year reflected the growth of what was known, in a simpler era, as "school spirit."

In February, the Board of Trustees officially adopted the coat of arms that had been drawn up by Loyd Haberly in collaboration with Dr. Kenneth Conant of Harvard University, who was a member of the Educational Policy Committee.[33] The first version of the coat of arms showed a simplified sketch of the Castle in white centered on a shield in bright red. As further campuses were added, the coat of arms was halved and then redesigned. In all the transformations, the institution's motto, *Fortiter et Suaviter*, chosen by Peter Sammartino, was placed in a supporting scroll beneath the coat of arms.[34] When Wroxton College was acquired, it received its own coat of arms.

Yet school spirit may, on occasion, mean something quite different from what is usually understood by the term. On March 24, 1950, forty students ensconced themselves in the Castle overnight. This was not a sit-in but an effort to prove or disprove the old legend that on that night each year the spirit of Mrs. David Ivison walked abroad Iviswold in sorrowful commemoration of her husband's death years before her own. At midnight, the lights un-

33. Paterson, N.J., *Call*, February 11, 1950.
34. When the Teaneck Campus was acquired (1954), the coat of arms was divided into an upper half, consisting of the white castle in a red field, and a lower half, consisting of a white swan on a blue field, symbolizing the swans kept in a pond at the new campus as well as the Hackensack River along which the campus is located. The acquisition of the Madison Campus in 1957 led to the creation of the still-current coat: a blue shield divided in the middle by a broad crenellated red band (for Rutherford) and with a white swan (for Teaneck) below, and three white roses (for Florham-Madison, "The Rose City") above the central band. A separate coat of arms was created in 1964, also by Haberly, for Wroxton College in England: a blue shield with a narrow crenellated gold border and containing a gold lion passant with two white fleurs-de-lis above the lion and one below, surrounded by a wide green border with a white rose between two white swans above, a white rose on the left and right sides and a white swan below the central blue shield. The central shield represents the Pope and North families, which long leased Wroxton, and the crenellation, swans, and roses represent the Fairleigh Dickinson campuses in the United States.

accountably went out, there were assorted shrieks from various parts of the Castle, and white and blue lights flashed through the building. Some students claimed they had heard a voice calling "David." As a result of these disquieting events, pandemonium broke out and the students fled out of the Castle in confusion.[35]

No adequate explanation of the real nature of these mysterious events has ever been supplied by any of the students involved.

In later years, the Castle has been used only for offices for the University's highest administrators. These have not noticed any unusual shrieks or other noises on March 24, although the day is only nine days after the date when annual contracts are distributed to the faculty.

Shortly before commencement, the newly established Textile Committee and Institute brought results in the form of a gift of $37,500 by the Edgar and Emily Hesslein Fund for the construction of a classroom building to be used for classes in the newly developed textile curriculum. The new building was planned to cost about $150,000 and would contain four classrooms and an office on the first floor, and a demonstration room, laboratory, and preparation room on the second floor.[36]

Students were interviewed to form a special pilot group to pursue the new textile curriculum in the building, and Edward T. T. Williams stated:

> I consider this the most important curricular development at the college during the last five years. We are situated in the most concentrated and most varied textile area in the country and it is only right that there be a collegiate textile training school within the State. The new building will give us the needed facilities for effecting a good course.[37]

On May 1, 1951, Sammartino and George Walker, Treasurer of the Hesslein Fund, broke ground for the new building. The college president officially thanked Mr. Walker for support by the Fund. Hilleboe also spoke and called the new building "a monument to community cooperation."[38]

The Seventh Commencement was held on June 1, 1950, in the not-quite-finished new gymnasium. Associate degrees for two years of study were awarded to 159 students. The first four-year class received a total of 159 bachelor's degrees; of these one was

35. Passaic, N.J., *Herald-News*, March 25, 1950. See Peter Sammartino, *Of Castles and Colleges*, pp. 145–46, for an explanation of these phenomena.
36. Paterson, N.J., *News*, May 4, 1950.
37. *Ibid.*
38. Hoboken, N.J., *Jersey Observer*, May 1, 1951.

awarded *summa cum laude* (Anthony P. Alessandrini), and two *magna cum laude* (Dorothy R. Egerton and John J. Propper).[39] The approval given two years earlier by the State had been vindicated and a four-year class successfully graduated.

Seven faculty members received citations in recognition of work for the college "above and beyond the call of duty."[40]

President Sammartino outlined the year's advances in courses and facilities and reported that the college's endowment was approximately $450,000.[41]

Dr. Allen B. DuMont, president of DuMont Laboratories, Inc., and a leader in the newly developing television industry, delivered the commencement address. He emphasized that television was bringing unprecedented possibilities in education, entertainment, advertising, and the diffusion of knowledge and news, and urged the graduates to become aware of and to make use of the opportunities offered by the new industry.[42]

The surprise of the ceremony was provided when 28 wives of male graduates were honored in recognition of their help to their husbands in earning their degrees. Each received an engraved certificate, signed by Dr. Sammartino and reading

> Fairleigh Dickinson College, in grateful appreciation for her help, sacrifices and inspiration while her husband was completing his college education presents this certificate to——[43]

Each graduate escorted his wife to the platform, kissed her after she had received her certificate, and escorted her back to her seat.

To a more "realistic" generation of college people such actions may seem bathetic, but who shall weigh the benefit such acts of recognition may have had for some of the marriages involved? Similarly, little handwritten notes of congratulations, condolence, or support sent by Sammartino to faculty members and others in the college community at critical or important moments in their lives, even when the institution and its faculty had become much larger, helped to maintain a mood of human concern.

The academic year 1950–1951 saw the introduction of a new curriculum, which was ultimately destined to give rise to the future University's first professional school. For more than a year,

---

39. *Ibid.*, June 2, 1950.
40. *Ibid.* Julius Luck, Sidney Kronish, Howard R. Mirkin, Louise M. Palladino, William G. Robinson, Leonard J. Smith, and John E. Vaughan.
41. *Ibid.*
42. *Ibid.*
43. *Ibid.*

negotiations had been under way with the State Department of Education and the State Board of Examiners and Registration in Dentistry for the establishment of a curriculum for the training of dental hygienists. Details were worked out by a Dental Hygienists Advisory Board.[44] The new curriculum was to consist of a two-year program including anatomy and physiology, bacteriology, dental histology, and pathology, oral prophylaxis, clinical practices, pharmacology, mental hygiene, dietetics and nutrition, and dental practice for hygienists. Other courses required of the future hygienists would include English, literature, contemporary society, economics, and psychology. In accordance with State Law, only girls could be admitted to the curriculum. Those completing the two-year course of studies successfully would receive an associate-in-arts and be eligible to take the state examinations.

The first director of the new School of Oral Hygiene was Dr. Roy D. Ribble.[45] The school was renamed the School of Dental Hygiene in 1951 and Dr. Ribble given the title of dean.

Another step into the field of the medical arts was taken during the same semester with the establishment of a training program for nurses to be carried on jointly by Beth Israel Hospital in Newark and Fairleigh Dickinson College. The plan had been proposed by Samuel Teiger, who was a member of the college's Board of Advisors and also a trustee of the hospital.[46]

The following arrangement was considered and approved by the Board of Educational Directors. During the first year of college work, the student spent one day a week at the hospital. Thereafter, the nurse candidate entered the hospital for two years of clinical training. During this period she received 64 college credits for her clinical work. In this way she would have a total of 99

44. Boonton, N.J., *Times-Bulletin*, June 13, 1950. The original Dental Hygienists Advisory Board was nominated by the New Jersey Dental Society and the Bergen County Dental Society and included: Dr. Murray Eltens of Rutherford; Dr. Robert Fear, Dr. Luther Heydan, Dr. Ray Morrow, and Dr. Walter Mossmann of Hackensack; Dr. S. M. Lyons of Summit; Dr. K. C. Pruden of Paterson; Dr. E. J. H. Schneider of Maplewood; Dr. E. C. Stillwell, Sr., of Glen Ridge; Dr. E. H. Wescott of Atlantic City; and Dr. Ray D. Ribble of Mountain Lakes. The representatives of the State Examiners Board included Dr. Walter A. Wilson, Secretary of the Board and, in later years, dean of the School of Dentistry of Fairleigh Dickinson University.

45. Mountain Lakes, N.J., *News*, August 10, 1950. Dr. Ribble graduated from the College of Dentistry of the University of Pennsylvania in 1912. He had been assistant editor of the *New York Journal of Dentistry* and was a Fellow in the International College of Dentistry, and Secretary of the New York Academy of Dentistry. Dr. Ribble was dean of the School of Dental Hygiene from 1951 to 1954. He retired with the title of Dean Emeritus of the School of Dental Hygiene.

46. Hackensack, N.J., *Star-Telegram*, May 25, 1957.

credits at the end of her third year and would receive certification as a registered nurse. At this point, she could either return to Fairleigh Dickinson for one year as a day student and complete the work for a bachelor's degree or could do so on a part-time basis in the evening. In order to encourage girls to enter the program, the college offered five $200 scholarships for girls in the uppermost tenth of their high school graduating class, and five $100 scholarships for those in the upper quarter.[47]

President Sammartino commented on this new program:

> This is a great step forward in the campaign to encourage more candidates for the nursing profession. There are always many girls in high schools who do not know whether to select college or nursing. This program combines both. . . . It is also important because many administrative positions require a college degree and those students who have a strong inclination for promotion can now go ahead.[48]

For 1950–1951, the Board of Trustees adopted a budget totaling $445,370. A total of $25,000 was set aside for the new Hesslein Textile Building, which was estimated to cost $150,000. For new equipment $29,000 was set aside and an additional $15,000 for new equipment for the new curriculum for dental hygienists. Faculty salaries were expected to total $228,500, and administrative and clerical salaries another $47,120. The sum of $18,000 was allocated for the library. To meet these expenditures, the Trustees expected to receive $382,500 income from approximately 900 day students, paying a tuition rate of $450, and an additional $63,000 from 700 evening students, for a total income of $445,500.[49]

If income and expenditures remained at the projected levels, the college would avoid any loss for operating expenses. One problem in this equation was the fact that no money had been set aside for the interior finishing of the new Hesslein building but only for completion of the outward structure.

Another step in preparing for the new academic year was the appointment of a dean of the college, a position that had been vacant since the retirement of Dean Wood four years earlier. The choice fell upon Ray A. Miller, who began his duties in the summer of 1950.[50]

---

47. *Ibid.*
48. *Ibid.*
49. Passaic-Clifton, N.J., *Herald-News*, August 5, 1950.
50. Dean Miller (B.S., M.A., and Ph.D. in education, New York University) held the position of dean from 1950 to 1957, when he was named administrative vice-president. The next year he accepted the presidency of York Junior College (later York College) in Pennsylvania.

Dean Miller proved to be a real asset for the burgeoning new four-year college. Ceaselessly active, intelligent, with a charming, outgoing personality, he paid close attention to every administrative detail without losing the broader view. He made it a point to get to know the strong and weak points of individual faculty members through personal acquaintance. When necessary, Miller was able to enforce discipline effectively upon faculty or students without resentment on either side.

The new academic year began on September 18, 1950, with 978 students registered for day and 1,623 for evening classes. These figures represented increases of 5% for day and 20% for evening registrants over the previous year. The total enrollment of 2,198 showed an average increase of 14% over 1949.[51]

Although strenuous efforts brought some improvement, the lack of adequate parking areas in Rutherford continued as a basic problem and, as enrollments rose, exercised an ever-greater pressure for the acquisition of other facilities elsewhere to relieve the situation.

One immediate result of the problem was a recommendation by the Board of Educational Directors to limit the college's day enrollment to 1,000 students. The grounds advanced were that excess of that number would decrease the services and guidance available to the individual student.[52] Yet such a recommendation, if it had been implemented, would have disrupted the momentum in Rutherford that led to the eventual development of the multicampus institution. For many years some members of the original Rutherford faculty felt that that would have been a good idea.

The international interests of the college were advanced during the fall semester by visits to the campus and speeches by Dr. Ali Sastroamidjojo, the Indonesian Ambassador,[53] and by Mrs. Perle Mesta, American Minister to Luxembourg.[54] Both diplomats were awarded citations. Dr. Sastroamidjojo's contact with the college was among the first of many by him and by a large number of other diplomats associated with the United Nations. Dr. Sastroamidjojo later lectured to a group of Fairleigh Dickinson students when they visited Indonesia.

During the spring semester, General Carlos Romulo, Philippine delegate to the United Nations, spoke at the college on the aims of

51. Hill, p. 92.
52. Rutherford, N.J., *Republican and American*, November 30, 1950.
53. Hackensack, N.J., *Bergen Record*, November 11, 1950.
54. New York, N.Y., *Herald-Tribune*, November 21, 1950.

the world organization, and was awarded a citation.[55] He. too, was to return many times to Fairleigh Dickinson and to become an enthusiastic friend of the institution.[56]

These visits by persons in the field of international affairs were climaxed by a visit, in May, by Alexander Kerensky, which had been arranged by Dr. Raditsa. The first Russian premier after the March 1917 Revolution, who was living in New York City, delivered no prepared speech but, in a lively, personal way, answered questions posed by the students. Kerensky was convinced that free election in Russia would return only five percent of the Communist candidates.[57]

The ability to bring in speakers of this type for a one-day program was another benefit conferred on the college by its proximity to New York City.

On the day after New Year 1951, Maxwell W. Becton died at the age of 83 in his home on Ridge Road in Rutherford.[58] His unfailing, calm, and resolute support of the college had been a great source of strength. Despite his age, he had made it a practice to attend many of the significant college ceremonies. He was the first of the original incorporators and trustees to pass from the scene. As a final act of generosity, he left his beautiful home on Ridge Road as a residence for the college president.

Maxwell Becton was succeeded as a trustee by his son, Henry, who continued the paternal tradition of concerned and faithful support of Fairleigh Dickinson.[59]

In connection with registration for the 1951 spring semester, a survey was held of the personal backgrounds of the 940 day students. Forty-four percent were residents of Bergen County, while substantial groups came from the neighboring counties of Passaic and Essex. Only 34 students came from outside the state, and nine of these were from foreign countries, either in Latin America or Europe.

Those who listed religious affiliations included 352 Protestants, 343 Catholics, 94 Jews, and 18 Eastern Orthodox. Among the

55. Hackensack, N.J., *Bergen Record*, February 8, 1951.
56. Rutherford, N.J., *Republican and American*, February 15, 1951.
57. Paterson, N.J., *Call*, May 3, 1951.
58. New York, N.Y., *World-Telegram and The Sun*, January 3, 1951.
59. Henry P. Becton (B.S., Yale) has been with Becton, Dickinson and Company since 1937. He later became chairman of its Executive Committee and a director. During the Second World War he served with the U.S. Army. He is a vice-president and a director of the National Community Bank in Rutherford, and chairman of the New Jersey Television Broadcasting Corporation.

Protestants, first place was held by Presbyterians, while Lutherans and Episcopalians were tied for second place. There were no day students under 17 years and only twelve over 31 years of age. More than a quarter were enrolled in the business management curriculum. Pre-professional curricula enrolled 156 of the approximately one thousand day students, while engineering included 107, accounting 92, merchandising 66, advertising 66, medical arts 37, and secretarial studies and journalism had 30 each.[60]

Practically every category—geographical origin, religious affiliation, age grouping, curricular choice—reflected the fact that the student body was composed overwhelmingly of the sons and daughters of the solid, general, middle- and working-class population of northeastern New Jersey. In the absence of dormitories and of efforts to recruit students more widely, and in view of the curricular arrangements, this result was a foregone conclusion.

The college's cultural life received another new facet during the spring of 1951 through the presentation in the gymnasium of a shortened version of the opera *Carmen,* by Miss Estelle Liebling of the Metropolitan Opera Company, who was also a famous teacher of piano and voice. Miss Liebling brought six of her students to the campus to sing *Carmen,* and the program was a great success. This program inaugurated another long-lasting relationship for the college that benefited all concerned, since Miss Liebling returned frequently, year after year, to present a variety of musical programs.[61] The presentation of several operas became a regular feature of the college year.

The Eighth Commencement was held on Tuesday evening, June 5, 1951, in the gymnasium auditorium. A total of 302 graduates were granted degrees, 120 becoming bachelors of arts or of science, and 182 receiving associate-of-arts degrees.[62]

An audience of more than 2,000 heard the commencement speaker, Roy T. Hurley, president of the Curtiss-Wright Corporation, who had just received the college's third honorary degree, ask for the cooperation of industry and government in solving the nation's problems.[63]

President Sammartino, in his remarks, stressed the establishment of the school of dental hygiene, of the hospital nursing pro-

60. Hackensack, N.J., *Bergen Record,* March 7, 1951.
61. *Ibid.,* March 8, 1951.
62. Union City, N.J., *Hudson Dispatch,* June 2, 1951.
63. Passaic-Clifton, N.J., *Herald-News,* June 6, 1951.

gram, and the construction of the new Hesslein building. He also reported that $35,000 had been obtained for a new library and that the endowment fund had reached half a million dollars.[64]

The academic procession was led, for the first time, by a pipe-and-drum band of six dressed as Highlanders and playing a marching tune on their picturesque and (to some) inspiring instruments. At the close of commencement, the pipers played "Auld Lang Syne" while all the graduates joined hands and sang.[65] This old Scotch practice became traditional at commencements and at other ceremonies at which the pipers appeared.

In order to carry out the symbolism of the Castle, a corps of spear-bearing student "Knights," dressed in chain mail over which they wore a tabard with the college's coat of arms, was formed. In the manner of the Swiss Guards escorting the Pope and Cardinals, the "Knights" escorted guests, trustees, and administrators at college ceremonies. Later, academic processions were also led by the college mace, donated by Mrs. Leo Pollack. It had been made in Sheffield, England, during the eighteenth century. The honorary doctors wore red robes and caps.

The whole ensemble of Highlanders, "Knights," red-gowned honorary doctors, and the administration and faculty in their, more or less, colorful academic gowns, depending on their degrees and institutions, made a picturesque spectacle indeed.

Inevitably, some of the more sober-minded and practical criticized so much display. But, for many who participated and who watched, it satisfied the hunger for color, ceremony, and tradition that are so noticeable by their absence in our great industrial and commercial society oriented principally to practical goals and built on republican simplicities.

The summer session of 1951 recorded the largest summer enrollment in the history of the institution. A total of 927 students registered for the two six-week sessions, during which they could earn a whole semester's credit. Of this number, 613 were veterans and 314 civilians. An important component of the summer enrollments was comprised of students who lived in the local area but who went away to college for the academic year. When home for the summer, students at such institutions as Notre Dame, Vermont, Bucknell, Ohio Wesleyan, Syracuse, and Bowdoin were perfectly satisfied to attend Fairleigh Dickinson's summer ses-

---

64. *Ibid.*
65. *Ibid.*

sions.[66] Constantly growing summer enrollments were of great financial help to the institution.[67]

What did the Fairleigh Dickinson students do who did not attend summer classes? A survey conducted by Industrial Coordinator Warren L. Duncan for the summer of 1951 showed that 176 female and 644 male students had found employment. The males earned from $150 to $1,500 for three months' work, averaging $450. The employed co-eds earned from $100 to $600 for an average of $275. The students did every conceivable kind of work, including that of assembly line worker, salesman, life guard, laboratory technician, social worker, truck driver, and waitress. Many of the students who had neither studied nor worked during the summer had not been completely idle. Students had traveled in eighteen foreign countries in Europe, the Middle and Far East, and Latin America for an aggregate total of 619,560 miles covered.[68]

Nor had the faculty been idle. Besides those who taught the summer sessions, others had traveled widely. Dr. and Mrs. Sammartino traveled in England, France, Switzerland, Luxembourg, and Italy. In Luxembourg, they had been guests of Perle Mesta in the American Legation. In his regular report to the Trustees, the college president emphasized:

> More than ever our philosophy at Fairleigh Dickinson of preparing for useful living must be emphasized. We should embark on a policy of getting our students and teachers to visit other parts of the world, and we should arrange for foreign students to attend American colleges. . . . We should continue to develop our plan of bringing in speakers from other countries to explain the point of view of other people.[69]

In September, a special conference was held at which Sammartino, Sidney Kronish, Dr. Philip C. Newman, and John E. Vaughan reported on their summer travels.[70] Kronish had visited western

---

66. Paterson, N.J., *News*, July 9, 1951.

67. This summer session marked the completion of three years of service by Julius O. Luck as director of the evening session. Luck holds an A.B. in physics from New York University, and an M.A. from Columbia University. He joined the faculty of Fairleigh Dickinson College in 1948. He continued to serve as director of the summer session until 1954. From 1971 to 1972 he served as provost of the Rutherford Campus. Luck was succeeded as director of the evening session by William Fewkes, who served in the post until 1954. Fewkes held an A.B. and an Ll.B. from the University of Buffalo, and an M.A. from Columbia University.

68. Paterson, N.J., *News*, October 5, 1951.

69. Hackensack, N.J., *Bergen Record*, August 29, 1951.

70. Hackensack, N.J., *Star-Telegram*, September 14, 1951.

Europe. Newman led a student group that studied the comparative economic situations in western Europe and Yugoslavia. Vaughan had visited his native Wales and reported on the development of British industry and the socialization program.[71]

This varied and busy summer was followed by another academic year characterized by further growth, also in facilities. A report on the library revealed that 8,000 volumes had been added during the past year, so that for 1951–52 a total of 20,000 volumes were available.[72]

Before fall classes began, Dean Miller released the results of a survey of veteran enrollments at the institution since the G.I. Bill had gone into effect. A total of 4,533 veterans had registered since the end of the war. Of that number, 1,304 were still active and would attend the fall semester. There had been a continuous increase in the number of veterans attending and no drop was expected for the coming year.

Dean Miller commented as follows upon the report:

> The veteran brought to the college an older personality, a more mature individual who had experience, military and civilian, that could not be matched by students whom we looked upon as traditional college entrants.
> With this more mature person came a more serious purpose, a clearer direction for his efforts. This seriousness of purpose has had a decided influence on the younger students and has tended to spur them to greater application to their course of studies.[73]

This analysis goes a long way in explaining the silence of the student generation of the "Silent Fifties."

Classes began on September 17, 1951, for a total of 2,583 students (960 day, 1,623 evening). Day enrollment declined less than two percent, while evening enrollment rose by one-third from the previous year's figures.[74] The college was becoming much more

---

71. *Ibid.* John E. Vaughan (B.S., State Teachers College, Bloomsburg; M.S., Bucknell University; Ed.D. in business, New York University) joined the faculty in 1947 and held the following positions: acting vice-president, 1964–1967; vice-president for development, 1967–1970; vice-president for governmental affairs since 1970.
Sidney Kronish (B.S., M.A., New York Univ.; Ph.D., New School for Social Research) joined the faculty in 1949 and rose to full professor before his departure in 1963. From 1956 until 1961 he was chairman of the Social Science Department.

72. Paterson, N.J., *News*, August 6, 1951. Since a separate history of the Fairleigh Dickinson libraries is being prepared by Althea C. Herald, for many years librarian at the Teaneck Campus, and also associated with the library of FDJC, this aspect of the institution's growth is not dealt with extensively in the present work.

73. Hackensack, N.J., *Bergen Record*, August 23, 1951.

74. Hill, p. 92.

of a part-time evening institution as far as the number of students was concerned.

The students found greatly improved laboratory facilities, which had been installed during the summer at a cost of $38,000. As Clair W. Black explained:

> The increasing demand for training in physics and chemistry and new advances in the physical sciences, particularly nuclear fission, made all the new equipment necessary. We are keeping pace with the new discoveries and facilities for measuring in these fields.[75]

The students also were made aware that a definite limit was being set to the development of Fairleigh Dickinson athletic teams for intercollegiate competition beyond the existing ones in basketball, baseball, and fencing. Late in September, Sammartino announced that the faculty, the Board of Educational Directors, and the Parents' Council had all agreed that the college should not have any football, and he explained why:

> First of all, football is expensive for all except a few of the extremely large universities, and any money spent for football has to come from other educational budgets. Secondly, very few of our students have enough time for football, especially since a great many of them are on the work-study plan.
>
> While we have teams in all other sports, participation in team activities is definitely secondary to the student's work in his particular career field. Every team member must have a definite career objective and is dropped immediately if he falls down in his work.
>
> The emphasis in athletics at Fairleigh Dickinson College is on two things: 1) intramural activities which have lifetime value. We also try to encourage those activities which have a social-recreational possibility, such as square dancing, social dancing, and bowling.
>
> We want our faculty to accept this point of view. Last year the faculty volley ball team participated in the intramurals the same as any other group. (Strangely enough, they won first place!) This summer about twelve members of the faculty learned how to play golf and are ready to give student golfers a tussle.
>
> People often ask us, "Why don't you try to get the crowds out to the basketball games?" It seems hard for many laymen to understand that a college is not in the entertainment field. We're not interested in putting on shows. And it would be foolish for any parent or any high school graduate to choose a college on the basis of "teams."
>
> We encourage students to take part in sports at college, feeling

---

75. Passaic-Clifton, N.J., *Herald-News*, August 30, 1951. New chemistry equipment included a colorimeter, polarimeter, hydrogen ion meter, specific gravity meter, vapor density meter, and molecular weight apparatus. New equipment for physics included a constant deviation spectrometer, a cloud chamber, Geiger counter, radiation sources, and potentiometers. Biology equipment additions consisted of a PH meter, an electric wash bath, new microscopes, embedding ovens, a microtome, a basal metabolism machine, and two boxes of human bones!

that a college should prepare a student for life on the broadest scale and not in terms of facts and figures. Athletic activities contribute toward the student's health and his ability to get along well with others. But it is our policy never to let team competition become the student's ultimate reason for being here.[76]

The statement clearly stated what remained essentially the institution's principles and policy, specifically with regard to football, and areas of inter- and intramural athletics in general. Only during the last years covered by this history was football introduced, and then in the form of "club football."

As if to compensate for the lack of a football team, the basketball team, under the able coaching of Richard Holub, consisting of thirteen returning veterans players and four promising new recruits, began a highly successful season. For the first time, Fairleigh Dickinson entered the New Jersey Intercollegiate Athletic Conference.[77] The basketball team also played the teams of such institutions as New York University, Pace College, and Yeshiva University outside the State.[78]

Beginning December 3, 1951, the tenth anniversary of the seminal meeting at the Elks Club in Rutherford was observed with a number of affairs. At a convocation in Grace Church, Edward T. T. Williams and Fairleigh Dickinson, Jr., spoke for the trustees, Edward DiMiceli for the Educational Directors, Dr. Metz for the Industrial Advisors, Dr. Messler for the faculty, and Eugene Sidor for the Student Council. Sammartino was given a surprise citation. A dinner followed the convocation.[79]

Some days later, Sammartino was given the Townsend Harris Medal "for distinguished contribution in education as founder and president of Fairleigh Dickinson College" by the Alumni Association of his *alma mater*, The College of the City of New York.[80]

Later during this month of anniversary celebrations, a dinner for more than 600 Rutherfordians was held at the college. Judge Guy F. Fake, the principal speaker, stressed the value of Fairleigh Dickinson for Rutherford. Loyd Haberly announced the formation of the Rutherford Town and Gown Society, which would include faculty members and residents of the borough.

76. Hackensack, N.J., *Star-Telegram*, September 23, 1951.
77. Passaic-Clifton, N.J., *Herald-News*, November 14, 1951. Holub (B.A., Long Island University; M.A., Columbia University) was first appointed to teach English in 1949. He served as coach of the basketball team during the remainder of the period covered by this work.
78. Paterson, N.J., *News*, November 2, 1951.
79. Passaic-Clifton, N.J., *Herald-News*, December 8, 1951.
80. Paterson, N.J., *News*, December 7, 1951.

Members of the society would be invited to all the cultural affairs at the college and would be able to use the college facilities.[81]

These celebrations were given a special luster by the information, received during the last week of November, that the Middle States Association of Colleges and Secondary Schools had granted accreditation as a four-year institution to Fairleigh Dickinson College.

The inspection committee had taken the institution's objectives and fundamental philosophy, its organization and administration, and the quality of its faculty, finances, library, and other facilities into account. Fairleigh Dickinson was the first four-year institution accredited by the Middle States Association in thirteen years, and it received its four-year accreditation in a shorter time than any other New Jersey college.

The Ninth Commencement was held on June 3, 1952, in the gymnasium auditorium, before an audience of 2,000. A total of 320 graduates received degrees; 194 of these became bachelors of arts or science, while the remaining 126 were awarded the associates-in-arts degree. Clair Black awarded curricular honors to 32, and Dean Miller administered the graduate pledge to the graduating class.

Four honorary degrees were conferred and the recipients of two of these gave this commencement a strongly political aspect, which was widely noticed in the press. Honorary doctor of laws degrees were awarded to the Governor of Nebraska, Val Peterson; to the Governor of New Jersey, Alfred E. Driscoll; to Dr. John H. Bosshart, retiring Commissioner of Education of the State of New Jersey; and to Joseph Brunetti, president of Columbia Protektosite Company, who was a leading member of the Textile Institute.[82]

In his annual commencement report, President Sammartino pointed to full Middle States accreditation as a four-year institution, and inclusion in a group of five colleges selected for study by President Truman's Advisory Committee on Education.[83]

A fifth honorary doctorate was conferred upon Mrs. Perle Mesta on June 24, 1952, at a ceremony at the State Department in Washington. The United States Ambassador to Luxembourg had been voted "Woman of the Year" by the Fairleigh Dickinson student body and was to have received the degree at commencement but

81. Passaic-Clifton, N.J., *Herald-News*, December 15, 1951.
82. Hackensack, N.J., *Bergen Record*, June 4, 1952.
83. Paterson, N.J., *Call*, June 4, 1952.

was not able to be present. Sammartino, accompanied by trustees and faculty, therefore traveled to the national capital to award the degree. The ceremony was widely noted in the press, particularly in Washington.[84]

Another event that was becoming traditional was the annual alumni dinner-dance on the Saturday following commencement. On June 7, 1952, a large attendance at the affair, held in the basement of the gymnasium set up as a night club, gave proof that alumni were increasing in number and dedication to their *alma mater*. After dinner, at a short business meeting, the officers of the Alumni Association were nominated and elected. After brief humorous talks by outgoing officers and the college president and dean, the audience of alumni, administrators, and faculty spent the remainder of the evening dancing.[85]

Those who, through the years, attended the many affairs of this and of other types held by the institution became aware that a spirit of involvement, community and, when appropriate, of downright good humor and enjoyment prevailed. It is difficult to put such an intangible thing as spirit or mood into words, but those who experienced it on so many varied occasions will testify that the institutional motto, *Fortiter et Suaviter*, "Bravely and pleasurably," can best describe what happened. More was being built than merely brick-and-mortar and student enrollments.

Yet, educational institutions depend upon their enrollments in a basic way, and those for the summer sessions of 1952 were encouraging. A total of 349 enrolled for the interim four-week session from mid-May to mid-June.[86] The first six-week session was attended by 732 students, of whom 293 were veterans. The day division supplied 163 of the total, while more than 70 colleges were represented among the 102 students, home for the summer, who were taking courses during that season at Fairleigh Dickinson.[87] Thus, practically two-thirds of the summer students were regular Fairleigh Dickinson College evening students during the academic year. As time passed, these proportions in summer sessions among day students, evening students, and transfer students gradually changed until the last category ultimately accounted for forty percent. Since summer enrollments kept increasing year after year, this meant that transfer students increasingly found

84. Boston, Mass., *Christian Science Monitor*, June 24, 1952; Washington, D.C., *Star*, June 24, 1952; Washington, D.C., *Post*, June 24, 1952.
85. Hawthorne, N.J., *Press*, June 5, 1952.
86. Passaic-Clifton, N.J., *Herald-News*, June 12, 1952.
87. Hackensack, N.J., *Bergen Record*, July 1, 1952.

Fairleigh Dickinson a good institution at which to study while home for the summer. Although there was no effort to proselytize, some of the summer transfer students invariably decided to remain at Fairleigh Dickinson in the fall.

New appointments for the academic year 1952–1953 included Willy Ley, Dr. George E. Nelson, and Mrs. Olive Foster. Willy Ley, who was originally a paleontologist, had been one of the founders of the German Rocket Society in 1927, and Dr. Wernher von Braun's first tutor in rocket research. When Hitler came to power, Dr. Ley came to the United States, where he was active in rocket research and wrote a number of books on rockets and space travel.[88] At Fairleigh Dickinson, Ley served mostly on a part-time basis due to many commitments. However, at many seminars and programs, his presentations on rockets and their possibilities for space travel, years before this became a fact, were fascinating and even incredible. The present author well remembers wondering at the time, after a personal conversation with Dr. Ley during which he prophesied that men would reach the moon in a few years, whether the scientist was really *compos mentis*. Time proved him a true prophet, although Dr. Ley did not live long enough to see his prophecy turn into fact.[89]

Dr. George E. Nelson, who was appointed as librarian in August, brought with him great experience in this area. Through the years, he guided the growth of the library at Rutherford and then, as new campuses were acquired, the further growth of what had been the library of Bergen Junior College at Teaneck, and the establishment of a new library at the Madison campus.[90]

Mrs. Newton Foster was appointed director of public relations in July and continued in this post for the remainder of the period

88. Paterson, N.J., *News*, July 1, 1952. Ley had studied at Berlin University and held the Sc.D. from Adelphi College. He was appointed as professor of science at Fairleigh Dickinson and held this appointment until his death in 1961.

89. Pittsburgh, Pa., *Post-Gazette*, December 30, 1957. In 1957, at a science conference held at Buhl Planetarium, Pittsburgh, Pennsylvania, Dr. Ley set the following time table for placing the first man on the moon: 1963— first manned satellite to circle the earth; 1967–1975—landing of a man on the moon. Actually, Neil A. Armstrong became the first man to set foot on the moon on July 20, 1969.

90. George F. Nelson (B.S., M.S., College of the City of New York; Library Certificate, McGill University; Ph.D., Columbia University) served as librarian from 1952 until 1954. Upon the acquisition of the Teaneck Campus in 1954, he was given the title "Director of Libraries." He supervised all libraries, including that on the Madison campus, until his retirement in 1960. A year before, Nelson's title was changed to "Dean of Libraries." No new all-university officer for this area was appointed after Nelson's retirement.

The Teaneck-Hackensack Campus by the nineteen seventies. The large new Dental School building is on the Hackensack side of the river. The Zorach mural is visible on the Library on the Teaneck side. Part of the huge parking lot can be seen to the right. The campus extends down to the Anderson Street bridge.

Day of Dedication of the Teaneck Campus, Sunday, October 3, 1954. Williams and Sammartino are immediately behind the Knights. In the file following Dr. Sammartino: Dean Ray Miller, Dean Louis A. Rice, Mr. Scaramelli, Mr. Blauvelt. The faculty in the front row are, from left to right: Dr. Samuel A. Pleasants, Dr. Heinz F. Mackensen, Prof. Pauline Kaiser, Prof. Fred Meystre; in the second row: Dr. Eileen Costello Balassi, Dr. Gerhard Schmidt, unknown, Prof. Curtis Thomas.

At the dedication of Williams Hall at the Teaneck Campus in 1955: Guy Hilleboe, Louis J. Scaramelli, Edward T. T. Williams, Peter Sammartino.

The William Zorach sculpture on the Weiner Library at the Teaneck Campus.

covered by this work. She had first become associated with the college on a part-time basis as an English instructor a year before her appointment as public relations director. Sammartino instructed her to try to get at least one item of major interest about the college inserted into the public information media each week. In those days, this meant chiefly the newspapers. In attempting to reach this goal, Mrs. Foster sought to diffuse news items that would add dignity and prestige to a young institution.[91]

Classes began on September 17, 1952, for a student body of 2,635 (1,040 day, 1,595 evening).[92] This was an overall increase of only two percent over the previous year, since day enrollment had grown by nine percent, while evening enrollment had declined by two percent.

For the first time, there was a group of students on campus living in a dormitory owned and operated by the college. Since the war, the number of students boarding in private homes in Rutherford had been constantly increasing. Most of these students were men. Meanwhile, requests for college-controlled dormitory space for girls had been growing.

The dormitories of Fairleigh Dickinson began as modestly as everything else. In the spring of 1952, the college acquired a former private home adjoining the campus. The hotel and restaurant management students planned the interior of the former home as a cooperative dormitory for twelve girls. Each girl was made responsible for her own room and had one housekeeping chore for the whole house each week. The girls got their own breakfasts and, in teams of two, took turns preparing dinner once a week. The director of the evening session, Professor William Fewkes, and his wife occupied an apartment on the first floor and acted as mentors for the girls.[93]

One wonders whether the small group of twelve girls ever realized that they were the vanguard of many thousands of young men and women who, in later years, were to live in Fairleigh Dickinson dormitories, even in England. It is also true that the life-style and values reflected in the dormitory arrangements of 1952 were to change enormously in later decades, but such profound changes in student dormitory life were not unique to Fairleigh Dickinson.

Another project completed with the help of students in the

91. Interview with Mrs. Newton Foster, April 14, 1971.
92. Hill, p. 92.
93. Hackensack, N.J., *Bergen Record*, August 1, 1952.

fall semester of 1952 might have won the agreement of later student generations more quickly than the dormitory arrangements of those days.

The $130,000 that had been raised for the Hesslein Building only sufficed to pay for the construction of the outer shell of the building. Completion of the interior, including cinder-block interior walls, insulation of piping, laying of cement floors, and electric wiring, was estimated at $90,000.

Sammartino, in despair, wanting to have the building ready for the fall semester, appealed to the student body and faculty to help finish the job themselves. The 1,000 day students voted in favor by a margin of eleven to one. The faculty, inspired by a speech by Loyd Haberly, who had once built himself "a sort of medieval stone house," supported the project except for two dissenters.

Led by Sammartino, all who thought they could help went to work. Dean Miller served as foreman, while Harold Feldman kept a strict time schedule and Loyd Haberly supervised the mixing of the cement and did the intricate partition work. Sammartino, one muggy day, personally built a cinder-block wall.

By the fall, the interior was sufficiently complete to be ready for classes, and on October 24, 1952, the building was dedicated at ceremonies attended by about fifty members of the area's textile industry, the administrators, faculty, and students.[94]

Thus, in a period of six years, four buildings had been added to the small campus. A sort of quadrangle with buildings on three sides had arisen: Becton Hall on the west; the Castle and East Hall on the north; and the gymnasium and the Hesslein Building on the east.

Along with helping to build their own classroom building, Fairleigh Dickinson students were exposed to another rather unusual experience at this time. A group of four sociology students, all veterans, had spent several days living as "hoboes" in the Bowery in order to study the lives of the destitute at firsthand. They had gotten to know a group of the derelicts and brought them to the campus to visit their sociology class. The group rather surprised everyone, because it included a graduate from Hamilton College and Columbia University who had written a work on Shelley, and another with degrees from Cambridge University in England. The latter emphasized, "Why work six days a week when you can make an adequate living by working one day a week?" His companions agreed. The writer on Shelley

94. New York, N.Y., *Daily News Record*, October 24, 1952.

described the Bowery as a place where a man could live a free life, and said he neither smoked nor drank. Thereupon his four companions commented, "You don't deserve to live," and insisted they could stop drinking any time they wished.[95]

Still another unusual incident on campus this year was a personal visit by "William Shaksper" of Stratford-on-Avon in England. "Mr. Shaksper" (in the person of Jack Schrier, an FDC sophomore), dressed in Elizabethan clothing, was put on trial before a court presided over by Adriance Kipp, Jr., the college attorney, wearing judicial robes. "Mr. Shaksper" was accused of plagiarism, namely, that the works published under his name had really been written by his contemporary, the Earl of Oxford. "Shaksper" was defended by Dr. Samuel Johnson, Professor of English at New York University. The prosecution was conducted by Charlton Ogburn, who had written works maintaining the anti-Stratfordian position. After hearing both sides the jury, consisting of a group of writers, businessmen, and teachers, found for the defendant by a margin of one vote.[96]

Sociology and English students at Fairleigh Dickinson surely had unique possibilities at this time for studying their subjects.

A number of honorary degrees and citations were conferred during the year upon persons in public life. In November, the United States deputy representative to the United Nations, Ernest A. Gross, was honored.[97] In March, the head of the Indian delegation to the world organization, Madame Vijayalakshmi Pandit, received a citation for outstanding service to humanity after she had spoken to the student body at the weekly college community conference.[98]

Yet another honorary degree for an important United Nations personality was awarded in April. A group of 200 faculty and students, led by Dr. Sammartino and Dr. Canfield, traveled to the United Nations headquarters in New York City to confer the degree of doctor of laws *honoris causa* upon the organization's secretary-general, Trygve Lie, about to be succeeded by Dag Hammarskjold.[99] As a result of these actions, ties began to develop with the world organization that proved helpful in advancing the college's emphasis on international studies.

---

95. Rutherford, N.J., *Republican*, November 20, 1952; New York, N.Y., *Times*, November 19, 1952.
96. Passaic-Clifton, N.J., *Herald-News*, March 26, 1953.
97. Paterson, N.J., *Call*, November 22, 1952.
98. Newark, N.J., *News*, March 26, 1953.
99. Passaic-Clifton, N.J., *Herald-News*, April 17, 1953.

The Tenth Commencement was held on June 2, 1953, at the college for 238 bachelors of arts or science and 107 associates-in-arts. A touching moment was the award of the one degree earned *summa cum laude* to Dorothy Constance Pallas of Wood-Ridge. Miss Pallas had earned her degree through study at home, since a crippling disease confined her to a wheelchair.

Brigadier General David Sarnoff, chairman of the board of the Radio Corporation of America, was the commencement speaker. He stressed that "America must be strong" and predicted that radio, television, and atomic power would transform the face of the globe in half a century.

> We must maintain our confidence and courage, our national preparedness and leadership, our scientific advances and technical skill. By continually strengthening these girders in our spiritual, economic and political structure, we shall grow in power to fulfill our responsibility in the world.[100]

General Sarnoff, along with New Jersey State Treasurer Walter T. Margetts, Jr., and Oscar O. R. Schwidetsky, research director of Becton, Dickinson and Company, were awarded honorary doctorates.

President Sammartino, in his commencement report, stressed the success of the two-year nursing program, that faculty annuity plans were under consideration, and that there were an enlarged endowment and plans for a new curriculum in elementary education and for a reading clinic.[101]

The summer session, beginning immediately after commencement, succeeded in enrolling more than 800 students. Of the total, 260 were from the day session, and 206 were transfer students for the summer from other institutions, the largest contingent being from Rutgers University. About one-fourth of the registrants were veterans of the Second World War or of the Korean conflict.[102]

And so year had begun to follow year in an ever-deepening routine of new curricula—more students, more faculty, and more activities of every type. Although the mood remained vital and fresh, despite the increasing routine, it is conceivable that the institution might gradually have lost much of its original momentum and élan if the development of an entirely new aspect of its life had not begun at this time.

Before considering this new aspect, it will be instructive to

100. Paterson, N.J., *Call*, June 3, 1953.
101. *Ibid.*
102. *Ibid.*, June 19, 1953.

compare the institution as it existed at the moment when it had become a four-year college with the status it had achieved by the beginning of the academic year 1953–1954.

In 1948, the faculty had numbered 46 full-time members and special lecturers, of whom twelve held doctorates.[103] The administration consisted of one president, one administrative assistant, and five department chairmen.[104] Student enrollment totaled 1,310 (710 day, 600 evening).[105]

By September 1953, the faculty had increased threefold to 126 full-time faculty and special lecturers with thirty—or one-quarter—doctorates. The administration included a president, a dean of the college, a dean of the school of dental hygiene, an administrative assistant for the president, six administrators with the title "director," five departmental chairmen, a faculty council, and thirteen standing faculty committees for various areas.[106] Student enrollments for September 1953 amounted to 2,807 (1,200 day, 1,607 evening), more than twice as many as when the junior college had become a four-year institution five years before.[107]

Moreover, the college had grown not only in numbers but in areas of study. In 1948, twelve curricula had led to the associate-in-arts degree and five to the bachelor of arts degree.[108]

By 1953, the college, fully accredited by the Middle States Association, offered nineteen curricula leading to the associate-in-arts, nineteen leading to the bachelor of science and three leading to the bachelor of arts degree.[109]

---

103. *Bulletin of Fairleigh Dickinson College, 1948–1949* (Rutherford, N.J.: Fairleigh Dickinson College, 1948), pp. 3–4.
104. *Ibid.*
105. Hill, p. 92.
106. *Bulletin of Fairleigh Dickinson College, 1953–1954* (Rutherford, N.J.: Fairleigh Dickinson College, 1953).
107. Hill.
108. *Bulletin of Fairleigh Dickinson College, 1948–1949*, p. 1. Two-Year Terminal Career Courses: engineering, textiles, accounting, journalism, photography, advertising, secretarial, business administration, merchandising and fashion, hotel management, laboratory technique, medical assistant. Four-Year Courses: liberal arts, engineering for industrial management, business administration, accounting, medical arts.
109. *Bulletin of Fairleigh Dickinson College, 1953–1954, passim.*
Associate-in-Arts curricula: accounting, advertising, business management, chemistry, dental hygiene, electronics, engineering for transfer, executive, hotel and restaurant management, industrial management, journalism, liberal arts, medical assistant, medical technician, nursing, retail merchandising, secretarial, textiles, traffic management.
Bachelor of Science curricula: accounting, advertising, business management, chemistry, chemistry-textiles, elementary education, hotel and restaurant management, industrial management, journalism, liberal arts, mathematics, medical assistant, medical technician, physics, pre-law, preprofessional (dentistry, medicine, retail merchandising, optometry, pharmacy, veterinary medicine), social science.
Bachelor of Arts curricula: economics, history, psychology.

Physical facilities had expanded to keep pace with the growth in numbers of faculty and students working in these many fields of learning. In 1948, the Castle, Becton Hall, and East Hall had stood upon the campus. By 1953, the gymnasium and the Hesslein Building had been added. The first dormitory had been established.

But the problems caused by student parking on the streets due to limited space on the small campus were causing increasing difficulties with many townspeople.

In view of the phenomenal success of its first eleven years in growing from nothing by way of a small junior college for girls to a large, bustling, many-faceted four-year college, many another institution might have begun to rest on its hard-earned laurels.

In judging the life and growth of any institution, the statistics of its material aspects in numbers, finances and property tell only one side of the story. There are also the intangible factors of the human personalities involved and of the spirit that human interaction in any activity generates. These are, perhaps, the most fundamental considerations when seeking to evaluate the growth of an institution and they are also the most difficult to judge and to describe.

At Fairleigh Dickinson College, there was to be no rest after attaining full accreditation as a four-year college. Instead, what would prove to be the single most decisive step in the institution's history was about to be taken.

7

The Two-Campus College, 1953-1956

The institution's twelfth year of classes began in routine fashion on September 16, 1953. A total of more than 2,800 had registered; 1,200 in the day and 1,607 in the evening session, the largest enrollment to date.[1] Orientation programs for the entering freshmen had been held as usual, and at the first faculty meeting President Sammartino welcomed and introduced 14 new faculty members.[2] Students who had traveled abroad reported on their experiences in England, and in Italy while visiting Rome and while having an audience with the pope.

Then, on November 23, 1953, this series of fall events of the type that had become almost routine in the college's activities was suddenly interrupted by a development of profound and basic importance for the institution's whole future. On that day Edward T. T. Williams announced to a surprised Bergen County that the trustees of Fairleigh Dickinson College and the trustees of Bergen Junior College in Teaneck had agreed to merge the two institutions into one under the name "Fairleigh Dickinson College." Dr. Peter Sammartino would continue as president while Dr. Walter Head, president of Bergen Junior College, was to be the provost of what would be known hereafter as "The Teaneck Campus of Fairleigh Dickinson College."[3]

---

1. Walter Hill, *Fairleigh Dickinson University: Some Aspects of Its Growth* (Rutherford, N.J.: Fairleigh Dickinson University, 1961).
2. Hackensack, N.J., *Bergen Record*, September 11, 1953.
3. *Ibid.*, November 23, 1953.

BERGEN JUNIOR COLLEGE IN TEANECK

Bergen Junior College was founded in 1933 by Charles L. Littel in Hackensack, the county seat of Bergen County, about ten miles north of Rutherford. For the first three years, classes were held in the Young Men's Christian Association building on Main Street, Hackensack. In 1936 Bergen Junior College acquired a campus in Teaneck on the Hackensack River's east bank, just across the river from the town of Hackensack.

The county seat had been prominent in Bergen County even before the Revolution. During the Revolutionary War, General Washington briefly established his headquarters in Hackensack. In contrast, Teaneck had been an inconspicuous adjunct of the town across the river from it. Only after the First World War did Teaneck begin to experience a certain growth. By the nineteen thirties it was recognized as one of the finest residential communities in the state and, in 1949, it was chosen as "The American Model Town" in a national competition.

The campus of Bergen Junior College in Teaneck consisted of two pieces of property. The larger of about thirty acres, known as "1000 River Road," was bounded by the Hackensack River on the west; by a private estate, the Davenport West property, on the south; and by a wide, busy, tree-lined thoroughfare, River Road, on the east. Along its northern flank ran New Jersey Route 4, which led eastward to the George Washington Bridge only five miles away, and westward to the Garden State Parkway and several small shopping areas. These were later expanded into huge shopping centers. Access to the campus was swift and easy from all directions.

Besides the 1000 River Road property, Bergen Junior College had also acquired another area of about ten acres located about a quarter of a mile to the south of the main campus. This southern extension, known as "Linden Campus," was also bounded by the Hackensack River on the west and River Road on the east. The Teaneck junior college had also acquired several smaller pieces of property east of River Road, or to the south of the Linden Campus.

The new campus brought about thirty acres to Fairleigh Dickinson College as compared to the roughly fifteen in Rutherford. There would be land on which to build the needed extra facilities. If the land between the 1000 River Road and Linden areas could also be acquired, a campus of about eighty acres would result, which would form a compact area. Further, its location on the fringes of the town prevented the campus from interfering in any way with the daily life of the townspeople of Teaneck.

During the years until 1954, Bergen Junior College had made use of the approximately 30 buildings it had found on its properties and it had added several others. At the time Fairleigh Dickinson had acquired East Hall from Camp Shanks, a recreation hall had been acquired from the same camp by Bergen Junior College. At government expense it had been dismantled, transported to the 1000 River Road property and reconstructed as a gymnasium. Similarly, a former officers' barracks had been reerected at the Teaneck site and, after receiving a brick veneer, had been transformed into a library. The other principal buildings consisted of the old Phelps homestead at 1000 River Road and the residence of the late Congressman Albert Hart on the Linden Campus. The latter structure was built in the style of a southern mansion, with white columns in front. There were also a number of private houses on the Linden Campus, which had been converted into dormitories and offices, and several barracks units, identical with East Hall in Rutherford, which had also been converted into classroom structures.[4]

The condition of the buildings of various ages and styles, and of the grounds, the scattering of offices in many small locations, and the generally poor organization of space as well as the prevalence of over-age or unused equipment caused problems.[5]

As a result of the postwar GI wave, enrollments at Bergen Junior College had risen to a high point of 1,493 for the academic year 1948–1949, with about one-third attending during the day and the remainder in the evening. Thereafter enrollments decreased. The chief reason was undoubtedly the failure of the junior college to earn accreditation from the Middle States Association. Application was made twice but, after study by the Association, accreditation each time failed of being granted.[6]

By the fall semester of 1953, the enrollment of Bergen Junior College stood at 197 day students and 297 evening students, a total

4. Interview with Milton C. Cooper, June 16, 1971. Cooper was a student at Bergen Junior College, 1935–1937, earning the B.S. and M.S. degrees at Hofstra College. From 1941 until 1942 he was a science instructor at Bergen Junior College and, after his return from service in 1944, became business manager of the college until its merger with Fairleigh Dickinson College. He was then appointed business manager of the merged institution and continued in the post until this writing (1971).

5. Peter Sammartino, *The President of a Small College* (Rutherford, N.J.: Fairleigh Dickinson College Press, 1954), pp. 154–63.

6. Interview with Milton C. Cooper, June 16, 1971.

of 495.[7] In five years the enrollment had dropped to one-third of its maximum size.

Dr. Littel, the founder and first president, retired in 1950 with the title "president emeritus." He was succeeded as president by Dr. Walter Head. The dean since 1948 had been Albert F. Carpenter.

Due to the steady decline in enrollments, Bergen Junior College found itself in ever-greater financial difficulties. By the summer of 1953 the situation was very serious. To provide needed funds, not forthcoming from operation of the school, some of the real estate was sold from time to time.

The board of trustees of Bergen Junior College, after many meetings to consider the future of their institution, decided that the best course would be merger with another institution. Arthur A. Kron, chairman of the board, was authorized to head a committee for this purpose.

THE MERGER WITH
FAIRLEIGH DICKINSON COLLEGE

Several different possibilities were explored. However, the advantage of merging with Fairleigh Dickinson College became clearly apparent during preliminary talks. The boards of both institutions, after a meeting at President Sammartino's house in June and a meeting in December between Edward T. T. Williams, Fairleigh Dickinson, Jr., and Arthur A. Kron, approved the following terms for the merger: that the assets and liabilities of Bergen Junior College would be assumed by Fairleigh Dickinson College, that the Rutherford institution's name would be used for the whole institution and that Dr. Sammartino would be president, while Dr. Head would be provost and Professor Carpenter would be dean of the new Teaneck campus.

In his initial announcement Edward T. T. Williams stated that the trustees of Bergen Junior College had initiated the talks in August. He said that a substantial building program for the next two years would take place, including a new classroom building and modernization of laboratory facilities.[8]

Arthur A. Kron, chairman of the board of trustees of Bergen Junior College, stated:

---

7. Paterson, N.J., *Call*, November 24, 1953.
8. *Ibid.*

This is a great day in educational history. By merging the campuses we are providing the finest possible educational opportunity for the youth of our county and this entire area. The future of Fairleigh Dickinson is now practically unlimited. The Teaneck property lends itself to considerable expansion. The members of our board of trustees congratulate the trustees of Fairleigh Dickinson College upon this important development. The merger is of mutual benefit to both institutions.[9]

As a first step in the integration of the two institutions, Hiram B. D. Blauvelt and Arthur A. Kron of the Bergen Junior College board were added to the board of trustees of Fairleigh Dickinson College.[10]

But how could the faculties and students be brought together? A "Welcome Teaneck Day" was held at Rutherford on December 2, 1953. The faculty and students of the Teaneck institution traveled to the Rutherford Campus for a tour of buildings, conferences, and a general orientation to the programs and activities of Fairleigh Dickinson College. They were personally welcomed and guided by Rutherford faculty and students amid scenes of great enthusiasm.

On the following day, December 3, the twelfth anniversary of the organizational dinner in the Rutherford Elks hall, an academic procession, headed by Dr. Sammartino and Dr. Head, proceeded from the Castle to Grace Episcopal Church for a chapel service attended by trustees, administrators, faculty, and students representing both institutions.[11]

In his remarks President Sammartino stressed that there would be six areas for the development of the Teaneck Campus: 1) financial rehabilitation, 2) beautification, 3) modernization of all facilities, 4) new construction, 5) widening and enrichment of

---

9. Rutherford, N.J., *South Bergen News*, November 24, 1953.

10. Hiram B. D. Blauvelt of Oradell, N.J., was a graduate of Princeton University, president of the Comfort Coal-Lumber Company, and a director of the Bergen County Chamber of Commerce, the Hackensack Trust Company, and the New Jersey and New York Railroad. He was known as a world traveler and had been a war correspondent who had interviewed Field Marshal Jan Smuts and the Emperor Haile Selassie of Ethiopia. He was a member of the trustees of Fairleigh Dickinson from 1954 until his death in 1958.

Arthur A. Kron of West Englewood, N.J., has been in the advertising field since 1916 in a variety of executive positions, including board membership of the Advertising Association of New York and the vice-presidency of the Gotham Advertising Company. He had been a member of the board of trustees of Fairleigh Dickinson until this writing (1972). He has traveled in many countries to study advertising. He was chairman of the board of trustees of Bergen Junior College from 1945 until the merger.

11. Paterson, N.J., *News*, December 3, 1953.

curricular offerings, 6) expansion of student services. Sammartino concluded his chapel address with these words:

> I have been elated with the enthusiasm shown by the faculties and staffs of both the Rutherford and Teaneck campuses. Those with whom I have discussed projects have wasted no time in planning and working for a greater college now that financial help and four-year status are available.
>
> Yesterday's meeting of the two student bodies was one of the most thrilling experiences we have ever had. As the Teaneck students arrived at this campus and were met by Rutherford students, they interlocked arms and marched into the gymnasium to the strains of the college band and resounding cheers of the students. There was such a feeling of solidarity, of willingness to share, of rejoicing in the new turn of events, no one could remain insensitive to the stirring emotions of the moment.
>
> With the union of the two campuses under one banner, there now exists in this area the greatest single phalanx of college-trained young men and women ready to use their influence for the strengthening of good within their communities. Already this force with their families reaches over twenty thousand; it will increase geometrically in the future. For industry, it means the greatest single pool of trained manpower in the northern part of New Jersey.
>
> And now there is more work to be done. And we shall do it. I can only end by repeating our college motto—*fortiter et suaviter,* "bravely and pleasurably," because that is the way we're going to share our resources and our experiences with the proposed new campus in Teaneck.[12]

And indeed resources and experience were shared with the new campus. A group of administrators and faculty descended upon the Teaneck institution. Courses, text-books, and laboratory and library facilities were revamped on a transitional basis to prepare for the beginning of classes under Fairleigh Dickinson auspices on February 1, 1954. The faculty and staff of Bergen Junior College were retained and were relieved to know that their salaries would be regularly paid. Later a few of the small faculty from Bergen Junior were not continued, due to differences in educational philosophy or lack of qualifications. The great majority, however, made the transition with no difficulties.

There were some problems in introducing the strict Fairleigh Dickinson dress standards, ban on fraternities and sororities, and other policies to the Teaneck student body.

There were three fraternities and two sororities at the new campus, with a total of 86 members, roughly half of Bergen Jun-

---

12. Peter Sammartino, "Address at Merger Chapel Exercises of Fairleigh Dickinson College and Bergen Junior College, December 3, 1953," typewritten MS.

ior's day enrollment.[13] The Teaneck students were informed by letter from Dean Carpenter that the fraternities and sororities had legally ceased to exist along with Bergen Junior College on January 20, 1954, the date of the official merger, and that such organizations were not permitted by Fairleigh Dickinson College.[14]

A number of Teaneck student leaders now demanded of the trustees that fraternities be permitted to continue for the 150 day students at Teaneck. This request was not granted.

In order to clarify the situation, a special meeting of the Teaneck student body was called. What was the students' surprise, after waiting for some time for the administration's spokesman to appear, when a short but somewhat broadly built medieval knight in shining armor strode onto the stage of the Teaneck gymnasium with his visor down! It was only when the knight began to speak that the students recognized the voice of their new president, who was a collector of armor. Sammartino had long had a suit of armor standing in his office, but no one had noticed that it was an exact fit.

Raising his visor, Sammartino told the students that he had come prepared for any brickbats they might throw at him because of the policies that had just been introduced, particularly the ban on fraternities. He then explained the reasons for the ban and also stated that those Teaneck students who were qualified would be able to graduate with a diploma from Bergen Junior College dated January 20, 1954. Those students who wished and were qualified could be admitted to Fairleigh Dickinson College as transfer students and could receive their associate-in-arts degrees in June, since Fairleigh Dickinson College was a fully accredited institution. Sammartino also emphasized that all possible steps were being taken to equalize the offerings at the two campuses, and pointed out the advantages of being students at a four-year college.[15]

At the close of the previous chapter the thesis was advanced that the acquisition of a second campus was the most significant step in the institution's history. This claim was not made because of the obvious reason that the acquisition of the Teaneck Campus finally provided the space for further expansion, which was blocked

13. Hackensack, N.J., *Bergen Record*, January 23, 1954. The fraternities and their members were: Zeta Iota Pi, 19; Phi Beta Chi, 20; Chi Sigma Phi, 15. Sororities included Phi Sigma Delta with 20 members and Alpha Tau Omega with 12.
14. Teaneck, N.J., *The Sunday Sun*, January 24, 1954.
15. Hackensack, N.J., *Bergen Record*, February 1, 1954.

at Rutherford. Nor was it made because the Teaneck Campus would add something different in spirit or quality. This thesis has long been debated in faculty lounges and lunch rooms.

The reason that the acquisition of the Teaneck Campus was so decisive for the institution's future was that it set a pattern. And that pattern, repeated several times, created a multi-campus institution with an increasing variety of programs and emphases. In fact, the multi-campus nature of the institution led imperceptibly to a multiplicity of institutions. Yet, during the remainder of the first quarter of a century, a strong central leadership supported by the all-university faculty body that ultimately appeared was to succeed in holding the many centrifugal elements in one cohesive institution.

The policy governing the relationship between the two campuses enunciated by Sammartino at this time was that of "co-equal campuses." This policy served as the basis of Sammartino's conduct of university affairs as they pertained to the various campuses and their interrelationships until the end of his administration. In a work written on the subject some years before his retirement as president, he set forth his interpretation of the term:

> Fairleigh Dickinson University has adopted the concept of co-equal campuses. No word is ideal to describe 'campuses,' and 'co-equal' may create false impressions. Our campuses are not exactly co-equal because each one may have certain attributes the other does not have. . . . But all are co-equal to the extent that they have equal, although not identical, educational facilities and services. Each campus is a community of faculty and students with a feeling of professional identification; each campus stands on its own feet.[16]

But before Teaneck could stand on its own feet the previous decline in enrollments at what had been Bergen Junior College had to be reversed. This was done almost instantly with the spring 1954 term. For that semester 170 day and 428 evening students enrolled for courses at Teaneck.[17] The total of 598 represented an increase of forty percent over the registration of Bergen Junior College for its last semester of operation.[18] Yet some of this increase, especially in evening students, reflected partly the transfer of Rutherford students to the new campus because they found it more convenient for a number of reasons, particularly for ease in commuting. Thus Rutherford's loss was Teaneck's gain. Yet one

---

16. Peter Sammartino, *Multiple Campuses* (Rutherford, N.J.: Fairleigh Dickinson University Press, 1964), pp. 58–59.
17. Hill, p. 92.
18. Hackensack, N.J., *Bergen Record*, February 8, 1954.

reason Teaneck had been acquired was to ease the parking problem, particularly at night, at Rutherford.

The increase at the new campus necessitated the immediate hiring of 19 new instructors for both day and evening classes. This group, along with the faculty remaining from Bergen Junior College and some transfers from Rutherford, formed the nucleus of the Teaneck Campus faculty.

The Teaneck students quickly began to share in the varied programs and activities that had proliferated at Rutherford.

Early in the spring semester Miss Estelle Liebling brought her group to perform, at the weekly College Community Conference (now also introduced at Teaneck), the abbreviated version of Puccini's *La Boheme* that had been such a success at Rutherford.[19] This was an example of how programs from one campus could be used at the other.

The academic year 1953–1954, which had seen the first great step toward the institution's new destiny, came to a close with the Eleventh Commencement on June 9, 1954. Except for the presence of administrators and faculty from the Teaneck Campus and of several former Bergen Junior students who received Fairleigh Dickinson associate-in-arts degrees, the event was still inevitably a wholly Rutherford affair, at which campus it was held.

A total of 408 degrees were awarded: 44 bachelors of art, 199 bachelors of science, and 165 associates-in-arts. Led by Robert Davis of Ridgewood and Melvin Pukatch of Passaic (both *summa cum laude*), 57 were graduated with academic honors.

The commencement speaker was Dr. Ralph A. Burns, chairman of the Education Department at Dartmouth College.[20] Honorary degrees were conferred upon the commencement speaker and upon Leonard Dreyfuss, Loyd Haberly, Louis J. Scaramelli, and George W. Walker, a Rutherfordian who was president of the Hesslein Company and had been instrumental in bringing the Hesslein Building into being.[21]

The summer session of 1954 reached an enrollment of 925 students. This figure represented an increase of about six percent over the previous summer.[22] In view of the fact that Teaneck was

19. *Ibid.*, February 27, 1954.
20. Passaic-Clifton *Herald News*, June 10, 1954.
21. Rutherford, N.J., *South Bergen News*, June 17, 1954. Leonard Dreyfuss was State Director of Civilian Defense at this time. From 1965 until 1967 he was a member of the Fairleigh Dickinson University Board of Fellows, and from 1967 until his death in 1970 a member of the Board of Trustees.
22. Paterson, N.J., *News*, June 29, 1954.

now available, there was not the same pressure for classroom space as in previous summers. The representation of summer transfer students from other institutions continued to increase. About a quarter of this summer's students were in this category.[23]

By now it was becoming almost traditional that some unforeseen new development would be initiated during the summer. The previous summer had been marked by the beginning of negotiations for the merger with Bergen Junior College. What would the summer of 1954 bring?

In July Dr. Sammartino visited the Instituto Edison in Havana, Cuba, a secondary school with 2,000 students. As a result of negotiations with this school, an agreement was signed that provided that Fairleigh Dickinson College would be responsible for the English and business administration curricula at the Instituto. Dr. Elwell F. Kimball was to be the administrative head of the program, which would bring Fairleigh Dickinson faculty to the Cuban school for periodic teaching visits and in order to give examinations. Graduates of the Instituto's commerce curriculum would be eligible for transfer to either one of the Fairleigh Dickinson campuses in New Jersey.[24]

Thus the long-held plans for a working relationship with a foreign educational institution in order to advance the foreign studies and international aspects was finally realized in fact. The relationship with the Instituto Edison was principally valuable for the business administration faculty because of the opportunities it afforded for becoming familiar with a school and students in their field in Latin America. After Fidel Castro came to power in Cuba in 1959, this institutional link with an American college was soon terminated.

EVALUATION OF FACULTY

During this summer the Fairleigh Dickinson College Press published Sammartino's book on the insights and experiences he had gained as "the president of a small college."[25] At the moment of publication the term *small college* had already become an anachronism for Fairleigh Dickinson.

The book treated, in a clear, common-sense style, the practical

---

23. *Ibid.*
24. Hackensack, N.J., *Bergen Record*, July 31, 1954.
25. Peter Sammartino, *The President of A Small College* (Rutherford, N.J.: Fairleigh Dickinson College Press, 1954).

Robison Hall, the building dedicated to science and dentistry on the banks of the Hackensack. The river bank was extended much farther into the water in later years to gain space for parking.

A scene in the clinic of the dental school in the Robison Building.

The Twombly estate, "Florham," when acquired by the University in 1957. The Mansion is in the center of what was to become the Florham-Madison Campus.

The Mansion at the Florham-Madison Campus. It is modeled on Hampton Court Palace.

problems of organizing and developing a small institution. One chapter, dealing with the evaluation of instructors, reproduced the students' rating sheet for evaluating the teaching effectiveness of instructors and described the manner of its use. Every year the students in two of the instructor's classes chosen at random were asked to fill out the forms. The president, dean, and department chairman read the sheets, which could also be seen by the instructor if he wished. A scoring system was also used. Three points in one of the five categories was for above average, two for average, and one for below average. Fifteen was a perfect score, while anything below eleven was considered as revealing deficiencies.[26]

Reaction to this system of rating among the faculty varied greatly. In general, effective teachers had little to fear. The students' anonymous written comments were sometimes useful in eliminating minor defects in teaching methods, as, for example, speaking in too low a voice or writing illegibly on the blackboard.[27] In later years the system was sharply curtailed upon faculty request. Still later, newer variants were restored as a result of strong student pressure. The first system had the advantage of simplicity and a balanced numerical rating of five basic categories: command of subject matter, enthusiastic attitude toward the subject, ability to explain clearly, sympathetic attitude toward students, and effective personality.

Looking back over the past twelve years' experience, Sammartino, in an epilogue, set forth the philosophy of *Fortiter et Suaviter* —brave, efficient development and operation in a spirit of amiable, cooperative companionship:

> I believe I can best sum up what a college should stand for when I state that it is a gathering of teachers, nonteaching workers, and students where all are active to provide the greatest possible opportunities for all to mature and where everyone is striving to be as

26. *Ibid.*, pp. 47f.
27. The evaluation sheet contained the following:

FAIRLEIGH DICKINSON COLLEGE
Student's Rating of Instructor
This is an unusual responsibility! Be fair and accurate!
Name of Instructor   Subject   Date

	Above Average	Average	Below Average
Command of subject matter			
Enthusiastic attitude toward subject			
Ability to explain clearly			
Sympathetic attitude toward students			
Effective personality			

State any exceptional qualities of the instructor or any difficulties you may be having

friendly and as considerate as possible to his fellow man. It is as simple as that. But if there isn't an underlying feeling of idealism, of service and of companionship, then everything else is of no avail. But I hasten to add that in order to provide the best opportunity for these goals to be realized, it is important to pay attention to the mechanics of everyday operation. A college president must almost be all things to all men. His life will find the greatest meaning in the spirit of service; it will find the greatest peace of mind through an orderly solution of everyday operations.[28]

DEVELOPMENT OF THE TEANECK CAMPUS AND OF GRADUATE EDUCATION

As the summer drew to a close, Edward T. T. Williams made known that the endowment fund had passed the million dollar mark, reaching a total of $1,142,857. There had been an increase in scholarships ranging from $100 to $500 per student. The college had distributed $41,931 in scholarships and grants-in-aid the previous academic year. "While the increase is very gratifying," Williams commented, "with the addition of the Teaneck Campus the needs of the college are greater than ever before."[29]

In fact, the program of developing the Teaneck Campus had gotten under way with a number of new projects. In order to hide the original barn of the estate, a row of twelve flagpoles (eleven more than at Rutherford) was erected on the semicircular entrance road and the flags of foreign students attending the campus, or various forms of the American flag since its beginning, were displayed, creating something of a festive mood. The administration building, gymnasium, and the existing laboratories received extensive interior remodeling and modernization.

The first major new construction undertaken by Fairleigh Dickinson College at the Teaneck Campus was a classroom building. This structure, called Williams Hall in honor of the board chairman, was to have fourteen classrooms, of which two would be for large lecture sections and two for small seminar groups. An unusual feature was the pond over which Williams Hall was partly built, resting on several large pillars. This pond was part of the solution devised for dealing with a marshy area near River Road. A small brook also resulted from the new landscaping.

The campus pond, over which Williams Hall was cantilevered, was soon endowed with a supply of swans by a friend of the

28. *Ibid.*, pp. 152–53.
29. Paterson, N.J., *Call*, August 9, 1954.

college. However, instead of swimming quietly on the pond as they were supposed to do, the birds succeeded in escaping onto nearby River Road. Luckily no automobile accidents occurred before scampering maintenance men were able to recapture them. A new fence thereafter kept the swans in place. For one frantic morning, however, motorists on River Road had the exhilarating experience of dodging swans.[30] After the experience of traffic while crossing River Road, there was no doubt in anyone's mind that the swans were the proper symbol of the Teaneck Campus, and one swan was inserted in the lower part of the new, halved coat of arms designed by Lord Haberly to represent the two-campus college.[31]

On May 14, 1954, the State Board of Education authorized Fairleigh Dickinson College to confer the degree of master of business administration. Plans were at once developed to take the first step into graduate education with the fall semester of 1954. Dr. Harry A. Sprague was appointed as educational consultant for the new graduate program. Graduate classes were to be limited to the evening at the Rutherford Campus. The first graduate faculty included Dr. Canfield, Dr. Forrest Irwin, Dr. Raditsa, Dr. Gerhard Schmidt, and Dr. Harold S. Sloan.[32] A group of 60 comprised the first students of the Graduate School. Half were graduates of Fairleigh Dickinson College. Of the remainder, four were graduates of the City College of New York, three each came from New York University, Pace College, and Seton Hall University,

30. Interview with Louis A. Rice, March 24, 1971.

31. It was soon noticed by the students that the swans preferred the company of co-eds and the birds were named "Romeo" and "Casanova." Their numbers did not increase until the introduction of a "coeducational" element among the swan population in the pond. Another problem was wild ducks that moved in occasionally for free food.

32. Dr. Sprague, who had been the president of Montclair State Teachers College, later served as dean of the Graduate School until his retirement in 1965.

Forrest Irwin (B.S., Northwestern Univ.; M.A., Teachers College, Columbia Univ.) had been president of Jersey City State Teachers College. At Fairleigh Dickinson he became professor of education in 1954 and was dean of the College of Education from 1958 until his retirement in 1963, when he was awarded the title "dean emeritus."

Gerhard Schmidt (Ph.D., Univ. of Berlin) had been on the faculty of Bergen Junior College. He remained with Fairleigh Dickinson until this writing, receiving the emeritus title in 1968.

Harold S. Sloan (B.S., A.M., Columbia Univ.; LL.D., Univ. of Denver) was vice-president of the Alfred P. Sloan Foundation from 1936 to 1945 and had been on the faculties of Teachers College, Columbia University, and of New York University. At Fairleigh Dickinson he was appointed professor of economics and was chosen a member of the Board of Trustees in 1964. He retired as a trustee in 1971.

while Lehigh University and Rutgers University each contributed two to the total. The rest came from a wide assortment of colleges in the New York metropolitan area. Thirty-seven were pursuing the business management curriculum, 16 were in economics, and six in accountancy. Their ages ranged from 24 to 55 years, with about half in the 24- to 34-year group.

Graduate education at Fairleigh Dickinson began as everything else at the institution had begun—on a small scale. Administrative leaders long hesitated at expanding the graduate programs because of the anticipated greater costs. Yet despite such hesitations, the graduate enrollment and courses and curricula began to grow as various departments entered the field.

Classes for the academic year 1954–1955 began on September 15. The addition of another campus made itself strongly felt in the undergraduate enrollment statistics, as follows (percentages represent increases over previous year) :[33]

	Day	Evening	Total
Rutherford	1,445 (19%)	2,011 (25%)	3,456 (20%)
Teaneck	456 (17%)	1,217 (184%)	1,673 (180%)
Total	1,901 (40%)	3,228 (50%)	1,673 (50%)

Both campuses had registered marked increases, but the increase at Teaneck, the site of an institution that had been forced to end its existence due to decreasing enrollments, was phenomenal. Fairleigh Dickinson College was now the third largest four-year college in the state.

With its greatly expanded student body and faculty, its renovated facilities and new construction in progress or planned, the Teaneck Campus after little more than half a year since its acquisition had become a vital and quickly growing part of Fairleigh Dickinson College.

In order to give public recognition to this fact, Sunday, October 3, 1954, was set aside as the Day of Dedication for the Teaneck Campus, on the model of the original Day of Dedication at Rutherford, September 12, 1942. More than 700 guests attended and afterwards inspected the campus. Representatives of the state and local governments, of education and industry, participated in the ceremonies involving trustees, administrators, faculty, and students. A procession from the library to the gymnasium led by the Highlanders and Knights began the observance, during which Sammartino, in speaking of the Teaneck Campus, said:

33. Hill, p. 92.

Much has been accomplished. A splendid faculty has been gathered together, a student body of excellent quality and numbering 1,673 has been enrolled, the existing buildings have been remodeled, a new class room building is almost completed and the grounds have been beautified. Two new buildings will be started soon and, altogether, a million dollars are being spent. We felt the moment of dedication had arrived. Good seeds have been planted, and now strong roots will grow in this community as they have in Rutherford.

Fairleigh Dickinson has become a large college with an enrollment of 5,140 students, to be exact, making it the third largest in New Jersey, and, of the 1,800 colleges in the country it is about 80th in size. . . .

Students come from about 200 high schools, from eight States and 18 foreign countries.

We strive to give them the best guidance possible so that they will become a phalanx of outstanding citizens residing here in this vital northeastern part of New Jersey. . . .

Our work in Teaneck will go on. We have not solved all of our problems. One of our most pressing problems, that of making the land area along the river usable for building and an athletic field, is not solved, but we are confident that there are enough competent and able men in these communities to advise us well in this matter. This, and other projects will be accomplished with your help.

We, the trustees, the faculty, the students dedicate ourselves to building this new campus—an institution of permanent pride for Teaneck, for Bergen County and for the State of New Jersey.[34]

On December 3, 1954, the thirteenth anniversary of the organizational dinner meeting at the Rutherford Elks hall was observed at an afternoon ceremony in Christ Episcopal Church, at which Edward T. T. Williams was awarded an honorary degree of doctor of laws.[35]

In his response, Williams explained the quick growth of the college by the fact that

we worked upward from the needs of the individual and have been able, in effect, to frame a new pattern—a pattern whose success is attested to, not by our endowment funds or building programs, but through the 5,000 students who came to us to participate in what we have to offer.[36]

A few weeks later, on Wednesday, January 5, 1955, the newly completed classroom building in Teaneck was dedicated as Williams Hall.[37] At the same time, plans were announced for a new library at Rutherford costing $350,000 and designed for 150,000 books.[38]

34. Paterson, N.J., *Call*, October 5, 1954.
35. Passaic, N.J., *Herald-News*, December 4, 1954.
36. Jersey City, N.J., *Jersey Journal*, December 4, 1954.
37. Rutherford, N.J., *South Bergen News*, December 30, 1954.
38. *Ibid.*

ARCHITECTURE — ANCIENT AND MODERN

Still another new building projected at this time for the Teaneck Campus was a girls' dormitory to be built in the northeast corner near River Road and just north of Williams Hall (the building erected over the swan pond). The dormitory was planned to house 80 girls. The total dormitory capacity at Rutherford in converted private homes accounted for only 60 beds at this time. Clearly, Teaneck's student body was destined to become more residential in character than Rutherford's. The size and the character of Teaneck's topography and landscape made it more attractive and practical for residential purposes.

Sixteen bids for the girls' dormitory were received from builders. Sammartino, ever fundamentally the teacher, determined to use the consideration of the bids as an opportunity to instruct the Teaneck students in this field of business procedures and to involve them in the decision regarding the new building destined for their campus. He had done this previously at Rutherford.

As a result, the whole Teaneck day-student body of almost 500 convened in the gymnasium auditorium. Among those on the stage with Sammartino were a member of the federal government's Housing and Finance Company, representatives of the contracting firms, student representatives, and Mr. Roland Wank, who was the architect for a great many of the institution's buildings.[39]

Dr. Sammartino explained to the audience how the bid applications had been submitted. Then the bids were opened one by one by Charles Mallory, vice-president of the Teaneck Campus Student Council, were read by another student, and were entered on the blackboard by a member of the faculty. There was a difference of $70,000 between the lowest bid and the highest, which latter amounted to $335,000. The students then moved and voted that the lowest bid be accepted. The contract was thereupon awarded to Baskin and Freeman Construction Company of Hackensack for a price of $264,234.[40]

As more and more structures in what might be called Wank's "contemporary, international, functional style" arose on the various campuses, they created an ultra-modern, unified, and, at the

---

39. Mr. Wank was connected with the firm of Fellheimer and Wagner in New York City. His basic architectural style was "contemporary," with inspirations from the Bauhaus school.
40. Hackensack, N.J., *Bergen Record*, January 6, 1955.

same time, aesthetically satisfying mood. The buildings succeeded in incarnating the spirit of the institution quite well in brick, mortar, cement blocks, and lots of glass.

The feeling of aesthetic harmony created by many buildings in the same style was further enhanced through the years by the acquisition and display of a number of outdoor sculptures and statues and of many paintings hung everywhere inside the buildings, even in the offices used for clerical purposes. The paintings came from all schools of art, from the traditional to modern abstract. The outdoor sculptures and statues were chiefly in the more recent modern idiom, although a group of copies of free-standing ancient Greek and Roman statues, inherited from the previous owners, adorn the garden to the south of the Mansion at the Madison Campus.

All these works of art, in their variety, were also expressive of the spirit of the institution and added to the almost festive aesthetic mood. Sammartino, himself a connoisseur and collector, who has willed his collection to the University, believes that art should be placed everywhere on the campus so that all may, consciously and unconsciously, experience and be affected by it.

Despite the chief emphasis on new, contemporary construction, old buildings (including one later in England of medieval origins) have not been ignored or neglected when available.

This other aspect of the institution's attitude was really established at the beginning, when Iviswold, a late-Victorian edifice, was transformed into the college's first building, "The Castle."

This trend was continued in January 1955, when Fairleigh Dickinson College closed an agreement with Mr. James H. Smith, Jr., to purchase from him the historic Kingsland-Kettell House, only about two blocks from the Rutherford Campus. The building was erected in 1670 by one of the first settlers in Bergen County, which had been an integral part of the New Netherlands until their occupation by the English four years before the house was built. It was one of the two oldest buildings in Bergen County, there being a controversy over whether it was the oldest. The Kingsland-Kettell House was an early example of the Dutch Colonial settler's house built everywhere in the Hudson River Valley.

A low, red sandstone dwelling, two stories high, it has a peaked roof that sweeps down to cover a front porch and a single-story rear extension. Almost inevitably, George Washington was believed to have had lunch there. Professor Kathleen Hoagland, history instructor at the Rutherford Campus, who was named historical custodian of the house by Sammartino, believed that the story was most likely true, since the house had belonged, during the Revolution, to the solitary "patriot" in what had been, to no one's surprise, solidly Tory Rutherford.[41]

The college bought the house for $45,000. It also bought from Mr. Smith an area of approximately 200 feet by 140 feet next to the house, which could serve perfectly as a parking lot.[42] The college announced that it planned to transform the house into a classroom center for the study of American history. The historical character of the building would be carefully preserved and the classrooms would be equipped with suitably "historical, colonial" furniture, prints, and maps. For the adjoining area, the college requested from the Rutherford Board of Adjustment a variance to construct a parking lot for seventy cars.

Again, some neighbors opposed the variance. They were not so effective this time. It became known that if the deal with the college failed, then the house and area would be purchased by a company that planned to tear down the Kingsland-Kettell House and replace it with an apartment house, including provision for parking for the tenants, for which the site was already zoned. Faced with this alternative, opposition declined and the college was able to acquire another classroom building (its oldest structure in the United States) and another parking lot to alleviate the situation in Rutherford.

About half a year later, the college was given the Outwater House by Becton, Dickinson and Company. This farmhouse had been built in red sandstone in 1720. For many years it had stood boarded up on the edge of the Becton-Dickinson plant in East Rutherford. The company was planning to erect a new building on the site.

The Outwater House was moved to Rutherford stone by stone and reerected next to Kingsland House, to which it was joined, thus adding several more classrooms and enlarging the colonial historical area created by the college.[43]

As if to strengthen the links with colonial and even pre-colonial America, several weeks after acquisition of the Kingsland-Kettell House, the rank of honorary chief was conferred upon President Sammartino and Trustee Blauvelt by the Shinnecock Indian Tribe

41. New York, N.Y., *The New York Herald-Tribune*, February 28, 1955.
42. Rutherford, N.J., *South Bergen News*, January 13, 1955.
43. Rutherford, N.J., *South Bergen News*, June 16, 1955. It was first erroneously called "Ackerman House," but an old map proved that the name was in error. Rutherford, N.J., *South Bergen News*, May 24, 1956.

at a ceremony at the Teaneck Campus. The tribe still owned its reservation, located in the elegant resort town of Southampton, Long Island, and occasionally conferred the feathered headdress of honorary chief upon men it believed worthy of becoming brother members of the tribe.

Princess Nowedema presided at the ceremony, assisted by six chiefs of the tribe, at which seven Bergen residents, including Blauvelt and Sammartino, were honored. Loyd Haberly spoke solemnly about Indian lore, and the guests were welcomed to Fairleigh Dickinson College by their new brother, Chief Wy Bennett, who happened to be president of the college as well.[44]

For the first time in a number of years, registration for a spring semester revealed a slight decrease in total enrollment over the fall instead of an increase. But the figures for February 1955 also showed that, whereas enrollment at Rutherford had decreased, thus causing the slight total decrease, there had been an increase in both day and evening students at Teaneck.[45]

The growing Teaneck student body encountered a new administrative face at the head of their campus as they began spring classes. Professor Albert Carpenter, who had been the dean of Bergen Junior College and had continued as dean of the Teaneck Campus of Fairleigh Dickinson College, had resigned to accept an appointment elsewhere. Louis A. Rice succeeded him as associate dean of Fairleigh Dickinson College, with particular responsibility for the Teaneck Campus.[46] A year later, in a move indicating a first limited step toward greater campus self-government, Rice's title was changed to "Dean of the Teaneck Campus."

Descended from pre-Revolutionary stock, Lou Rice, in his patriarchal way, was reminiscent of an older, more rural America. Rice quickly began to create a feeling of identity and community among the Teaneck faculty and student body. Eminently honest and fair with everyone, the best-known illustration of these char-

---

44. Paterson, N.J., *News*, January 24, 1955.
45. Teaneck, N.J., *Sunday Sun*, February 27, 1955.
46. Louis A. Rice (B.C.S., B.S., M.A., New York University) had been president of Packer Collegiate Institute in New York City and had held other administrative and faculty positions. He first came to Fairleigh Dickinson in September 1954, as teaching evaluator for evening instructors at both campuses. He held the following positions at Fairleigh Dickinson: associate dean for Teaneck, 1955–1957; dean, Teaneck Campus, 1957–1958; associate professor, business administration, 1958–1963; professor, 1963–1964; emeritus professor since 1964. In 1959, Professor Rice transferred from the Teaneck to the Madison Campus. The cherry-paneled lounge in the Madison Recreation Building was remodeled and then renamed "Louis A. Rice Lounge" in his honor.

acter traits was Dean Rice's appearance before the Teaneck Student Court to answer a summons placed on his car by a student marshal for parking in a prohibited spot. The dean of the campus quietly pleaded guilty and paid his one-dollar fine. No one could miss Dean and Mrs. Rice at the many college affairs, which they assiduously attended. Both towered over everyone else, looking like reincarnations of George and Martha Washington, and acting with the kindly dignity one hopes was also typical of the Father of his Country and spouse.

In handling administrative matters, Rice was quite deceptive. His seemingly slow, somewhat hesitant manner of operation actually resulted in everything's finally getting done, and getting done well. There was not the hustle and busyness many another administrator exudes as he "handles the situation." In moments of crisis, Rice was as calm and reliable as the proverbial Rock of Gibraltar.

The ceremonial high point of the spring semester of 1955 was the awarding of honorary degrees to Burl Ives, the ebullient, well-known folk singer and actor, and to Dr. William Jansen, Superintendent of Schools of New York City for many years, who was soon to retire and who presented a cool Scandinavian contrast to the effervescent Ives, although one who had the privilege of knowing Dr. Jansen personally will gladly testify that his dignified exterior concealed a humanity of considerable vitality combined with a deep religious seriousness about everything he did.[47] He was a devout and faithful attendant at the Lutheran Church in the Bronx, where he had been confirmed as a youth.

Ives was cited as "The Troubador of the American Nation," Jansen "for maintaining a sense of administrative justice and good-humored balance" in one of the most difficult educational administrative posts in the world.[48]

After the ceremony in Grace Episcopal Church, a reception was held in President Sammartino's residence on Ridge Road. The occasion was long remembered for the good fellowship created by Ives through his personality and singing, the latter accompanied by Sammartino at the piano. At the close, the whole company, rather encouraged by the refreshments, were enthusiastically led by Ives through a community songfest of old and new American favorites.

47. Passaic, N.J., *Herald-News*, February 19, 1955.
48. *Ibid.*

REPORTS AND STUDIES ON THE GROWTH

Shortly before commencement, the American Institute of Management published a report that received wide attention. The Institute had been alerted to the growth of Fairleigh Dickinson College through statistics released by the Federal Office of Higher Education. According to these, the New Jersey college during 1954 had been the fastest-growing college in the country.[49]

The Institute's audit was subdivided into nine sections: academic function, corporate structure, health of growth, development program, alumni analysis, fiscal policies, operating efficiency, trustee analysis, administrative evaluation, and academic leadership.

Under the heading "Academic Function," the report placed Fairleigh Dickinson College "within the broad definition of a liberal arts institution, with strong emphasis upon career preparation."[50] The almost totally local, commuting nature of the student body was cited to reveal the market being served, as well as the fact that there was no local competition.[51] The report also stressed that the college had as its secondary aim preparation for a professional or business career, which led it to put emphasis upon the manners, speech, and appearance of a student as well as upon his mind.[52]

Under "Corporate Structure," the report noted the various boards and committees, and expressed the thought that greater delegation of administrative authority and a still larger measure of faculty participation in governance had become desirable.[53]

Under "Health of Growth" the Institute found cause for satisfaction with the past and expected a bright future for the college.

---

49. "Fairleigh Dickinson College," *Management Audit*. Special Audit no. 130, 5, no. 2 (New York: American Institute of Management, May 1955):1.
50. *Ibid.*
51. *Ibid.*, p. 2. "There is no other comparable institution in the northern part of New Jersey, despite the fact that the population within a small radius of the college is over one million."
52. *Ibid.*
53. *Ibid.*, p. 3. "It is inevitable in an institution as new as this that too much administrative responsibility be placed upon the president. The American Institute of Management believes that in the very near future it will be incumbent upon Dr. Sammartino, the active and able president of Fairleigh Dickinson since its founding, to delegate certain authority either through the appointment of additional college officers or by permitting even greater participation of the faculty at the policy level."

By the time competition were to appear, the institution would be so firmly established that it would have nothing to fear.[54]

However, the report saw the acquisition of a second campus as a "mixed blessing," despite the strong efforts to create coequal campuses.[55] A finger was, thus, early laid upon an area of relationships that was to become more complex and difficult as the institution became multi-campus in character.

Under "Development Program" the growth in curricula, laboratories and physical facilities was cited. Library facilities at both campuses were considered adequate, although the Rutherford Campus library was viewed as lacking sufficient book and study space for the students. The construction of a new library for $350,000 at Rutherford was noted.[56]

The report stated the obvious about the alumni situation: that they were still few in number and young in age and achievement. More effective communication with the alumni and an expansion of the placement bureau were recommended.[57]

Under "Fiscal Policies" the report pointed out that the college had never had an operating deficit and that the current operating budget of about one-and-a-half million dollars was only slightly in excess of income. "This is particularly to the credit of the administration, since the tuition charged by this college (now $525 per year) is much lower than at most comparable institutions."[58] It was considered probable that trustees and other private sources would not continue as the major contributors indefinitely, and instead the creation of a long-range program for public fundraising was recommended.[59]

The college received marks of "above average" for insurance and pension plans, hospitalization, and health insurance.[60]

---

54. *Ibid.* "By the time additional colleges may be established in this area, which might possibly represent a drain on the potential student body of Fairleigh Dickinson, the college will have achieved a place and a tradition that will guarantee it an adequate number and quality of students."

55. *Ibid.* "From a management and policy standpoint, the geographical separation has brought about certain growing pains which remain still to be overcome."

56. *Ibid.*, p. 4. "With the constant expansion of physical facilities, and with the even greater selectivity of students which will be possible before any saturation point of enrollment is reached, there can be no concern about the future development of this institution. Furthermore, this development will be in terms not only of measurable financial and educational growth, but in the solidification of the college's place in the communities it serves."

57. *Ibid.*

58. *Ibid.*, p. 5.

59. *Ibid.*

60. *Ibid.*

With regard to operating efficiency, the survey concluded that administrative and operational procedures had developed through evolution rather than by planning. This was considered natural, given the nature of the institution's founding and early growth. Recommendations were made for the further delegation of responsibility for noninstructional personnel and business decisions through creation of the position of personnel manager and by expansion of the authority of the business manager.[61]

The efficient utilization of the physical plant, its carefully planned multi-functional nature and efficient and relatively inexpensive maintenance and housekeeping were praised.[62]

The report found no fault with the small size of the Board of Trustees, since this prevented the need for committees and guaranteed full attention by the Board to the problems brought before it as well as quick decisions. The fact that the college president was secretary of the Board and represented effective liaison with the operating administration of the college was considered a positive factor. The seriousness and devotion of the Board members to their work were praised.[63]

A chart revealed that the average age of the Trustees at this time was 53 years. Six of the eight were industrial leaders, while two (Hilleboe and Sammartino) were in the field of education.[64]

The report recommended that the college president be given more administrative assistance.[65] The college dean also needed more assistance, since he was also functioning as dean of the faculty, as did the registrar, who was also the director of admissions.[66]

The existing smooth flow of administrative action resulted, according to the report, "more as a result of harmony at the top levels than because of structural sufficiency."[67] A word of warning was spoken regarding the potential administrative problems caused by the existence of separate campuses. "It is suggested that the

---

61. *Ibid.*, p. 6.
62. *Ibid.*
63. *Ibid.*, p. 7.
64. *Ibid.*, p. 6.
65. *Ibid.*, p. 7. "He [Sammartino] has generally in the past been required by the circumstances to handle too much of the operational responsibility of the institution. Although he has carried these burdens ably, the situation should be remedied as soon as possible, to avoid the dual evil of placing too great a strain upon Dr. Sammartino and of localizing in him an excessive amount of the flow of authority which should properly be generated through a well-organized staff."
66. *Ibid.*
67. *Ibid.*, p. 8.

final authority over each area [of operation] be established in a central office."[68] The location of these could be split between the two campuses. An elaborate chart for unified administration was also included.[69] It gave no recognition whatsoever to the existence and development of the campuses as separate entities.

In the area of academic leadership the report felt that the college's policies

> for procurement of faculty members, for granting them tenure, for encouraging the kinds of accomplishment which warrant promotion, and for providing security in the form of retirement, insurance and pension plans are well conceived and carried out.[70]

The fact that less than ten percent of the faculty held the rank of full professor was considered as operating "to the advantage of the institution in that promotion to top levels is possible in practically all departments."[71] The faculty were praised for taking their responsibilities seriously, for visiting the students at their homes, for furnishing advice and counsel as required, and for promoting a cooperative spirit between faculty and students. Faculty salaries were comparable with those at other institutions, the report found.[72]

The management audit attracted considerable attention in the local press. An editorial entitled "An Interesting Study" appeared in several papers and made a number of points much more vividly than the audit report had done and, inevitably, highlighted certain problems as seen from the local perspective.

> Fairleigh Dickinson College has mushroomed with such speed that it is almost unbelievable that the South Bergen College was founded but 14 years ago. . . .
> This college . . . which purchased its original home from the Rutherford National Bank for a mere $20,000, according to the survey, . . . now, since Bergen Junior College was absorbed, has a combined value of $4,000,000!
> What happens when recognized college facilities are thrown open to the neighborhood, was demonstrated by the results in Bergen Junior. Just before its acquisition by Fairleigh Dickinson, Bergen Junior had an enrollment of 453 students. Last February, the number of

---

68. *Ibid.*
69. *Ibid.*, p. 7.
70. *Ibid.*, p. 8.
71. *Ibid.*
72. *Ibid.* "The pressing problem of faculty remuneration is dealt with as realistically as the college's resources permit. Faculty salaries are comparable with those at other institutions. They may be augmented by the faculty members through consulting services, professional writing, and other such avenues, so long as these activities do not abridge their teaching function."

day and night students had soared to 1,860. . . .

. . . Folks who thought they were moving into residential areas have found themselves alongside what amounts to an academic industry—and one that goes day and night.

The story of the college demands sympathy, help, encouragement. But somebody still has to find out why a small segment of the population—the area in Rutherford which has been inundated by the college parking and traffic needs, and the borough itself, which must carry the ever-growing physical plant tax-free,—should stand the burden of cost.

The trustees and the administrators of the college are fully aware of the problems. The management audit just made can help to make the rest of us more aware of them.[73]

It was very hard for some of the older community leaders, whose ideas had been formed before the First World War, to understand the profound social and economic changes that had made possible the growth of a college like Fairleigh Dickinson in the middle of an old town like Rutherford. They saw the rapid expansion of housing developments, shopping centers, and industrial plants in the areas of the county all around them that had been farmland in their youth. And, repelled by much they saw, they determined to keep their old town forever in the year 1905. They failed to realize that the almost total motorization of the American people during the intervening half century had made "suburbanization," with all its attendant benefits and problems, inevitable.

The Twelfth Commencement was held on June 8, 1955, in the Rutherford gymnasium, and 424 degrees were awarded.[74] More than half the total consisted of bachelors' degrees given for the full four years of study. Fifty-six of the graduates received academic honors. The senior farewell was delivered by Helen Krogull of Paterson, the only graduate *summa cum laude*.[75]

Honorary degrees were conferred upon the commencement speaker, Colonel Ben C. Limb, South Korean Ambassador to the United Nations; and to Ellsworth Tompkins, Chief of the Secondary School Division of the United States Office of Education; Dr. Allen B. DuMont, president of Allen B. DuMont Laboratories, Clifton; Dr. Forrest E. Lang, professor of education at New York University; and Raymond P. Lansing, vice-president of Bendix Aviation Corporation.[76]

---

73. East Rutherford, N.J., *Leader-Free Press*, June 2, 1955.
74. Passaic, N.J., *Herald-News*, June 7, 1955. They were distributed as follows: bachelor of science—215; bachelor of arts—32; associate-in-arts—177.
75. Newark, N.J., *News*, June 9, 1955.
76. Passaic, N.J., *Herald-News*, June 9, 1955.

Colonel Limb, who was to be a frequent visitor at Fairleigh Dickinson, emphasized the great strides forward the Republic of Korea had made since the end of the Korean War, and called for more cultural and trade exchange between the United States and his country.[77]

In his commencement report, President Sammartino featured the planned establishment of a dental school and advances in the engineering program.[78]

The School of Dental Hygiene held separate ceremonies, at which twenty graduates of the curriculum were capped. This was the fourth such class to be graduated since inception of the program in 1949. President Sammartino and Dr. Roy D. Ribble, Dean Emeritus of the School, extended greetings.[79] Dr. Walter Mosmann presented the caps to the graduates.[80]

The 1955 summer session set a new high with total registration of 1,109, the first summer enrollment to reach four figures. Classes were held at both campuses.[81]

Placement activities always accelerated in the spring and summer. Warren L. Duncan, the director of the Placement Bureau, in his annual report published in August, revealed that 141 different companies had been in touch with the college during the academic year 1954–1955 in their search for candidates. Forty-six of the companies had sent representatives to the campuses to interview applicants in person. The companies had included insurance firms, government agencies, sales organizations, and industry. The situation was good. Duncan commented, "There are many more positions than there are applicants, but the real problem is getting the right person to do the right job."[82]

As the summer drew to a close, 43 new faculty appointments were made known.[83] Among these, Margaret L. Coit had a national

77. *Ibid.*
78. *Ibid.*
79. Ray D. Ribble (D.D.S., University of Pennsylvania) was dean of the School of Dental Hygiene from its inception in 1949 until his retirement in 1954, at which time he received the emeritus title.
80. Walter Mosmann (D.D.S., Northwestern University; Diplomate, American Board of Orthodontics; F.A.C.D.) was director of the School of Dental Hygiene from its inception until its inclusion in 1957 in the School of Dentistry. Since that year, Dr. Mosmann has been professor of orthodontics and chairman of the department of orthodontics.
81. Rutherford, N.J., *South Bergen News*, July 21, 1955.
82. *Ibid.*, August 4, 1955.
83. Teaneck, N.J., *Sunday Sun*, September 18, 1955.

reputation. Miss Coit had won the Pulitzer Prize for her biography of John C. Calhoun.[84] Appointed to teach English and American history, she added a vital, creative note to these fields, and to the humanities in general, at the Rutherford Campus. Many works flowed from her pen in the years that followed. Her comments at faculty meetings became known for the trenchant, often strongly humorous manner in which she could characterize situations or persons.[85]

The growing department of nursing received a new chairman at this time in the person of Miss Mary Topalis, R.N. The former chairman, Miss Alice Rines, R.N., who had helped to initiate the nursing program two years before, resigned in order to complete the work for the doctorate.

Miss Topalis was to head the nursing department for eleven years. During this time, in her quiet, reliable, and friendly way, she developed the program to a level widely recognized for the quality and effectiveness of the nurses. Under her leadership, the cooperative arrangements with local hospitals for nursing education were extended and strengthened.[86]

Classes for 1955–1956, the institution's last academic year as a college, began on September 14 for 6,755 graduate and undergraduate students. They were distributed as follows (percentages show increase over previous year):

	Rutherford	Teaneck	Total
Day	1,655 (15%)	791 (73%)	2,446 (29%)
Evening	2,310 (14%)	1,861 (52%)	4,171 (29%)
Graduate	138 (new)	—— —	138
	4,103 (18%)	2,652 (59%)	6,755 (32%)[87]

The figures clearly reveal that Rutherford was continuing to grow but that Teaneck was taking giant steps, particularly in its day enrollment, to come abreast of the older campus.

---

84. Margaret Louise Coit, *John C. Calhoun, American Portrait* (Boston: Houghton Mifflin, 1950).

85. Margaret Louise Coit (A.B., Litt.D., Women's College, University of North Carolina), had risen to the rank of professor of history by the time of this writing.

86. Mary Topalis (R.N., New York Hospital School of Nursing; B.S., M.A., Teachers College, Columbia University), was associate professor of nursing and chairman of the department until 1966, at which time she left to accept a similar position at a college in New England.

87. Hill, p. 92.

The new Rutherford Campus library, built in contemporary style and joined to the Castle's southwestern corner, was now finished. During the fall semester, it received a welcome addition in the form of a donation of his law books by Milton B. Ignatius, a New York City lawyer, who was a long-time resident of Rutherford. Mr. Ignatius had taken a great interest in the college from its beginnings. His legal library, valued at $40,000, contained volumes on essential cases, decisions, and texts. About 1,000 volumes were devoted to New York State law and cases, and another 2,000 to United States law. The complete Corpus Juris was also included and Mr. Ignatius also contributed the steel shelving for housing the books.[88] At the time and later, there has been speculation that this gift could serve for beginning a law school, but nothing ever resulted.

The library was named in honor of Dr. W. Allen Messler, who had had a varied career as scholar, teacher, college founder, and president.[89] He served as an educational consultant from the founding of Fairleigh Dickinson College until his death on January 12, 1956. Dr. Messler was also one of the original faculty of the junior college, beginning in September 1942, on a part-time basis. At his death, he was the last remaining member of the original faculty group who was still connected with the institution. Dr. Messler's wisdom and scholarly, gentle nature made a great impression on anyone with whom he conversed.

During the preceding and this semester, the Fairleigh Dickinson Chapter of the American Association of University Professors, as the result of a membership drive, increased its membership to include ninety percent of the faculty. The group had started in a small way in 1952 and Clair W. Black and Sidney Kronish were among its early presidents. Its stated purposes were: to improve and increase faculty usefulness through evaluation of the college in terms of its contribution to the development of student intellectual maturity and personal behavior, and through improvement of the professional status of the faculty. Julius O. Luck and Eileen Costello were elected, respectively, president and secretary for 1955–1956.[90]

88. Rutherford, N.J., *South Bergen News*, November 3, 1955.
89. W. Allen Messler (A.B., 1898; M.A., 1903; Rutgers University: M.Ed., 1912; D.Ed., 1915; New York University). Dr. Messler taught in rural, one-room schoolhouses and in the Jersey City public schools. He was the founder and principal of the Jersey City Normal School. Upon the transformation of the institution into the Jersey City Teachers College, he became its president.
90. Rutherford, N.J., *South Bergen News*, November 10, 1955.

The AAUP Chapter proceeded to form committees on academic standards, professional status, salaries, and health and welfare. Their reports were discussed at the regular monthly meetings of the Chapter, taking into consideration the stated objectives of the AAUP.

Based on the committees' work, recommendations for achieving the goals were formulated. The report containing the Chapter's recommendations was presented to the college president and Board of Trustees on March 15, 1956, the same day on which the annual contracts were distributed.

The document is significant, since it reflects faculty concern at certain aspects of the institution's policies and operations which, until this time, had not found expression in any official documentary form.

The report was divided into three sections: one on academic standards; one on professional status; and one on salaries.[91]

The report called for a study of the admissions policy since, it claimed, half the freshman class was admitted from the lower half of high school graduating classes.[92] Student load and class sizes, perennial sources of faculty concern, were considered too large.[93] There was a similar proposal with regard to the number of student advisees assigned for guidance to a faculty member. It should not exceed fifteen. The claim was made that some advisors were assigned more than double that number.[94] "In addition to teaching a basic load and guidance, instructors should not be encouraged to teach extra hours and perform minor clerical duties for extra income."[95] In order to help with such tasks as grade recording at the end of semesters, it had become customary for faculty to come in and assist with this job. The custom was in keeping with the early pioneering tradition where everyone helped in whatever

---

91. *Progress Report* (mimeographed typewritten document of seven pages). Progress Report Committee (Clair W. Black, Eileen Costello, Harold Feldman, Robert Frederick, Kathleen Hillers, Sidney Kronish, Julius Luck, Malcolm Sturchio), Fairleigh Dickinson College Chapter, The American Association of University Professors.

92. *Ibid.*, p. 1. "1.1. *Admission Policy.* The admission policy of the college needs to be studied. The policy of admitting a freshman class, 50 per cent of whom are from the lower half of their high school class, tends to lower the academic standards of the college. The student of average and above-average ability is frequently not challenged."

93. *Ibid.*, pp. 1 f. "When classes are so large that teachers in their full-time schedules work with more than 125 students, it tends to create a situation where course requirements will be minimized."

94. *Ibid.*, p. 2.

95. *Ibid.*, p. 2.

way he could, but as the institution and its faculty had grown, this practice had met ever more opposition.

There was a request for more office space.[96] An expansion of the administrative staff was also recommended to help both administrators and faculty.[97]

The section in the AAUP report on professional status made strong statements regarding salary levels, number of full-time faculty as compared with part-time, secretarial help, and faculty meetings.[98]

---

96. *Ibid.* "1.5. *Office Space.* At the present time there is not enough space devoted to faculty-student needs. It is almost impossible to find a room where a student can be given guidance in private."

97. *Ibid.*, p. 3. "1.6. *Administrative Assignments.* Each administrator has too many responsibilities, and the administration staff is so small that many administrative tasks are assigned to faculty members or fall on their shoulders by default."

98. *Ibid.*, pp. 3 f. "2. Professional Status.

"2.1. *In the college.* The general impression is that the administration does not recognize the individual instructor as a member of a profession. Some factors that contribute to this feeling are:

"2.11. Salary. The administration does not provide an adequate salary for a full-time faculty position. Additional work is provided at part-time rates that are high enough to persuade the faculty member to work over-time at the college; and low enough so that the tasks are performed for about half their full-time value.

"2.12. Total Full-Time Staff. It is recommended that by September 1956, the full-time teaching staff should be at least doubled. The present full-time staff of under 70 is so small that an undue burden of administrative and clerical duties is placed on each staff member.

"2.13. Secretarial Help. A minimum of one full-time secretary should be employed for each department on each campus. At the present time no secretarial help is provided a faculty member even when the correspondence concerns his administrative duties.

"2.14. Faculty Meetings. There is a tendency to talk down to the faculty, and an insufficient opportunity for faculty participation. Policies that affect the faculty are rarely determined by faculty action.

"2.15. Clerical Duties. The grading-recording procedures should be re-evaluated in an attempt to eliminate the necessity of assigning clerical duties to the faculty. It is also recommended that responsible Grants in Aid be assigned to collect tickets at the weekly College Community Conference.

"2.2. *In the Community.* In general, faculty members are expected, by the college and the community, to make professional contributions to the community. They should have the time, the income, the housing, and the clothing of professional people. The average full-time salary of the Fairleigh Dickinson College faculty is under $4,800. This is about $700 less than the average high school teacher's salary in the metropolitan area. The average income of our students' families is even above the average salary of the Fairleigh Dickinson College faculty. We are interested to note that the annual earnings of the General Motors and General Electric factory workers is in excess of $5,000 a year."

A proposed salary guide was included.[99] Reduction of the basic teaching load to twelve instructional hours was recommended.

When this AAUP report is compared with the report by the American Institute of Management examined above, a difference in tone emerges as the chief contrast between the two documents. The latter reflects the calm, objective nature of a management survey; the former the involved, emotional tone of a group who are deeply immersed in the institution, the policies of which affect their professional and personal lives profoundly. Yet the matters brought up by both reports are much the same: need for more administrative and clerical staff, improvement of the salary situation. The difference in content relates to such matters as faculty status and participation in governance, class sizes, and lack of office space.

On the matter of admissions, Sammartino pointed out that during the war there was open admission at Fairleigh Dickinson, as there was at almost every college in the country. During the veteran influx, admission was based on a mental maturity test, since it would have been absurd to think in terms of high school records

---

99. *Ibid.*, p. 5

Salary Guide

Title	Minimum Qualifications	Salary Range
Asst. Instructor	B.S. degree or equivalent experience	Open
Instructor	M.A. or equivalent experience, except in specialized curricula	$4,500-$6,000
Asst. Professor	Three years of college teaching experience	$5,400-$7,800
Associate Prof.	Six years of college teaching experience	$6,600-$9,300
Full Professor	Six years of college teaching experience in rank above instructor	$8,400-$11,100
Visiting Professor	Full-time teacher— possibly retired from another institution	Open
Prof. Emeritus	Part-time teacher— possibly retired from another institution	Open
Adjunct Professor	Part-time teacher employed as a full-time professor at another institution	Open

that might antedate a veteran's five-year service to his country.
But during the early fifties, Sammartino began to think in terms
of upgrading admission standards about three percent per year.
Three criteria were used: college boards, high school record, and
intelligence quotient. Sammartino explained this to the high school
principals and to the guidance counselors. It was during this period
that he established the Reading and Study Institute in East Rutherford to take care of those students who could not meet the ever-
higher standards. The Institute was later moved to Wayne. But
as the endowment increased, he devoted practically all of its income to providing scholarships for top students. He fought tooth
and nail for the establishment of state scholarships, and there was
hardly a week that he was not seen escorting legislators around
the campus. Later these same legislators elected him vice-president
of the New Jersey Constitutional Convention. Slowly but surely,
in the sixties, the fiftieth percentile was passed and later the six-
tieth. But he went a step further and established the Honors'
College, referred to elsewhere. No community problem escaped his
attention and long before it became fashionable to do so, he began
a campaign to take care of minority groups, whether they had
money or not, and secured the help of leading industrialists in
discerning among their employees black workers who might profit
from evening college work.

While the faculty salaries had been low during the forties, as
most college salaries were, during the fifties there was a gradual
upward climb. There was an added factor which probably did not
exist at any other institution: the faculty fund. Sammartino had
always felt that, since salary schedules and budgets had to be
made up during the spring for the following year, in view of the
uncertainties of income the tendency was always to be conserva-
tive. But, during the spring of the actual year of income and
spending, the situation would be much more realistic. It was
therefore decided that each spring an allotment would be made
toward the faculty member's retirement, over and above the regular pension. This allotment would be based on the finances of the
college for the year. It has varied from five to nine percent of
the salary.

Indeed, by the sixties, the salary schedule had improved to the
point that Fairleigh Dickinson was included in the A.A.U.P. 1963–
1964 honor roll of institutions with relatively high grades of
compensation scales. Considering the fact that there were 2,500
colleges and universities in the United States and only about 200

on the A.A.U.P. list, it meant that Fairleigh Dickinson was in the 90 percentile salary-wise. But the early faculty members were not forgotten. They had served at low salaries and during the forties without the benefit of T.I.A.A. pension. At the suggestion of Sammartino, they were guaranteed fifty percent retirement benefit based on their terminal salaries, and a special fund was created to guarantee the pension.

Besides these outward matters, there were, perhaps, deeper, more inward sources for the dissatisfaction in the 1956 AAUP report. Even in nature, the process of growth is never painless. At the age of fourteen, adolescence, with all of its new challenges and accompanying difficulties, begins. Occasionally such problems actually destroy a youth, whether physically or morally.

Fairleigh Dickinson College had reached adolescence after fourteen years of rapid growth. It was about to signal its recognition of the still greater possibilities it faced by a change in its status and name. But a period of questioning and seeking was also about to begin, which would lead ultimately, despite all the intervening painful and difficult problems—or perhaps because of them—to a final period of maturity and stability as the institution's first quarter of a century gradually drew to a close.

8

The Three-Campus University 1956-1960

The Thirteenth Commencement was held on June 12, 1956, at the Rutherford Campus. It was to be a memorable occasion. An audience of more than 3,500 witnessed the awarding of degrees to 563 graduates, among them eight masters in business administration, the first graduate degrees awarded by Fairleigh Dickinson College. They were also to be the last ever awarded by the *college*.

Honorary degrees were awarded at the outdoor evening ceremonies to Guy E. Hilleboe, Leon Canfield, Forrest A. Irwin, and Dr. Albert E. Meder, Jr.[1]

The Commencement address was delivered by Guy Hilleboe, who had returned briefly from service on an educational mission to India sponsored by the International Cooperation Administration of the Federal Government. In his vital, energetic way Hilleboe praised American aid as an important factor in that country's evolution toward a "self-sufficient democracy."[2]

The evening's most dramatic moment came, however, during President Sammartino's commencement remarks. He informed the audience that just before the ceremony, he had received confirmation from the New Jersey State Board of Education that it had approved university status for the institution as of that day. Fairleigh Dickinson College had just become Fairleigh Dickinson University.

1. Dr. Meder was dean of admissions of Rutgers University at the time. In later years he became dean of graduate studies at Rutgers.
2. Passaic-Clifton, N.J. *Herald-News*, June 13, 1956.

184

After a moment's silence, during which his news sank in, the whole audience of trustees, administrators, faculty and graduates and their friends and relatives, broke into a loud cheer and prolonged standing applause.[2]

Sammartino added that preliminary approval for the step had also been obtained from the Middle States Association and that final approval would be a formality. He explained that a college was entitled to become a university when it had reached a certain complexity of organization and scope of studies, and was awarding graduate degrees. All of these qualifications were met by Fairleigh Dickinson. Besides having a graduate school it would have a school of dentistry, scheduled to begin classes in the fall. Moreover, the new University, besides these two graduate schools, would be organized into three undergraduate colleges: liberal arts and sciences, engineering and science, and business administration.[3]

Thus the institution stepped onto the highest rung of the academic institutional ladder. In 14 years it had moved from junior college to university status.

How correct was Sammartino's statement that the institution now deserved the title *university*? If complexity of organization, size of faculty and student body, variety of studies, and scope of physical facilities are the criteria, then Fairleigh Dickinson was as well qualified as many another American institution carrying the designation.

Let us consider numbers first. The student body of the 1956–1957 academic year totaled 7,823. Of these the new dental school accounted for 46. As it is just entering class. Another 646 students were enrolled in the Graduate School, indicating a modest increase of only seven students over the previous first year of graduate studies.

The students were distributed as follows (percentage indicates change over the previous year):

	Day	Evening	Graduate	Dental	Total
Rutherford	(3846 +4%)	(3223 –1%)	—	—	(7069)
Teaneck	(1703 +40%)	(2373 +58%)	—	(46 new)	(4122 +46%)
	(7823 +42%)	(5844 +44%)	(646 +1%)	(2,169)	(7823 +13%)

2. *Ibid.*
3. *Ibid.*
4. Venter Hill, *Fairleigh Dickinson University: Some Aspects of Its Growth* (Rutherford, N.J.: Fairleigh Dickinson University, 1961), p. 2.

The total of 191 graduate and dental students composed slightly more than two percent of those studying for degrees at the newly designated university, yet the graduate degrees this small band was pursuing included the doctorate (Doctor of Dental Surgery).

The statistics reveal that Rutherford's growth in students had come to a standstill, but that Teaneck was making phenomenal strides to come abreast of the older campus. Two "coequal" campuses, at least in student numbers, were almost a fact at the new university.

A similar growth in numbers of faculty had taken place. The newly designated university listed 206 faculty members in its catalogue, of whom about one-fourth held doctorates.[6]

The administrative structure at the moment of achieving university status included a president, three deans, one administrative assistant, ten directors, and five department chairmen. The last-named group supervised academic departments, including the faculty on both campuses. Very shortly this administrative structure was expanded to consist of a president, two vice-presidents (one academic, one administrative), one campus dean, five deans of colleges and schools, 13 directors, two administrative assistants, and five department chairmen.[7]

The establishment and dedication of a dental school had taken place seven months before Sammartino emphasized the school's importance at the 1956 commencement as a factor in acquiring university status, although the first dental students did not begin their studies until the fall 1956 semester. On November 16, 1955, an audience of 600 listened as the governor of the state, Robert Meyner, hailed the establishment of the first school of dentistry in New Jersey.[8] The only other such school was to begin opera-

6. *Bulletin of Fairleigh Dickinson College, 1955-1957, Teaneck and Rutherford* (Rutherford, N.J.: Fairleigh Dickinson College Press, 1955), pp. 11-22.

7. Dr. Ray Miller was named administrative vice-president. Dr. Clarence R. Decker (A.B., Carleton College; Ph.D., University of Chicago), was named academic vice-president. He had been president of the University of Kansas City and had come to Fairleigh Dickinson in 1955 as professor of English. Dr. Decker's title was changed to "vice-president" after Dr. Miller left to become president of York Junior College. Dr. Decker remained vice-president until his retirement in 1967. During 1959-1960 he was also dean of the College of Arts and Sciences and was the first (*ex-officio*) chairman of the University Council from 1961 until 1963. He died in 1969.

The following were appointed first deans of the newly created colleges and schools: Clair W. Black (engineering and sciences), Harold Feldman (business administration), Harry A. Sprague (graduate), Walter A. Wilson (dentistry).

8. Newark, N.J., *Newark Evening News*, November 17, 1955.

tions simultaneously at Seton Hall University, also in the fall of 1956. Thus the Fairleigh Dickinson University School of Dentistry was one of two "firsts" in the Garden State. At the ceremony in Teaneck the new dean of the dental school, Dr. Walter A. Wilson, stated:

> We dedicate ourselves to provide for the community, state and nation graduates so trained in the basic sciences that they will possess a foundation of knowledge which will enable them not only to integrate their scientific learning with their clinical practice, but which will equip them for further post-graduate studies.[9]

Representatives of the dental profession who spoke at the dedication included Dr. Gerald T. Timmons, dean of the Temple University School of Dentistry, and Dr. John A. Campi, president of the New Jersey State Dental Society, who was the official representative of the American Dental Association.

Dr. Sammartino officially dedicated the new professional school

> to serve the state and the dental profession and to enable the immediately neighbouring communities to achieve a higher degree of dental health.[10]

The dental school was housed on the lower floors of the new Science Building, later known as Robison Hall, which was erected on the rise of the river bank overlooking the Hackensack Valley to the west and south, near the northern center of the Teaneck Campus.[11]

Perhaps the most striking thing about the dental school for the nonprofessional was the sight of fifty dentist's chairs arranged in rows in a huge room on the building's first floor, with fifty clinical patients being treated by fifty dental students under the expert guidance of the school's faculty. It was a most unusual classroom.

The establishment of an anatomy laboratory, replete with cold

9. *Ibid.*
Walter A. Wilson (D.D.S., F.A.C.D.) was secretary to the New Jersey State Board of Dental Examiners from 1939 until 1955. He remained dean of the School of Dentistry of Fairleigh Dickinson University until his retirement in 1971.
Dean Wilson is writing a separate history of the dental school.
10. *Ibid.*
11. Robison Hall was named after Adolf C. Robison, long a member of the University's Board of Fellows, an advisory body to the Trustees. He was Director-President of the Robison Textile Company in Fairview, N.J. Mr. Robison was chairman of the Board of Fellows from 1967 until 1970. Mr. and Mrs. Robison were most generous in their support of the University's development, especially at the Teaneck Campus. Their contributions to the University included their own time and the influence of their creative and vital personalities.

storage facilities for the cadavers being dissected, caused many a chill at night to freshmen trying to sleep in the Teaneck dormitories, as well as macabre jokes among the male faculty and students trying to prove that they were undismayed by the contents of the new facility on campus. The Teaneck faculty were soon impressed by the high professional standards of the new dental faculty colleagues in their midst, who were very much alive.

The establishment of the dental school, in addition to the beginning of graduate studies in other fields and the establishment of the College of Engineering, was probably the chief justification on an academic basis for the redesignation of the institution as a "university." The old medieval criteria for establishing a *studium generale* for an institution, at which all the major fields of study are represented, had not been met. Whole areas of thought and study were still unrepresented on the graduate level. But the criteria for an *universitas*—complexity of structure, wide scope of studies a certain size, even the growth of a doctorate (D.D.S.) —these now existed at Fairleigh Dickinson University.

Even before the granting of university status, the growing significance of Fairleigh Dickinson had been recognized by the Ford Foundation when, around Christmas 1955, it distributed half a billion dollars in gifts to universities, colleges, hospitals, and medical schools throughout the nation. Fairleigh Dickinson received over one million dollars, the second-largest amount given to an educational institution in New Jersey, Princeton University being awarded the largest.[12]

The University's material assets had continued to increase. By 1956 they amounted to approximately six million dollars in buildings and grounds on two campuses, and to an endowment fund in excess of two million dollars.[13]

Nor was a halt called to continuing growth at this time in the area of physical facilities. In December 1956 the university bought for $75,000 a farm of 265 acres in Chester Township in Morris County in the north central part of the state. Ten buildings stood on the acreage, one of them a sizable home that had just been completed by its previous owner, a builder in Essex County, who had died intestate. Sammartino announced plans to utilize the farm for a research and development program in organic farming, and remarked:

12. North Arlington, N.J., *Leader*, December 15, 1955.
13. Rutherford, N.J., *South Bergen News*, September 20, 1956.

I have always believed that good food and good eating are consistent with good nutrition and have never allowed candy or carbonated beverages to be sold on our campus.[14]

It was indeed true that Sammartino had long held strong views in the area of nutrition. For years a special bread of unbleached flour had been made especially for Fairleigh Dickinson and was on sale in the institution's bookstores. Carlton Fredericks, well-known radio commentator and consultant in the area of nutrition, had begun to teach at the Teaneck Campus during the 1956 spring semester.[15] He continued to give courses in nutrition at the Teaneck Campus for a number of years.[16]

The Chester farm was, in fact, used for several faculty conferences and picnics before it was sold for a profit some years later.

This incident principally has importance because it showed that the University had plans for further expansion in real estate and facilities and that these plans centered in Morris County.

The year 1957 began with the gift of a three-century old silver mace to the University by Mr. and Mrs. Leo Pollak of New York City, who were long-time friends and supporters of the institution. The mace was of English provenance, made by a silversmith in Sheffield during the seventeenth century.[17] Used at commencements and other formal ceremonies, the mace symbolized the authority exercised by the University in its various functions. Its English origin was a totally unplanned link with a future development of the University, which no one at the time foresaw.

On February 2, 1957, Louis J. Scaramelli died in his sleep at his house on 229 Montross Avenue in Rutherford, on the porch of which house the plan had first been formed to found the institution.[18]

Scaramelli had attended the 1956 Commencement, at which the granting of university status had been announced. In a conversation with a group of faculty after the ceremony, he had revealed his deep satisfaction at the growth of the school that he had helped to found fourteen years before. It was obvious to those who heard him speak on that occasion how much the institution had come to mean to him and how pleased he was by the results.

14. Newark, N.J. *News*, December 12, 1956.
15. Rutherford, N.J., *South Bergen News*, March 1, 1956.
16. Carlton Fredericks (A.B. Alabama; M.A. New York University) had also taught at New York University, Brooklyn College of Pharmacy, Columbia College of Pharmacy, and several other institutions.
17. Paterson, N.J., *Call*, January 16, 1957.
18. New York, N.Y. *Herald Tribune*, February 2, 1957.

Only a few months later Guy L. Hilleboe, the Commencement speaker in 1956, succumbed to a heart attack while in Bangalore, India, where he had been serving as deputy director of the International Cooperation Administration.[19]

Both Scaramelli and Hilleboe had seen the institution attain the highest academic status, that of a university.

These two deaths left only Sammartino and Williams alive of the original group of five founders and incorporators. The two survivors, occupying the university's key positions, continued to work effectively and in mutual supplementation of each other's abilities during the decade still ahead of them.

The institution's first academic year as a university proved to be among the quietest experienced during the first quarter of a century. The round of classes, and educational, social, and ceremonial affairs of all kinds unrolled in the ways that had become customary.

Even the Fourteenth Commencement, held on June 5, 1957, at the Rutherford Campus, was a relatively quiet affair in contrast with the previous year's dramatic announcement of university status. Of the 720 students who received degrees, 62 were graduated with honors. Paul Arts of West Paterson, Barbara Buhlman of Allendale, and Robert Lofts of Bogota were awarded their degrees *summa cum laude*.[20] A new factor first noticeable on a larger scale at this commencement was the ever-greater proportion of graduates who had studied at the Teaneck Campus rather than at the Rutherford site.

No guest speaker had been scheduled.[21]

Dr. Sammartino also reported on the institution's work during its first year as a university, and showed how it had been growing into new stature in faculty, curricula, and facilities. He concluded by reading a message from President Eisenhower, which ended with the words:

> Tell them that I would like nothing better than to be one of the thousands graduating from college this year. Tell them also that they will never appreciate anything unless they work for it.[22]

According to Warren L. Duncan, placement director and industrial coordinator, the 1957 graduates were having little trouble in finding jobs. Representatives of 111 companies had conducted

19. Newark, N.Y., *News*, May 8, 1957.
20. Hackensack, N.J., *Bergen Record*, June 6, 1957.
21. Passaic-Clifton, N.J., *Herald-News*, June 3, 1957.
22. *Ibid.*

interviews with Fairleigh Dickinson seniors at the two campuses and a great many graduates had been hired. Some companies were still looking.[23]

The summer of 1957 unrolled in the same quiet, constructive manner as the whole preceding year.

In order to reinforce the Board of Trustees diminished by the deaths of Hilleboe and Scaramelli, election of Samuel J. Silberman was announced on July 1, 1957. Mr. Silberman had been associated with the Consolidated Cigar Company since 1934 and its president since 1949. During the Second World War he served with the Coast Guard, emerging with the rank of Lieutenant Commander.[24] A native of Hartford, Connecticut, Silberman through his succeeding years as a trustee continued to exemplify the calm, constructive tone that had been characteristic of the academic year of his election.

The summer session of 1957 further exemplified the mood of quiet, continued growth with an enrollment of 2,790 students, of whom 421 came from 161 different institutions just for the summer. In this category of summer transfer students there was a drop in percentage compared with the previous summer. The total number of summer students was, however, considerably higher, since Teaneck's enrollment had increased by seventy percent over that campus's previous summer. The total summer enrollment was almost evenly divided between the two campuses. Thus the summer session of 1957 represents the point at which the newer campus, after only three-and-a-half years of operation, drew abreast of its elder sister in student population.[25]

Margaret Coit was featured at a writers' conference at the University of New Hampshire because of her newly published biography of Bernard Baruch, which was ultimately chosen by the Book-of-the-Month Club as its December 1957 selection.[26]

Only 214 of the 720 graduates were awarded the Associate-in-

23. Rutherford, N.J., *South Bergen News*, August 22, 1957.
24. Paterson, N.J., *News*, July 1, 1957. Silberman was also chairman of the board of Michigan Peat, Inc., a member of the advisory committee of the Bankers Trust Company in New York City, and a director of the National Community Bank (formerly the Rutherford National Bank). He participated in many civic activities, including a vice-presidency of the Federation of Jewish Philanthropies of New York and chairmanships in fund-raising campaigns for that organization and for the Greater New York Fund, the YMCA, and the Cerebral Palsy Campaigns. His clubs included the Harvard, Quaker Ridge Golf in Scarsdale, and yacht clubs in San Juan, P.R., Middletown, Conn., and St. Croix, V.I.
25. Paterson, N.J., *Call*, 1957.
26. Keene, N.H., *Daily Sentinel*, August 31, 1957. Philadelphia, Pa., *Bulletin*, November 24, 1957.

arts degree for two years' study. The students were in increasing proportions pursuing the full four-year course for the bachelor's degree.

Honorary degrees were awarded Dr. Harry A. Sprague, the former president of Montclair State Teachers College, who had become the first dean of the Fairleigh Dickinson University Graduate School, and to H. Lee Moss, who had been a trustee of Bergen Junior College and had helped with the negotiations that led to the merger of the Teaneck school with Fairleigh Dickinson.[27]

A new feature at this commencement was the presentation by the newly appointed deans of the graduates of their various colleges and schools to the university president for the awarding of degrees, thus visibly illustrating the movement into the more complex structure of a university.[28]

In his remarks President Sammartino announced that the 14 acres of the Davenport West estate, "Red Towers," in Teaneck just to the south of the 1000 River Road property, had been acquired by the university.[29] This acquisition increased the size of the Teaneck campus by about twenty percent and was an important step forward in the process of joining two parts of the campus into one coherent whole. The transaction also brought the institution a building that was used for office space. It was later torn down to make room for the present library.

The classical languages had been introduced into the ever-growing list of courses and subjects available for study at Fairleigh Dickinson University and Professor Walter Freeman, who became the institution's resident classicist, announced early in July that courses in Latin and Greek were being expanded for the fall in response to growing student demands.[30]

In the area of graduate studies, Dr. Sprague announced that same month that the New Jersey State Department of Education had approved graduate programs at Fairleigh Dickinson University leading to master of arts degrees in history, English, and psychology. The courses for these degrees would be offered at the Teaneck Campus.[31]

27. Moss later served as placement director and industrial coordinator at Fairleigh Dickinson University from 1952-1957.

28. *Ibid.*

29. Passaic-Clifton, N.J., *Herald-News*, June 6, 1957.

30. Rutherford, N.J., *South Bergen News*, July 1, 1957. Prof. Walter H. Freeman (A.B., M.A., Ph.D., Harvard University) came to Fairleigh Dickinson in 1956 as professor of English. He continued to teach his popular classes in Latin and Greek even after his retirement as emeritus professor in 1961.

31. Ramsey, N.J. *Journal*, July 25, 1957.

The Class of 1958 is about to begin its march onto the field near the Friendship Library, the site of the first commencement for the whole University at the newly acquired Madison Campus. A wing of the Mansion is at right.

Dr. Sammartino addressing the participants at the Fifteenth Commencement, June 4, 1958, the first held at the new Madison Campus. Dean of Libraries George Nelson holds the University's eighteenth-century Sheffield mace.

Wroxton Abbey from the air.

Street in Wroxton Village.

Later that summer, again in the mood of orderly growth, the creation of a fourth undergraduate college, that of education, was announced. This school, after the existing three undergraduate and two graduate schools, was the University's sixth. Dr. Forrest A. Irwin was named the first dean of the College of Education.[32]

The appointment of men such as Dr. Sprague and Dr. Irwin to high administrative positions at Fairleigh Dickinson, after they had retired from college presidencies elsewhere, revealed that older men could bring their great experience and still vigorous talents to a new, youthful institution and still contribute some years of constructive, useful work. They could begin the development of a graduate school or of a college of education from nothing, and avoid making some of the mistakes a younger, less-experienced man might make. The university's president meanwhile was there to provide creative momentum. The difficulty with this arrangement was to decide when the older man had fulfilled his task and should be replaced by a younger, more innovative, and possibly more independent administrator. Of course, such a man would also be liable to make greater demands and have greater expectations. The replacement of the old, reliable men in these posts by new men from outside of the institution was in the course of time to lead to a number of difficulties.

In early August the construction of a new ten-room classroom building in East Rutherford on land donated by Becton, Dickinson and Company was made known. The building, located at Hackensack and Cornelia Streets, would seat 300 students. The parking lots around it, used during the day by Becton, Dickinson employees, would be available in the evening for Fairleigh Dickinson students. Thus the new structure was to serve the greatly expanding evening enrollment and to decrease the parking problem around the Rutherford Campus.[33]

Although these developments of the summer of 1957 had a certain importance, they were not of the dramatic character that had marked previous summers. In view of the quiet preceding

---

32. Lodi, N.J., *Messenger*, September 5, 1957. Forrest A. Irwin (B.S., Northwestern University, M.A., Teachers College, Columbia University, LL.D., Fairleigh Dickinson University) had been vice-president and head of the department of education at Trenton State Teachers College from 1931 to 1942. He was president of Jersey City State Teachers College from 1946 until 1954. He joined the Fairleigh Dickinson faculty in 1954 and was placed in charge of teacher training. Dr. Irwin retired as dean of the College of Education in 1962.

33. It did so with effect for about twelve years, at which time the arrangement was discontinued because Becton, Dickinson needed the facilities for its own use.

academic year and the relatively uneventful summer, Fairleigh
Dickinson University watchers seemed justified in concluding
that the era of great surprises during the summer were over.

SUDDENLY — A THIRD CAMPUS:
FLORHAM-MADISON

Then, during the last third of August, a surprise of great importance again overwhelmed the institution with its possibilities
and challenges.

On August 21, 1957, Edward T. T. Williams announced that
Fairleigh Dickinson University had acquired 180 acres and a
100-room mansion in Florham Park, near Morristown in Morris
County, as a third campus. Mr. Williams explained the reason
for this new acquisition:

> The trustees were attempting to look ahead several decades and make
> proper provision for the eventual needs of the university. If we look
> at some important institutions today, for example, Columbia, Yale or
> Brown, it is evident that what seemed a great deal of land genera-
> tions ago is inadequate [to] present-day university requirements.[34]

The university had acquired, with its third-campus land, buildings and a tradition. The new campus was about five times the
size of the Teaneck Campus and more than ten times the size of
the Rutherford Campus. Besides the mansion with 100 rooms,
there were also a large carriage house (later transformed into a
science building), a recreation building with swimming pool and
an indoor tennis court (transformed into a gymnasium), an
orangery (transformed into a library), and a series of smaller
buildings that were adapted to a variety of new uses. The mansion
at first housed the offices, classrooms, and dormitory facilities of
the new campus.

What the university had acquired was "Florham"—the buildings and about one-fourth of the grounds of the estate established
by Mr. and Mrs. Hamilton J. McKeown Twombly during the
Gilded Age.[35] Mrs. Twombly was one of the granddaughters of
Cornelius Vanderbilt, who had married still more wealth. Her
marriage to Twombly was one of the social highlights of the
Gilded Age.

In order to live in suitable quarters, the Twomblys had built

34. New York, N.Y., *Times*, August 22, 1957.
35. The remainder of the real estate, about 700 acres, was acquired by
the Essex Research Corporation, which built a laboratory on the property.

for themselves their huge mansion modeled after Hampton Court Palace. A magnificent park, gardens, and lawns surrounded the building and broad, wooded acres stretched beyond. The play house, with swimming pool, tennis court, and paneled music room with grand piano, was built to help their daughter enjoy her favorite recreations.

After the death of her husband sometime before the First World War, Mrs. Twombly continued her role as society matriarch with great energy until her death at an advanced age in 1952. Her daughter survived her by only a few years, dying in 1956. Thereafter the buildings and grounds were vacant.

How had the new campus been acquired?

As indicated in his announcement, Edward Williams had come to believe that more land to the west would be needed by the University. He therefore began to look around in Morris County. In this way Florham had come to his attention.

When the acquisition of the Madison Campus was proposed by Williams, the trustees were at first generally in favor. Dr. Sammartino, however, pointed out the difficulties that would be encountered. The University was still trying to develop its second campus. A third campus would retard Teaneck's growth. There would be a further dispersion of personnel and resources. As a result of this discussion, the trustees voted not to go ahead with the acquisition.

After the meeting, Mr. Williams and Mr. Dickinson, in a private discussion, concluded that "the wrong decision had been made for the right reasons." There was the example of other universities, such as Columbia, which had hesitated too long in acquiring additional land and now could acquire more near their present campuses only with great difficulty. Florham. Park-Madison was located at the spot in New Jersey that promised the greatest increase in population during the next twenty years. It could be the home of a new, beautiful, ready-made campus. The buildings available could be altered for educational purposes. Once lost by an impulsive decision, the property could never be acquired and no other remotely approaching it was available.

Before the group of trustees dispersed, Mr. Williams asked Mr. Blauvelt to negotiate for the purchase of the property over an extended period of time, which would permit the University to carry the Twombly estate in reserve for three or four years, holding the operations down to the maintenance of buildings and grounds. Mr. Blauvelt, who had been enthusiastic about the site, was able to accomplish the negotiations within thirty days. The trustees then reconsidered the matter and decided to acquire the property, arranging the terms of acquisition to give Dr. Sammartino the time needed for the adjustment.[36]

The acquisition of the Madison Campus was second only to that of the Teaneck Campus in importance. The pattern of having more than one campus, which had been initiated in 1954, was thus continued and strengthened by the acquisition of Madison in 1957. The institution became even more varied and diverse in its components. The two older campuses were situated in similar socio-economic environments. They were surrounded by suburban towns close to New York City inhabited by working people or members of the middle class. Madison, in the nineteen fifties, still belonged to "exurbia." The population surrounding the new campus, besides including the middle class, also had wealthier and more socially advanced elements from the junior executive and executive layers of American society. Moreover, the beautiful grounds of the campus and the architecture of the buildings seemed as if made to order as a setting for the cultivation of the liberal, fine, and performing arts, and for a large dormitory population.

Another simple yet basic fact was the distance of thirty-five miles that separated the new campus from its two older sisters, which were themselves only nine miles apart. This greater distance was to exercise a subtle, almost unconscious, yet powerful influence upon the relationship of the Madison Campus to the rest of the institution.

The newest campus was first officially used by the University for its Commencement on June 4, 1958. The opening of the ceremonies was delayed twenty minutes due to the traffic jams caused by the crowd of 10,000 persons who drove to attend. When the academic procession began at 2:40 P.M., many participants and spectators were still arriving. A forty-piece band played appropriate music as the "Knights" with their chain mail and spears led the colorful procession of trustees, administrators, faculty, and students onto the large lawn to the southwest of the Mansion. It was an ideal spot for an outdoor commencement and the weather was perfect for it. The green stretches of the lawn were covered by long rows of folding chairs, gradually filled by the graduates. The trustees, administrators, and faculty sat on raised platforms

---

36. Interview with Edward T. T. Williams, August 21, 1962.

facing the audience, with the old orangery, which was being converted into Friendship Library, behind them. Magnificent old trees bordered the lawn toward the south, while the Georgian façade of "Florham," also known as "The Mansion," loomed above the festivities on the other side. The scene seemed to reflect the commencements of a much older institution. At its first commencement the Madison Campus looked as if it had served these academic purposes for half a century at least. For those who could remember the small, modest circumstances and setting of the first Fairleigh Dickinson commencement, the scope, setting, and attendance at this ceremony were awesome evidence of the institution's growth in numbers and outreach. Yet, those sensitive to such things felt that the same vital spirit that had been alive on those early and smaller occasions was still alive and strong at this greatly expanded event.

In his remarks President Sammartino apologized because all the mechanics had not worked smoothly, and stated that the new campus would be kept "as a small campus and daring educational experimentation center."[37]

He added:

> The great need today is for the American family to realize that not everyone can have a college education. Even in a democracy there are limits to universal education, limits dictated by ability. We must make sure that an adequate number of scholarships are provided to take care of students who could otherwise not afford to go to college. . . . Fairleigh Dickinson University will grow extremely slowly from now on, and only if there is a real community demand for increased facilities for qualified students, and if contributions received support this expansion.[38]

The emphasis upon keeping the newest campus small was ultimately to be changed, due to pressures from the communities surrounding it, and from the small, devoted administration and faculty that began to appear on the Madison Campus.

The man chosen as dean of the new campus. Dr. Samuel Pratt, was to lead Madison for ten years, almost until the end of the period covered by this history. He had taught business subjects and his wife, Lois, had taught sociology at the Teaneck Campus for several years before they undertook the challenging operation

---

37. Morristown, N.J., *Record*, June 5, 1958.
38. Paterson, N.J., *Call*, June 5, 1958.

of transforming an estate from the Gilded Age into a modern college campus.[39]

The Pratts were a hard-working, devoted couple who threw themselves fully into their task. Mrs. Pratt held a doctorate in sociology and soon emerged as an energetic force among the emerging Madison faculty. In his ten-year career as Madison Campus dean, Sam Pratt revealed a strong intellectual and analytic bent combined with considerable ability and drive as an administrator. He knew his own mind and never hesitated to speak it clearly. From the first day of his administration Pratt began to recognize and to expound the need for greater campus autonomy and to work and fight for it with considerable resourcefulness. The growing Madison faculty, firmly led by Pratt, supported him in this effort.

For the first few months Pratt had no desk and used a packing crate while repairs and reconstruction went on all about him.[40] Slowly the campus began to take form. It was possible to begin evening classes at Madison with 300 students by June 1958, at the time of the first commencement at Madison. By September 1958, evening enrollment at Madison had risen to 652 and an entering class of 304 full-time day students also began its studies.[41]

Several faculty members from the older campuses transferred to Madison.[42] The great majority were, however, employed by Fairleigh Dickinson University for the first time at the Madison Campus. The fact that most of the faculty came directly from other institutions was another factor, in addition to greater geographical distance, that tended from its beginning to give the newest campus a somewhat different tone and orientation.

Dean Pratt worked and fought for ever-greater control over its own curricula and destinies by Madison. A decisive victory was

---

39. Samuel A. Pratt (B.S., University of Connecticut, I.A., Harvard Graduate Business School; M.A., Michigan State University; Ph.D., University of Michigan) served as dean of the Florham-Madison Campus until the fall of 1966. In later years he was associated with Montclair State College, Montclair, N.J., where he began and developed the School of Fine and Applied Arts as its first dean until 1972. He has subsequently continued to teach at Montclair.

Lois Pratt (B.S., University of Connecticut; M.S., Michigan State University; Ph.D., University of Michigan) became Associate Professor of Social Sciences at the Florham-Madison Campus. In later years she joined the faculty of Jersey City State College.

40. Interview with Samuel A. Pratt, June 16, 1972.

41. Hill, p. 92.

42. Dr. Bernard Budish, Louis A. Rice, Malcolm Sturchio.

the gradual separation of the academic departments from control by chairmen located at one or the other of the older campuses.[43]

Another important step was the granting by the Trustees of the request that the sciences not be developed at Madison as two-year feeder curricula for the upper two years at the older campuses. The decision to permit Madison to develop four-year science curricula on its own not only made possible the construction of four-year programs in the sciences, but also implicitly permitted and encouraged the development of such curricula in liberal arts and business administration areas as well.[44]

Still another significant decision that gave Madison a character different from Rutherford and Teaneck was the construction of dormitories on a large scale. The completion of Twombly Hall at the Madison Campus in 1964 made possible the enrollment of 250 male and 225 female dormitory students. More dormitories were built in later years. These dormitory students proved to be more liberal arts-minded than most of the commuter students.[45]

Given its great architectural and natural beauty, its growing dormitory population, and its general environment and setting in Morris County, it was almost inevitable that the Madison faculty and students should develop a strong bent toward the liberal arts, and, under the encouraging guidance of Dean Pratt, a concentration on the fine and performing arts. Yet a sizable evening student body continued to study chiefly business subjects for practical reasons. Nor did the sciences lag. Biology, in particular, grew in scope and strength.

While preparations began at Madison for its opening of classes for the next year, the two older campuses began the academic year 1957–1958 with an enrollment of over 9,000 students. More than half were at the Teaneck Campus, which thus became the largest numerically, a position it has retained during the subsequent years. Graduate School enrollment grew to 375, about a sixty-percent increase over the previous year.[46] The Dental School enrollment of 93 was more than double the previous year's total. It reflected the admission of a class of first-year beginners who joined the students starting their second year. Dental School enrollment stabilized at about 200 by 1960, representing an average of 50 students for each of the four years of study.

---

43. Interview with Samuel Pratt, June 16, 1972.
44. *Ibid.*
45. *Ibid.*
46. Hill, p. 92.

With such growth in numbers, facilities, and intricacy of organization and operation, the need for a central university administrative body became strongly apparent. The need was met in October of 1957 by the formation of the Administrative Council. This body consisted of the president, vice-president, and deans.[47] It served as a cabinet for the president until the end of Sammartino's administration. Like all true cabinets, it was a confidential body built upon mutual trust and upon the fact that it consisted of officials who had been appointed by and were working in an administrative structure with the cabinet chief. It met monthly and whenever the president needed quick consideration of a problem. Again, on the model of cabinets everywhere, its proceedings were confidential and were not published or recorded in minutes. The decisions taken during its meetings were implemented by administrative action. Whenever faculty consideration was required, the various faculty committees and the President's Advisory Committee could be consulted. After the establishment of the University Council, matters proposed in the Administrative Council that required consideration by the faculty were referred to that body for study and recommendations. Thus ultimately something like the relationship generally prevalent between an executive cabinet and a parliamentary body emerged between the Administrative and University Councils.

During that same month the Board of Trustees was again decreased in numbers by the death of Hiram B. D. Blauvelt, who had played such a key role during the past summer in completing the negotiations for the acquisition of the Madison Campus in thirty days after the Trustees had made their final decision. In recognition of his work for the merger with Bergen Junior College, of which he had been a trustee, Blauvelt had been awarded an honorary degree of doctor of laws by Fairleigh Dickinson University earlier that year. His passing removed a colorful and active personality from the ranks of the trustees. Although he had served on the board for less than four years he was not quickly forgotten.

At the Rutherford Campus ground was broken in December by

47. Paterson, N.J., *Call*, October 7, 1957. The first members were: President and Chairman of the Administrative Council, Dr. Sammartino; Academic Vice-President, Dr. Clarence R. Decker; Administrative Vice-President, Dr. Ray A. Miller; Vice-President for Development, David Hammond; and the various deans of schools and campuses: Clair W. Black (science and engineering); Dr. J. Stephen Bloore (Teaneck Campus); Dr. Harold Feldman (business administration); Dr. Forrest A. Irwin (education); Dr. Harry A. Sprague (graduate); Dr. Walter A. Wilson (dental).

Administrative Vice-President Ray Miller for a new Student Union Building to be built on the site of East Hall. The new building, when completed, supplied the oldest campus with a new cafeteria, more office space, and meeting rooms. The faculty lunch room and lounge on the second floor, with fireplace and many carefully selected paintings from the University collections, proved to be a great success with the faculty and quickly became a favorite spot for meetings.

The Commencement on June 7, 1959, was again held outdoors at the Madison Campus, and for the first time the number graduating exceeded one thousand. Honorary degrees were conferred upon Robert B. Meyner, then Governor of New Jersey; Sir Pierson Dixon, G.C.M.G., C.G., who was United Kingdom Permanent Representative to the United Nations for many years; and to Dr. Ewald B. Lawson, president of a neighboring institution, Upsala College in East Orange, New Jersey.[48]

The principal commencement speaker was Edward T. T. Williams. The board chairman spoke to the huge audience in words that, for those who knew him well, reflected his own values and character:

> Men and women cannot ever feel secure if, on the one hand, they are plagued by fears and apprehensions, and, on the other, they attempt to buttress their defense with material possessions.
> It is entirely necessary for you to believe in the dignity of man, in the moral codes by which Western man has progressed, and in the ultimate triumph of orderly free governments. It is necessary for you to believe that the world is always ready to receive young people who have the spirit of adventure, who refuse to be discouraged, who grow in stature as they gain in years, because the horizon of their interests is broad, beckoning and stimulating.[49]

In order to advance the University's concern with international affairs and to deepen faculty competence in this area, the Board of Trustees, as proposed by Dr. Sammartino, arranged for an unusual study tour for the summer of 1959. The social science professors representing all three campuses were given a choice of a paid six-week study tour either to the Far East, or to West Africa, the Middle East, and Russia. Dr. Decker was designated as the groups' leader.

---

48. Paterson, N.J., *News*, June 8, 1959. Governor Meyner was cited for his devotion to the principle of frequent consultation of the people by referenda, Sir Pierson for his distinguished career for 30 years as a British diplomat, and Dr. Lawson for his outstanding performance at Upsala and his preservation of Swedish culture in America.
49. *Ibid.*

One group, consisting of Drs. Kuan I. Chen, Nasrollah Fatemi, Kenneth MacKenzie, and Clarence Weems, visited Japan, Korea, Formosa, Indonesia, Hong Kong, and India during June and July.

Meanwhile, the other group, led by Dr. Decker and including Profs. Anthony Alessandrini, Herbert Gutman, Sidney Kronish, Heinz Mackensen, Samuel Pleasants, and Bogdan Raditsa, toured Ghana, Nigeria, the Sudan, Egypt, Jordan, Israel, Syria, Turkey, and Russia.

The Fairleigh Dickinson University professors traveled approximately 40,000 miles by plane, bus, car, train, boat, camel, donkey, and on foot. At times they swam, but only for recreation. In the countries visited they spoke with all sorts and conditions of men. They interviewed American diplomatic and overseas personnel and foreign government officials. They met professors and students at universities, managers and workers in industrial plants, archbishops and archatheists, medical men and medicine men, princes and shoeshine boys.[50]

The group learned a great deal, especially about the educational value of travel. The writer, who was a member of the group, has been drawing upon the experiences and insights gained to enrich his teaching ever since. Most of the participants were inspired to continue their travels in later years. Thus, the international note that had been an aspect of Fairleigh Dickinson's development from the beginning was stimulated to further growth among the faculty.

The academic year 1959–1960 began with the following enrollments:

	Day	Evening	Graduate	Dental	Total
Rutherford	1589 (−2%)	2662 (+3%)	532 (+40%)		4783 (+4%)
Teaneck	2005 (+12%)	4109 (+10%)		186 (+30%)	6300 (+11%)
Madison	533 (+70%)	1021 (+57%)			1554 (+59%)
	4127 (+11%)	7792 (+11%)	532 (+40%)	186 (+30%)	12,637 (+12%)[51]

Madison had taken the lead in rate of numerical growth, as was to be expected of a campus beginning its second year of operation. Teaneck was also continuing to increase at a respectable rate, while Rutherford continued for the second year to show a decline

---

50. A film made during the tour, with narration by Dr. Heinz F. Mackensen, is on deposit at the Audio Visual Aids Center of the Teaneck Campus.
51. Hill, p. 92. Percentages show changes from the previous years.

in day students, which was balanced by a slight increase of evening students at that campus.

Turning to levels of education instead of campuses, these figures show that graduate students were the category increasing most rapidly.

The growth in the number of dental students was not far behind, reflecting the introduction of the third year in the Dental School. Graduate studies of all kinds were beginning to flourish at the University and the statistics reflected these developments.

The total University enrollment of almost 13,000 students placed Fairleigh Dickinson University among the ten largest private colleges and universities in the United States at the time.

9

The Development of a Constitution, *1960-1963*

So far in our narrative considerable emphasis has been placed upon growth in numbers, facilities, and programs.

Considering the nature of what happened during those years, such an emphasis was natural and inherent in the subject matter. An effort has also been made to convey something of the spirit and mood that had originally generated and continued to motivate the institution.

There were to be minor additions and subtractions, and the amplification of one aspect but, by the early nineteen sixties the major outlines of the University's physical plant was firmly established as it has continued, in the main, to exist.

What about the human beings who lived, taught, and learned, and had their being at these various locations? Of students, between 18 and 20 thousand now formed relatively stable enrollments, with about one-half at Teaneck and one-fourth each at Rutherford and Madison. These figures include part- as well as full-time students.

By 1962 the full-time faculty numbered 350. Of these, 149 held earned doctorates.[1] The full-timers were supplemented by close to 600 part-time faculty members. This sizable *corpus academicum* had a great variety in background and preparation. Their pro-

---

Issue, 1962-1963 (Rutherword–Teaneck–Madison, N.J.).
1. *Bulletin of Fairleigh Dickinson University, Undergraduate Catalogue*

fessional and scholarly interests covered an enormous scope, from the most practical and mundane subjects to the highly abstract and arcane. Moreover, their separation into three separate campuses helped, especially in the case of newcomers, to create an identification primarily with their local campus, and this often superseded identification with the institution as a whole. Campus allegiance tended to be roughly five times stronger than involvement with one's colleagues in the same discipline or college but at the other two campuses.

Moreover, since the new faculty members had joined a sizable institution rather than adventurously linking their fortunes with a struggling small college, their expectations, particularly in financial terms, were often greater than had been the case with the earlier faculty.

These factors contributed to the years of tensions and reexamination that occurred at Fairleigh Dickinson from 1960 until 1963. These years also witnessed the first relatively small waves of student unrest. These remained minor at Fairleigh Dickinson University, and the institution was spared the profound student disturbances that shook many other American and foreign universities to their foundations later during the decade.

The developments from 1960 to 1963 were met and solved with the same determination and élan that had created the institution and built it to that point. There were controversy and strife but, as in every struggle, good was produced as well as evil. The good that resulted consisted in the establishment of a working constitutional partnership between trustees, administration, faculty, and students, based upon: 1) broadened and strengthened structures and agencies of participation in the government of both the University as a whole and the individual campuses and colleges; 2) the expansion of the spirit of community and involvement also to the newer faculty; 3) a calm, detailed look at the current state of the institution and its possibilities and challenges for the future.

Possibly the greatest good that flowed from the events of these years was that Fairleigh Dickinson emerged strengthened from a time of troubles that it had been able to solve. It was thus well prepared beforehand to weather successfully the worldwide student crisis of the late nineteen sixties. This later crisis at Fairleigh Dickinson never attained major significance.

Sammartino had tried to keep all channels of communication open and continued to be active throughout the University. He became aware that certain problems were developing and summed up his concern in a special section of the annual *President's Report,* entitled "Dangers to the University," as follows:

What are the dangers that could face us, just as they face any other University?

1. Breakdown of communication among the segments of the University.
2. Emergence of vested interests or empires within the University which could absorb more than their just share of the income.
3. Flight from the economic facts of life so that the University would soon toboggan into financial chaos.
4. Forgetting that good teaching is the most important aspect of any educational institution.
5. Forgetting that the dynamic participation of the faculty in the development of an institution is the vital force that makes for progress.
6. Desire to grow too large.
7. Overbuilding so that the costs of operation will be out of proportion to the income.

Nevertheless, one cannot remain static. Our institution, Fairleigh Dickinson University, will, as finances permit, develop in the graduate field. It will increase its scope of services to the region it serves. It will enlarge the realm of research, making sure that, as it does so, it does not lessen the role of effective teaching. Above all, it will seek to maintain that esprit and elan among the faculty that has always been the life-blood of its growth and success.[2]

The appointment of two new deans from outside the closely knit University community helped to initiate the time of troubles.

When Madison began operations, the dean of the Teaneck Campus, Louis Rice, decided to relocate in Morristown and to teach at the new campus. Rice's two-and-a-half years at Teaneck had seen the growth of a cohesive and active campus faculty, among whom he had generated an amiable, comradely spirit, well reflecting his own personality.

In February 1957 the chairman of the English Department at Teaneck, Stephen Bloore, was appointed to succeed Rice.[3] Bloore, before serving briefly as chairman of the English Department at Teaneck, had been on the faculty of New York University. In both positions he had shown that he was a good teacher and scholar.

---

2. Peter Sammartino, *The President's Report* (Rutherford, Fairleigh Dickinson University, January, 1962).

3. J. Stephen Bloore (A.B., M.A., Columbia University; Ph.D., New York University) had previously taught English at New York University. He served as chairman of the English Department at the Teaneck Campus from 1956 until 1958, and as dean of the Teaneck Campus from 1958 until 1961.

Possibly his studies at an old established university with a great reputation such as Columbia and his faculty service at another long-established institution such as New York University caused Bloore to view the quite new, undeveloped Teaneck Campus, of which he now became Dean, with some inquietude. He occasionally expressed concern at the idea of calling such a young, rapidly growing, and still developing institution a "university." Moreover, Dean Bloore's personality stood in sharp contrast to that of his predecessor, Dean Rice. The latter had been all calmness, amiability, and quiet self-confidence, with an ability to keep a cool head when all around him others were losing theirs. Rice was readily accessible and easy to talk to and with. His personal involvement with the Teaneck faculty had helped to create a strong feeling of community.

Bloore tended to keep his own counsels. While his decisions may have been in the public interest, they were often criticized. His relations with other administrators and with much of the Teaneck faculty were soon strained, although some of the faculty gathered around the new campus dean.

Another new administrative face at Teaneck, also coming from outside the institution, was Vito L. Salerno, who was appointed to be dean of the College of Science and Engineering. He had been recommended for appointment by his predecessor, Dr. Clair Black, and brought with him a doctorate in aeronautic engineering and a reputation for achievement in his profession. Salerno did a good job in gaining accreditation for the growing programs in science and engineering.[4] The new dean had great plans for his college and wished to move ahead with them. He was an energetic, rather strong-willed personality. However, such plans meant growing expenditures for the University. After some years Dean Salerno came to believe that the university president was preventing the development of his college. Disagreements about projected programs and the finances involved began to increase. There seems also to have been a clash of personalities.

As a result of the sharpening of tensions involving these two important administrators, it became necessary to create a new situation. It was found best on both sides to terminate relations on comparatively short notice. The separation was effected with no hard feelings.

---

4. Interview with Dr. Clair W. Black, March 12, 1971.

Dr. Salerno was not reappointed as dean of the College of Science and Engineering but spent the next academic year on the Teaneck Campus as a consultant on matters pertaining to his former college.

Both men were replaced by successors who were to have long, distinguished careers at Fairleigh Dickinson University.

Marinus C. Galanti was one of the original founders of the institution as a member of the Board of Educational Directors.[5] He had also helped to establish the Textile Institute at the Rutherford Campus.[6] Since 1958 he had been director and since 1960 dean of the University's evening division, with his office at the Teaneck Campus. During his years in the evening office he had become well and favorably known to the Teaneck faculty, most of whom taught one or more evening classes.

Galanti was appointed dean of the Teaneck Campus as successor to Bloore. In this office, which he held for almost a decade, Galanti emerged as a remarkably capable administrator in terms of social and emotional cohesion. Close to twenty buildings were built at the Teaneck Campus during Galanti's leadership. Through many skillfully negotiated and executed maneuvers, the real estate in and around the Teaneck Campus was exchanged, acquired, and sold. Thus the cohesive campus of more than 100 acres was assembled, with the Hackensack River, as a sort of Grand Canal of Higher Education, flowing between two large compact areas, one in Hackensack and the other in Teaneck.[7]

But Galanti was also extremely effective in creating a cooperative spirit with and among faculty and students. When he announced his retirement as Teaneck Campus dean in 1969, the student government and body almost staged a demonstration to keep him in office, this at the very time when demonstrations and sit-ins were being held at many other institutions to get certain administrators out of office.

Another useful trait was Galanti's disassociation from any direct involvement with the academic aspects of the campus. This development he left largely in the hands of the college deans and department chairmen working together with the faculty.

Dr. Salerno was succeeded as dean of the College of Science and Engineering by Dr. Harold Rothbart. Dr. Rothbart remained

5. See above, chap. 2.
6. See above, chap. 5.
7. The two areas were ultimately joined by a bridge which brought the facilities on each side within walking distance of the facilities on the other side.

at the head of the College of Science and Engineering until 1972. During these years he did much to stimulate a spirit of creativity among the faculty of his college. His own interests ranged widely. He felt that scientists, like humanists, were under obligation to build intellectual and cultural bridges between the "two cultures." In an effort to foster such rapprochement he ventured into the field of poetry.

In the years of faculty controversy from 1960 until 1963, several areas emerged as of strong concern: 1) salary levels, 2) teaching loads, and 3) greater faculty participation in decision-making. An active group, particularly at Teaneck and Madison, began to agitate these issues during the academic year 1960–1961. These faculty members joined the three separate campus chapters of the AAUP that were now formed. Until 1960 there had been only one A.A.U.P. chapter covering all three campuses, but growing identification with their local campus, especially on the part of the newer faculty, made the reorganization into three separate chapters inevitable. Thus the A.A.U.P. foreshadowed the campus autonomy that was ultimately to grow larger and larger. Moreover, the local campus chapters tended to be much more active than their all-University predecessor.

A number of newer faculty were given terminal notice or contracts in the spring of 1961. Many of these faculty, along with others, became exceedingly active in pressing for an investigation of the University by Committee T of the national organization of the A.A.U.P.

In order to carry out its role as watchdog of the interests and concerns of faculty members, the national office of the A.A.U.P. had developed a set of procedures for the investigation, evaluation, and reporting of alleged violations of academic freedom and due process at American colleges and universities. Committee T was the Association's agency for these functions. Its reports were presented to the organization's national convention, which could vote censure of the institution if the report seemed to justify such action. Censure had no practical effect except to give the institution a black eye and to warn faculty members against seeking employment there.

In order to prevent misuse of its Committee T investigations for personal and other reasons, the Association conducted preliminary studies of the situation by a small special committee, which visited the campus to establish whether a full Committee T investigation was necessary.

During the years of intense involvement with the A.A.U.P. from 1960 to 1963, the A.A.U.P. procedure regarding Fairleigh Dickinson University never went beyond this preliminary stage. No Committee T investigation was ever held necessary and therefore obviously no censure was ever proposed or voted.

However, the actions and demands of the activists in the A.A.U.P. chapters did lead to a visit on February 26, 27, and 28, 1963, by a committee consisting of Louis Joughin and Bertram H. Davis. At the time, both men were associated with the National Office. For the two years previous to this visit there were frequent meetings of the A.A.U.P. officers and delegates with representatives of the trustees and administration. At the national conventions of the A.A.U.P. during these years, progress reports on the situation at F.D.U. were given by the chairman of Committee T and by the General Secretary, William P. Fidler. Delegates from the F.D.U. chapters and representatives of the administration spoke in committee meetings and on the floor of the A.A.U.P. conventions. As is inevitable in such controversial situations, the evaluations and reports varied greatly in emphasis, tone, and conclusions. Nor were obligations to confidential treatment of such documents as A.A.U.P. preliminary reports always observed.

Thus the New York Post published an article on June 7, 1962, which was supposedly based on the confidential A.A.U.P. report and repeated charges allegedly made by some faculty members regarding teaching loads, faculty turnover, student preparation and quality, and admissions standards. This action by some of their colleagues so greatly incensed a total of 97 of the full-time faculty who were members of the A.A.U.P. that they joined in signing a letter of protest to the editor of the *New York Post*.

What conclusions can be drawn from this involvement of the University with the A.A.U.P. from 1960 until 1963?[8]

The development of the institution from very small beginnings to greater complexity and large size within two decades inevitably produced certain growing pains. These had become stronger as the

---

8. From 1958 until 1959 the writer of this chapter (Dr. H. Mackensen) was president of the A.A.U.P. Chapter of F.D.U. After the division into three campus chapters, he was elected secretary of the Teaneck Campus chapter annually from 1959 until 1964. He attended the National A.A.U.P. convention of 1962, 1963, and 1964. These conclusions are based upon his personal involvement and knowledge, and upon study of the confidential A.A.U.P. and other documents. While he has used these documents and sources to form his conclusions, the writer is determined to respect their confidentiality and will not quote or cite them. Many of the documents on which these conclusions are based are in his possession.

multiple-campus system grew. It is hard to maintain the ease of communication and personal relationships that characterize a small institution on one campus when the faculty increases to almost a thousand members scattered over three campuses. Obviously a more formalized and widely articulated system of university government had become necessary.

Similarly, there was an obvious need for the formation of more definite and defined forms of government for the individual campuses and colleges.

Procedures through which faculty members and groups could formulate and advance their concerns needed to be spelled out.

After two decades of constant growth, a pause to consider what had been achieved, what the current problems were, and what should be done for the future was in order.

These purposes were served by the establishment of the University Council in 1961 and of the Committee on the Future in 1962.

THE PRESIDENT'S FACULTY ADVISORY COMMITTEE

In order to supplement his contacts with the Administrative Council and the old faculty members, Dr. Sammartino had established the President's Faculty Advisory Committee, consisting of newer and younger faculty. At a meeting of this committee on March 24, 1961, the president presented its origins and purposes:

> The President outlined the background and functions of this Committee. When the faculty was small in number, frequent meetings of the entire faculty were held and all decisions were made in these meetings. When the number grew, a faculty council was formed; its members were primarily persons who had been with Fairleigh Dickinson for some time. With further growth, most of these persons became administrators and the council became substantially an administrative council. The President's Faculty Advisory Committee was then created in order to give younger faculty members an opportunity to express their opinions. The present procedure for selecting the members was established by the Committee itself. Members are chosen by the President from nominees suggested by the entire faculty. Members are selected on the basis of campus, college, and other relevant factors, including the need for female representation. The Committee has its own rules; copies of these rules may be obtained from the President's office. The Committee may meet at such times as it may choose.[9]

9. "Meeting of the President's Faculty Advisory Committee, March 24, 1961," memorandum to all full-time faculty from the Office of the President.

At this meeting the president considered with the faculty members the points that were being raised by the A.A.U.P. chapters. On the subject of criticism of the existing practices and policies, it was agreed that any faculty member had the right to make suggestions, but that this must be distinguished from merely negative criticism. In all criticism the constructive aspect should be emphasized.[10]

The rates for teaching summer session classes were next considered, and it was agreed that the summer hourly rate of pay would be calculated on the basis of the contract salary for the next academic year rather than the past academic year, which had preceded the summer session. The benefit to be gained from this was that a faculty member's salary was higher for the coming year and he would therefore receive a higher summer rate.[11]

Aspects of university policy in the area of fringe benefits for faculty, such as grants for study for the doctorate and inclusion in the faculty fund for retirement, were considered.[12]

Doctoral Grant

The President outlined the University's practice regarding financial aid to faculty members who are working for a doctorate. Tuition will be paid for course work. A thesis grant, generally $2,000, is intended to compensate for the reduced pay which results from a reduced teaching schedule; this grant is paid at the rate of $100 per month during the year and $1,000 upon attainment of the doctorate within that year. The latter provision is intended to discourage procrastination. The Committee recommended that this information be published in the Faculty Manual and be given greater publicity.

Faculty Fund

The President described the Faculty Fund. It is intended to show appreciation for extra efforts given by the faculty members to further the work of the University. It is not salary; salaries should be as high as possible regardless of the Faculty Fund. In the spring of each year as finances allow, the Trustees decide a percentage of salary (it has been as high as 9%) to be added to the Fund for each faculty member who is included. This Fund is invested and is payable at retirement, as a lump sum or as an annuity. If a person leaves the faculty, the sum set aside for him is returned to the University treasury. A faculty member is eligible for the plan during the spring of his fourth year. About 80% of the eligible faculty members are included. The President further commented that retired teachers are usually permitted to teach one course, so that the income from pension, Faculty Fund and teaching can often equal the pre-retirement salary.

Still other faculty concerns brought up at this meeting were the number of faculty in each rank, criteria for promotion, classroom

---

10. *Ibid.*, p. 1.
11. *Ibid.*, p. 2.
12. *Ibid.*

observation and rating of new teachers, student evaluation of teaching, and the granting of tenure and the dismissal of faculty.[13]

The president and the committee agreed that a distribution of 25% in each academic rank from instructor to full professor should be the goal. As to promotions, they should be based upon the quality of teaching and of the academic degrees held, on research and publications, and on any other services performed by the faculty member. The committee and president concurred that new teachers should be observed in the classroom by competent evaluators and that every effort should be made to impress upon the faculty member that the evaluation process is to be constructive and not hostile. Moreover, the professor should be observed by more than one person.

With regard to student evaluations, the president brought out that no faculty member had been dismissed because of unfavorable student evaluations, but that the decision had always been made independently. In some cases faculty members had been retained because student evaluations had been favorable, although it had previously been decided to dismiss them. At any rate, comments by vindictive students stood out like "sore thumbs."[14]

Regarding tenure, it was agreed that a three-year probation period would be too short. It was ultimately set at seven years. As to dismissal, the president stated that the existing policy was to notify the faculty member of impending dismissal as soon as possible. On occasion he was kept on an additional year while looking for another position. After further discussion the president and committee unanimously agreed on the following schedule:

Notice of Dismissal of Faculty Members
    Notice of dismissal should be given as follows:
    Persons notified during their 1st year: 3 months before end of academic year
    Persons notified during their 2nd year: before December 15th
    Persons notified during their 3rd year: 1 year before end of academic year.[15]

This meeting of the President's Faculty Advisory Committee in March 1961 is informative as to the points of strong faculty concern during this period. It also clarifies the existing policies in the various areas at the time and the directions in which changes were being sought.

---

13. *Ibid.*, pp. 3–4.
14. *Ibid.*, p. 4.
15. *Ibid.*, p. 5.

Yet, a certain number of faculty members remained dissatisfied. They either left or gradually assimilated to the new constitutional structure which was built. In some cases those who had been among the most disgruntled finally realized that an honest attempt in good faith was being made to maintain and to expand the community participation in governance that had characterized the institution from its earliest days.

The events of these years underlined the need to expand the principle of faculty participation in governance, which had first been expressed through the weekly "town meetings" of all the faculty of the small junior college in the Castle, and had then grown into the Faculty Council and the President's Faculty Advisory Committee. There was now a need for an all-University forum, in which the central administration and the administrations and faculties of the various colleges and campuses, including representation from both senior and junior faculty, would meet regularly. In such a body the many divergent points of view could be presented, evaluated, and, if possible, compromised, and formulated into proposals for consideration by the Trustees.

ESTABLISHMENT OF THE UNIVERSITY COUNCIL

By 1961 it was clear that the time for the establishment of such a body had arrived. On September 23 of that year the University Council of Fairleigh Dickinson University held its first meeting in the Little Theatre of the Rutherford Campus.

The meeting was preceded by a dinner in the cafeteria of the Rutherford Gymnasium. At the dinner Dr. Sammartino emphasized that the new University Council was not the first such body at Fairleigh Dickinson. In the early years the concept of a weekly faculty conference had been borrowed from New College. Occasionally all-day meetings of the then-small faculty had been held to consider and settle important issues, such as the move from two- to four-year status. The Faculty Council had been organized but, as the college grew, its members had gradually entered the administration. A Tenure Committee, first organized in May 1953, soon changed its name to Administrative Advisory Committee as its role expanded. When the Administrative Council had been formed in 1957, the new President's Faculty Advisory Committee, consisting of sixteen of the younger faculty members, had been formed.[16]

Dr. Sammartino continued:

The time has now arrived to initiate a University Council. . . . Now there are certain things we should keep in mind:

1. This is one of the most important steps in the history of the University. It is a transition to a new pattern whereby the participation of the faculty in the development of the University is placed on a more formal basis. Great care should be taken during this transitional period not to disrupt the orderly business of the University.
2. We must have faith in each other. In all our deliberations we must seek to reach our decisions with equanimity and, above, all with a sense of humor, striving always to serve the greater interests of the University. We must be objective and judicial.
3. All of us understand, I think, that the University Council derives its authority from the Board of Trustees. It will function within the framework of the University. Its functions are not primarily administrative, nor can it exercise the responsibilities that the Board of Trustees is required by law to perform.
4. The Council has the power to recommend, either to the President of the University or to the Board of Trustees through its Secretary. It is to be hoped that most, if not all, of its recommendations may be adopted by the President if they are purely administrative or by the Board of Trustees if they are of such a fundamental nature as to require legal passage into the by-laws of the Board.
5. This year will be one of study and experiment with respect to the scope of the Council's activities and responsibilities. It will receive the reports of many important committees—beginning tonight. The present committee structure may have to be changed or reorganized as we proceed, in order to expedite the work of the Council.
6. Participation in the work of the University Council will require the expenditure of time and efforts on the part of all of us. I am confident that each member will carry his responsibilities completely and faithfully.

I want to thank all of you for your attendance here tonight. This first meeting will be another great step forward in the development of our University.[17]

According to the charter given to the Council by the Board of Trustees the academic vice-president was to serve *ex officio* as

16. "Introductory Remarks by Dr. Peter Sammartino at the Dinner Preceding the First Meeting of the University Council," *University Council Minutes* (hereafter indicated as *UCM*), 1:21.
17. *Ibid.*, pp. 3f.

Chairman of the University Council.[18] Dr. Clarence R. Decker in his after-dinner remarks quoted Benjamin Franklin to the effect that:

> persons of good sense . . . seldom fall into disputation, except lawyers, university men, and men of all sorts that have been bred in Edinburgh.

Decker confessed that, as a university man and as a man "bred, not in Edinburgh, but in the equally disputatious Midwest, he was happier in the role of deliberator than moderator, but was honored to preside over the Council's organizational meeting.[19]

Decker was chairman of the University Council during its first two years, from 1961 to 1963. His strongest activity proved to be the urbane and friendly manner in which he presided over the Council meetings. By refraining from giving the emerging committees of the Council too strong leadership, Decker permitted effective committee chairmen to emerge and to lead in developing the Council's activities and areas of responsibility.

After dinner the Council began its first formal session in the Little Theater on the Rutherford Campus. Dr. Eileen J. Costello was unanimously elected secretary.[20]

---

18. Charter of the University Council as effected September 23, 1961

1. The Board of Trustees through this Charter hereby authorizes for formation of a University Council to be composed of
   a. All Professors and all Associate Professors who have had at least two years of service at the University.
   b. Fourteen Assistant Professors who have had at least two years of service. These shall be elected by the Assistant Professors within the several colleges as follows: one from each of the undergraduate schools at each campus, plus one from the Graduate School and one from the School of Dentistry.
   c. Members of the Administrative Council.
2. The University Council shall be empowered to set up committees dealing with academic matters and student policies. These committees shall report to the University Council directly.
3. It shall be the function of the University Council to discuss academic matters and to make recommendations to the President if they are purely administrative and to the Board of Trustees through its Secretary if they are matters requiring legal enactment.
4. The University Council shall draw up its own bylaws for the conduct of its business. Such bylaws shall be within the framework of this charter.
5. The officers of the University Council shall be the Chairman, who will be the Academic Vice President, and the Secretary, who shall be elected.

19. "The Corporate Judgment of a University. Remarks by Dr. Clarence R. Decker, Vice-President," *UCM* 1:9.

20. Eileen Costello Balassi (B.S., Boston University; A.M., Ed.D., Columbia University) served as Secretary of the University Council from 1961 until 1963. She later attained the rank of Professor of Business Administration.

The membership of the new body totaled 76.[21] Three different principles were used to establish membership: office, rank, and election. The entire Administrative Council were members *ex officio*. Thus about a dozen of the institution's leading administrators, including the president, vice-president, and all deans were simultaneously members of the Administrative and University Councils. At first there was opposition by some faculty members to any, or to so many, administrators as members in the University Council. But as the faculty component grew in size, ultimately numbering almost 200, this objection faded. Moreover, the presence of the University's Administrative Cabinet at the meeting of the new all-university body soon proved to be extremely useful. Faculty Council members were in an excellent position to ask the whole

---

21. The University Council of Fairleigh Dickinson University, September 23, 1961:

Dr. Wesley O. Alven
Mr. Charles Angoff
Dr. Ernest Baden
Dr. Clair W. Black
Dr. Bernard E. Budish
Dr. Roy Bundy
Mr. Frank J. Cannizzaro
Dr. Maria Castellani
Dr. Hsin-hai Chang
Dr. William Clark Child
Mr. Patrick J. Conway
Miss Jane E. Cornish
Dr. Eileen T. Costello
Dr. Clarence R. Decker
Dr. Maurice Demar
Dr. John G. Dollar
Dr. Gladys Ellenbogen
Dr. Nasrollah S. Fatemi
Dr. Harold Feldman
Dr. Walter H. Freeman
Mr. Marinus C. Galanti
Dr. Theodor H. Gaster
Mr. George J. Geier
Dr. Francis Gimble
Mr. Salvatore P. Gimelli
Dr. Joseph Green
Dr. Herbert G. Gutman
Dr. Loyd Haberly
Dr. Samuel L. Hart
Dr. Warren H. Held
Mrs. Kathleen C. Hillers
Dr. John H. Hindle
Dr. Richard Holub
Dr. Forrest A. Irwin
Mr. Stanley A. A. Iwanski
Dr. Dolores E. Keller
Dr. Howard G. Kimball
Dr. William T. Kirscher

Dr. LeRoy L. Kohler
Dr. Frederick Kronenwett
Dr. Sidney J. Kronish
Mr. Ignatius E. Lawlor
Dr. Martin M. Lipschutz
Dr. John MacEachen
Dr. Heinz Mackensen
Dr. Kenneth M. MacKenzie
Mr. John Marshall
Dr. Andrew A. Pirigyi
Dr. Samuel A. Pleasants
Mr. Daniel Pliskin
Dr. Lois V. Pratt
Dr. Samuel Pratt
Dr. Bogdan Raditsa
Mr. Louis A. Rice
Dr. C. Russell Riggs
Mr. Bernard Rivin
Dr. Harold A. Rothbart
Mrs. Peter Sammartino
Dr. Amedeo G. Sferra
Dr. William E. Smith
Dr. Harry Sprague
Dr. Charles H. Stern
Mr. Malcolm L. Sturchio
Dr. Margaret C. Tavolga
Dr. T. Smith Taylor
Miss Mary Topalis
Dr. John E. Vaughan
Dr. Stanislaw Wajda
Dr. Warren T. Ward
Dr. John C. Warren
Dr. Harold Weinberger
Dr. Clair S. Wightman
Miss Sarah W. Wildebush
Dr. James D. Williams
Dr. Walter A. Wilson
Dr. Peter Sammartino, ex officio

administration or individual members thereof direct or indirect questions on a very broad range of subject at Council meetings. Administrators found the University Council an excellent forum in which to present and defend their actions and policies before a very broad audience.

The second type of Council members consisted of all full and associate professors, both tenured and untenured, who had served at least two years at the University. Thus the whole senior faculty were Council members, due to their rank and length of service. Their membership rested on the principle of personal achievement in academic terms.

In a sense the meetings of the Council for the senior members of the faculty constituted pure, direct democracy. Like an ancient Athenian citizen, every senior faculty member at Fairleigh Dickinson University was a full voting participant in the most important body at the institution, with the exception of the Board of Trustees. Even at the beginning, this element of the Council's membership was in the majority. It greatly increased in numbers as ever more faculty were promoted to the senior ranks.

The third element of the Council's membership represented yet another principle of choice, different from the *ex officio* principle of the administrators and the principle of rank used for the senior faculty.

Fourteen assistant professors were elected by their fellow junior faculty members on the basis of campus location and general academic subject matter areas. On each campus the junior faculty of each of the four undergraduate colleges elected one of their number. These twelve representatives were also joined by one assistant professor elected from the School of Dentistry and one from the Graduate School. These elected members were thus unique among the Council members in having constituencies to whom they were responsible personally instead of speaking for themselves, as was the case with the administrative and senior faculty members.

At the time, the thought that students, staff, and alumni should be members of such a body was not yet prevalent among the framers of university councils and senates in America. In fact, Fairleigh Dickinson University was somewhat unique in starting, as early as 1961, such a broadly based university parliament that also included representatives of the junior faculty. Some institutions did not institute such bodies until after the extremely damaging sit-ins and riots that took place during the latter half of the nineteen sixties. The fact that such a body as the University Council began its work almost a decade before the era of widespread university unrest may well have helped to keep such manifestations to a minimum at Fairleigh Dickinson.

THE UNIVERSITY COUNCIL BEGINS ITS WORK

Besides the election of its secretary, the business of the Council's first meeting consisted in receiving the final reports of four of the old standing faculty committees.[22]

Necessary steps were the establishment of a Committee on Committees to propose appropriate committees to serve the Council; the establishment of a Committee on Agenda; and the establishment of a Committee on Bylaws to begin the compilation of rules essential for the functioning of a parliamentary body.[23]

At its next meeting on November 18, 1961, in University Hall on the Teaneck Campus, considerable progress had been made by the Council in functional terms. The three committees established at the previous meeting had been appointed and had two weeks' notice to begin their work.[24] But this meeting was principally notable because, for the first time, an important all-university problem was considered by the Council and steps were taken to find a solution to the problem and to formulate a definite policy for the future. The problem had arisen from the efforts of a group of student leaders at Rutherford to bring to the campus a series of outside speakers who had been selected principally for their shock value. The Trustees were concerned about the basic questions raised by their action and at their meeting of November 15, 1961, decided to request the University Council to prepare recommendations on University policy concerning outside speakers.[25]

The Council reacted swiftly to this indication by the Trustees that they wished to make real use of its counsel in a very important matter of practice and policy. The Council authorized the Committee on Committees to appoint an *ad hoc* Committee on Speak-

---

22. Curriculum and courses (Dr. Wesley O. Alven, Chairman); Research (Dr. Adam M. Aguiar); Admissions (Dr. William F. Kirscher); Evaluation of Teachers (Dr. Joseph Green). *UCM* 1, no. 1 (September 23, 1961).
23. *Ibid.*, p. 1.
24. *Ibid.*, no 2 (Nov. 18, 1961):2f.
25. *Ibid.*, p. 2.

ers to prepare a policy statement.[26] The Council also spent some time in introductory debate on the matter.

The question of who may be invited to speak from outside the University has always been one fundamental consideration in establishing the extent of academic freedom in the discussion of any question on campus. If you can ban individuals from being heard on a campus because of their ideas, is not the next step to ban their ideas? Or is it not, in fact, effectively to back *some* ideas?

The views expressed in this preliminary debate revealed the existence of a spectrum on this question in the Council, ranging from total libertarianism to the point of view that insisted that an outside speaker must be at least a "responsible person" and that his views contribute to "academic achievement." More exact definition of who should be responsible for inviting outside speakers was also requested.[27]

The *Ad Hoc* Council Committee on Speakers presented an interim report to the University Council later that year, at its first meeting on the Madison Campus. Dean Black, the committee's chairman, reported that they had met and had considered a request by the staff of the Rutherford Campus newspaper, *The Bulletin,* and by the Executive Board of the Rutherford Student Council that Malcolm X, Lincoln Rockwell and Gus Hall be permitted to speak at the campus.[28]

The committee had heard the students' arguments in favor of inviting the speakers they had chosen. Since the committee felt that they could not draw up a set of principles and policy statement at their very first meeting and after very little study of the matter, they had decided to vote approval of rejection of the first of the three speakers available for the series, Gus Hall. The committee had also stipulated that a group of professors from the Social Science Department should be present on stage and ask Gus Hall questions after his speech. The committee had approved this proposal and the students had accepted this proposal. Dean Black now presented it to the University Council for approval.[29]

In later years such a student request, if handled ineffectively,

---

26. *Ibid.*
27. *Ibid.*, pp. 3, 4.
28. *Ibid.*, 2, no. 1 (Oct. 13, 1962) :6. All were highly controversial figures. Malcolm X was leader of the Black Muslims. Lincoln Rockwell was the head of the American Nazi Party. Gus Hall was the Secretary General of the Communist Party of the U.S.A.
29. *Ibid.*

easily led to sit-ins, demonstrations, and possibly the seizure of deans and buildings. But the new machinery of the University Council prevented such an escalation at Fairleigh Dickinson as early as 1962.

Yet, the Council did not approve the proposal first presented to it but decided that it was out of order because such specific action would constitute an act of administration. The Council Charter and Bylaws prohibited it from performing any specific act of administration and thus confounding the executive and legislative roles of government.[30]

Nevertheless, the discussion on the Council floor and a straw vote showed the appropriate administrative officers that the Council would support them if they proceeded along the practical lines that had been worked out with the Rutherford students by Dean Black and his committee.[31]

Thus what could easily have grown into a major crisis was settled in a sensible and conciliatory manner through the University Council. Much else of a practical nature would be dealt with successfully in this way by the Council in the years thereafter.

Yet, the Council would have become merely an instrument for the momentary expedient solution of a critical problem if it had not proceeded also to formulate an appropriate statement of general principles and policy in this area for future guidance. This did not prove to be an easy task and led to considerable controversy.

At the next Council meeting (December 8, 1962) the *Ad Hoc* Committee on Speakers presented a "Proposed Statement on Policy Regarding Outside Speakers," which included two brief paragraphs committing the University "wholeheartedly to those principles of free speech which are the fundamental hallmarks of our country."[32] It also came out for the traditional academic freedoms of research, teaching, and discussion, "which have always characterized universities when they have been at their best as vital, creative forces in the intellectual and scientific life of their time and place."[33] The Committee had also added some other criteria

---

30. Bylaws. 1. "The Council shall perform no administrative functions assigned to officers of the administration." *University Council Bylaws*, Article IV, Section 7.
31. *UCM* 2, no. 1 (Oct. 13, 1962) :8, 9.
32. *Ibid.*, no. 3 (December 8, 1962) :2.
33. *Ibid.*

that should be taken into consideration when choosing outside speakers.[34]

After brief discussion this report was tabled. But the subject of outside speakers was not yet a closed subject at this Council meeting. The tabling was soon shown to have been a maneuver for further action at this meeting on the subject under new business. Professor Kenneth MacKenzie of Rutherford distributed the following policy statement on outside speakers and moved its adoption.

> Believing, with Oliver Wendell Holmes, that "the ultimate good desired is better reached by free trade in ideas," Fairleigh Dickinson University asserts its faith in academic freedom. The University neither fears nor avoids competition in the market place of ideas, but rather encourages it. With the end in view of fostering an unremitting search for truth, a search free from pressures from without or from within, the University sets forth the following policy with regarding to visiting speakers:
>
> 1. Any faculty group or any recognized student group is free to invite to the campus any speaker of its choice.
> 2. No bar to the appearance of a speaker shall be offered based on his alleged competence. his membership or non-membership in organizations, his reputation, his past record, his past utterances, his being under suspension or indictment, his being at liberty pending appeal, or like factors.
> 3. No speaker shall be required to take a test oath, to submit in advance either an outline or text of his remarks, or to undergo prior restrictions on the content of his remarks.
> 4. Any faculty member is free to bring to his class anyone who, in that faculty member's opinion, will illuminate for his students the subject under discussion.
> 5. Neither the invitation to a speaker, whether or not he accepts it, nor the appearance of an invited speaker on the campus, shall imply endorsement of his views by the individual or group that invites him or by the University itself.[35]

Professor Stern of Rutherford then proceeded strongly to support the newly introduced statement. His remarks emphasized his

---

34. *Ibid.*

1. Does the speaker have a contribution to make which is worthy of an educational community?
2. Does the speaker subscribe to the principles of freedom of speech, not only for himself but also for others with whom he may disagree? Is he willing to submit to rebuttal?
3. Does he represent an organization which advocates the violent overthrow of our government?
4. Does he have a past which ought to disqualify him from addressing a university audience?
5. Does his presentation or presence incite to riot?
35. *Ibid.*, p. 13.

disagreement with the *Ad Hoc* Committee's statement that had just been tabled.

Soon the debate became intense and included the introduction of personalities, personal references, and the questioning of motives. Dr. Decker was kept busy trying to keep order. Clearly these were issues that deeply moved the faculty. The storm was mitigated for the moment when the council voted to return the matter once again to the *Ad Hoc* Committee on Speakers for further study, an action clearly much needed.[36]

This meeting revealed that the Council was an effective forum for the clash of strongly held and divergent views and for reasonable action to allay the momentary heat of intense debate and controversy with a minimum of rancor.

The *Ad Hoc* Committee continued its labors. It heard witnesses from administrators, faculty, students, and outside authorities. It presented a brief progress report to the Council in the spring.[37] But it was not until a year after it had first considered the matter and much heat had been dissipated that the committee returned, on October 19, 1963, to present to the Council the following policy statement on outside speakers:

> Fairleigh Dickinson University asserts its faith in academic freedom and in the underlying principles of free speech which are the fundamental hallmarks of our country. It wishes to be regarded as an outstanding proponent of the critical public discussion of ideas. Hence, the University encourages strongly competition of ideas, no matter how dramatically expressed and fosters a vigorous and continuous search for truth. Members of the faculty or a recognized student group are free to invite to the campus any speaker of their choice in their name. Neither the invitation nor the appearance of a speaker should be construed as an endorsement of his views, either by the University or by those responsible for the invitation.[38]

This forthright statement was adopted with almost no debate by the Council and has been the policy governing the invitation and selection of outside speakers at Fairleigh Dickinson University ever since.

There was so little debate at the meeting because a year of committee hearings, the previous Council debates, and informal discussions among the faculty during the year had clarified both issues and views on this vital subject. Many other problems and controversies in succeeding years followed these precedents of

36. *UCM* 2, no. 3 (December 8, 1962):2.
37. *Ibid.*, no. 4 (February 9, 1963):2.
38. *Ibid.* 3, no. 1 (October 13, 1963).

introduction into the Council, careful and sometimes lengthy committee work, and effective debate on the Council floor ending in formulation of a policy supported by the majority of the Council and agreed to by the President and Trustees. The fact that there were available mechanisms and, more important, that they actually worked and were respected by all concerned proved to be of incalculable benefit in bringing about changes in an orderly fashion and as they were needed.

Yet, the Council did not consider its job finished when it had formulated a policy. The recommendation of proper organizational structure and implementing procedure were also its concern. After five months further study the *Ad Hoc* Committee on Speakers returned with a proposal for procedure as follows, which was approved by the Council:

> THAT student groups inviting a non-FDU speaker should first consult their faculty adviser and then inform the Dean of the Campus.[39]

This procedure worked quite well in practice. Without any prohibitions or limitations on the freedom of student groups to invite outside speakers, it provided a mechanism by which the students would receive the benefit of the advice of their faculty advisor *before* inviting an outside speaker. Furthermore, the campus dean would know in advance what sorts of arrangements he might have to make for a prospective outside speaker.

Thus a potentially explosive issue had been handled at once, effectively, by the Council, a general policy had then been formulated after a year of committee work and study, and the implementing machinery had been established after still another half year's work.

After some preliminary tensions and misunderstandings, as is natural in any new relationship, the lines of communication between the Council and the president and trustees became clarified, well understood, and established among all parties concerned.

The statistics with regard to the recommendations made by the Council from its inception in 1961 until the end of Dr. Sammartino's administration reveal this quite clearly. Experience gradually showed that the Council's proposals and the replies to them should best be put in writing. The written Council recommendations sent to the president and Trustees and their written replies were circulated to the entire faculty in the Council minutes. This

---

39. *Ibid.*, no. 3 (March 6, 1964) :15.

**CAMPUS IN AN OXFORDSHIRE
JACOBEAN MANSION**

Dean Loyd Haberly and Wroxton Abbey.

*Procession to Wroxton Church on the Day of Dedication of Wrox-
ton College, June 30, 1965. Dean Haberly carrying the University
Mace is followed by Dr. Heinz Mackensen, University Council
Chairman, with the Wroxton College Banner. Behind the Bishop
of Oxford and clergy are Dr. Sammartino conversing with Lord
Harlech (partly obscured). In the file immediately behind Dr.
Sammartino are Edward T. T. Williams, Henry P. Becton, and
Umberto II, the last King of Italy.*

gave all concerned a clear picture of the contents, progress, and final disposition of the many proposals made by the Council.

Of the 128 Council recommendations made during the years from 1961 until 1967, only ten were vetoed by the Trustees. This is less than ten percent. Thirteen others, mostly referring to financial and related aspects, were received and thereupon studied further. In a number of cases, such further study, including consultation with administrative and faculty leaders and groups, ultimately led to the working out of compromise agreements. Thirteen proposals involving financial matters were approved as presented by the Trustees.[40] These included such important steps as the adoption of a major medical plan, long term disability insurance, free tuition for the immediate family of a faculty member, and free tuition for a deceased faculty member's minor children.

During 1962 the University Council considered and passed an amendment of its bylaws that changed the nature of the Council Chairman's position from an *ex-officio* post held permanently by the academic vice-president to one to be filled by a Council member elected for a two-year term. The trustees approved this amendment.[41]

In accord with this amendment the academic vice-president, Dr. Clarence Decker, felt that the election of the new Council Chairman should be held at the first meeting in the fall. At the Council meeting of October 19, 1963, at Madison, an election was held and Dr. Heinz F. Mackensen, who had served as parliamentarian and secretary of the Agenda Committee for the first two years of the Council's operations, was unanimously elected. He continued to be reelected to this post for the remainder of the period covered by this work.[42]

A further amendment to the bylaws extended Council membership to more junior faculty members by making membership automatic for assistant professors upon their receiving tenure.[43]

In practice this meant that all of the fourteen assistant professors elected to represent them by the junior faculty would be chosen, after this amendment, from the ranks of the untenured

40. Statistics derived from H. F. Mackensen, ed., *Motions and Resolutions by the President and/or the Board of Trustees* (Fairleigh Dickinson University, The University Council, 1968).
41. *UCM* 2, no. 5 (April 20, 1963) :6.
42. *UCM* 3, no. 1 (October 19, 1963) :2. Dr. Mackensen was reelected in 1965 and 1967, but decided in 1969 that there should be a rotation in office and did not run for reelection. Prof. Irving Halevy was elected in 1969. The University Council was superseded by the University Senate in 1970.
43. *UCM* 2, no. 5 (April 20, 1963) :5.

faculty. Thus, between the tenured assistant professors and four-teen elected untenured assistant professors, the junior faculty were represented in the Council by an increasingly larger delegation.

The election of its chairman and the increase in the ranks of the junior faculty were important first steps in broadening still further the base for the University Council's leadership and composition.

The University Council was required by its bylaws to evaluate itself every two years.[44] This was done by the appointment of a special evaluation committee by the Council Chairman. This committee, after spending about six months in studying the Council, reported its findings. In general, these committees recommended still further broadening of the Council's membership. It was as the result of the work of such an evaluation committee's report that students were added to the membership of the University Council's Committee on Student Life and Welfare in 1967. Evaluations of the Council on this pattern were held in 1963, 1965, and 1967.

ESTABLISHMENT OF THE COMMITTEE ON THE FUTURE

Another need that had emerged was a careful formulation of plans for the future development of the institution. This could not be done without taking a detailed look at what had been built during the first two decades.

On April 3, 1962, the establishment of the Committee on the Future of the University was publicly announced by Edward T. T. Williams. It had been authorized by the trustees in June 1961 and had begun operations in January of the following year.

Williams emphasized the feeling of the trustees that the period of growth in numbers was substantially at an end. The university would now go through a period of consolidation and of determining its strengths and weaknesses where necessary. One problem would be the increasing prevalence of junior colleges. Growing demands for graduate education could also be expected. Both of these developments would cause financial problems, Williams prophesied. He added:

We feel that a meticulous self study of this sort is entirely in keeping with the university's established tradition of educational innovation.

---

44. *The Bylaws of the University Council*, Article X.

In addition, it will undoubtedly establish the character of the university and its relations with the community for at least the next decade.[45]

The trustees appointed Fairleigh S. Dickinson, Jr., as chairman of the Committee on the Future of the University. The position of executive secretary was given to Dr. John Vaughan. In order to study the various areas, six subcommittees of the Committee on the Future were established: 1) Faculty Personnel Policies and Administrative Structure; 2) Students; 3) Community Services and Continuing Education; 4) Research; 5) Business Affairs, Buildings, Grounds and Finance; and 6) Educational Policy.[46]

Subsequently other subcommittees were added for: 1) Medical Arts, 2) Governmental Relations, 3) the Graduate School.

This committee and its subcommittees were essentially appointed working committees designed to do the research and to formulate the recommendations for change. Their reports were intro-

---

45. " 'Committee on the Future' of FDU Lists Areas of Study." News release, April 3, 1963.

46. The membership was as follows:
Committee on Faculty Personnel Policies and Administrative Structure: Chairman, Dr. Joseph Green. Dr. Bernard E. Budish, Madison Campus; Dr. Herbert G. Gutman, Teaneck; Dr. John H. Hindle, Rutherford; Prof. Vartkis Kinoian, Teaneck; Prof. Louis A. Rice, Madison; Dean Harold A. Rothbart, Teaneck.

Committee on Students: Chairman, Dr. Amedeo G. Sferra. Prof. John G. Dollar, Rutherford Campus; Mr. Leonard Granick, Rutherford; Dr. Harriet G. McCormick, Teaneck; Dean Samuel Pratt, Madison; Prof. Mary Topalis, Rutherford; Dr. John C. Warren, Rutherford; Dr. E. Wallace McMullen, Madison.

Committee on Community Service and Continuing Education: Chairman, Dr. Nasrollah N. Fatemi. Dr. Samuel Gordon, Madison Campus; Dean Loyd Haberly, Rutherford; Dr. Sidney J. Kronish, Teaneck; Dr. Ann Lucas, Teaneck; Dr. Heinz F. Mackensen, Teaneck; Dr. Kenneth M. MacKenzie, Rutherford; Dr. Carl E. Prince, Madison; Miss Evelyn F. Terhune, Rutherford.

Committee on Research: Chairman, Dr. Harold Weinberger. Dr. Adam M. Aguiar, Madison Campus; Prof. Charles Angoff, Rutherford; Dr. Roy Bundy, Teaneck; Dr. Philip Cooperman, Rutherford; Dr. Theodor H. Gaster, Teaneck; Dr. Gerhard Lang, Teaneck; Dr. Bernard D. Rivin, Teaneck; Dr. William E. Smith, Madison; Prof. William Struning, Teaneck; Prof. Mara Vamos, Madison.

Committee on Business Affairs, Buildings, Grounds and Finance: Chairman, Dean Marinus C. Galanti. Prof. Frank J. Cannizzaro, Teaneck Campus; Prof. Stanley A. A. Iwanski, Rutherford; Mr. A. Otto Iwen, Rutherford; Dr. Arnold Kaufman, Teaneck; Dr. Howard Kimball, Teaneck; Prof. John Marshall, Madison; Mr. Samuel J. Silberman; Dr. Warren T. Ward, Madison.

Committee on Educational Policy: Chairman, Dean Clair W. Black. Dr. Wesley O. Alven, Rutherford Campus; Prof. George J. Geier, Teaneck; Prof. Kathleen C. Hillers, Rutherford; Dr. John MacEachen, Teaneck; Dr. Lois Pratt, Madison; Prof. Malcolm L. Sturchio, Madison.

duced into the University Council for study and consideration before they were presented to the Trustees.

Consultants were also appointed by the Board of Trustees to assist the Committee on the Future with their counsel and experience. These were Dr. Frederick Redefer of New York University, and Dr. Harold Taylor, former president of Sarah Lawrence College.

For the next year these subcommittees worked at studying and analyzing the current structure, operations, and purposes of the institution. On the basis of these studies they then prepared reports on what they had found, which also contained recommendations for proposed alterations. These reports were then studied by the Committee on the Future of the University. After approval by this body they were presented to the University Council. The Council, after studying the reports, could propose revisions or refer the reports to its own parallel standing committees.

In this manner a thorough, detailed survey of the whole institution was made; proposals for changes were carefully formulated and then considered by the highest all-university body of administrators and faculty, the University Council, before being presented to the final authority of the Board of Trustees. All of the reports followed this route, and most were approved by the Trustees essentially in the final form in which they had been formulated by the Committee on the Future and recommended by the University Council. After approval by the Trustees, occasionally with slight modifications, the proposals were put into effect.

Consideration of the individual reports seriatim will provide the reader with a good grasp of the institution as it was in 1962–1963 and will also provide an understanding of the changes that the various joint administrative faculty committees and the University Council felt needed to be instituted.

Although all of the reports were significant documents, the reports of the subcommittee on Faculty Personnel Policies and Administrative structure loom among them as of basic importance for the years that followed.

Two documents of fundamental constitutional importance for the structure and functions of the University emerged from this subcommittee: 1) The Campus and College Structure, and 2) The Final Report of the Subcommittee on Faculty Personnel and Administrative Structure.

THE CAMPUS AND COLLEGE STRUCTURE

The Campus and College Structure document was approved by the Committee on the Future on October 18, 1962, after two major and several minor changes had been made.[47]

It was considered and approved by the University Council on November 10, 1962.[48] The Trustees approved the Structure on February 4, 1963, and it went into effect for the fall of that year.

In the discussion on the Council floor on November 10, 1962, the question of the advantages of the greater decentralization of administrative functions and authority proposed by the Structure over a centralized one was considered. Dr. Joseph Green, the subcommittee chairman, pointed out that an organization is generally more effective if its functions are clearly defined and then developed into the operative components of the entire organization that are closest to the functions and tasks involved.[49]

Another question asked was whether too many committees were not being created.[50] This indeed seemed to be a problem, since the University Council had 14 standing committees in existence at the time and the proposed Structure would create an additional 24 standing committees: one on the university level, 15 on the campus level, and 8 distributed among the colleges.

The formulators of the resolution for approving the Campus and College Structure had, however, foreseen this difficulty and had included provisions for articulation of the University Council Committees and the Committees proposed by the new Structure.[51]

The plan that was worked out reduced the number of Council standing committees to five, and linked them, through joint memberships, with the new committees of the College and Campus Structure. In this way a web of interconnected committees on the university, campus, and college levels was created, which served

---

47. "Minutes of the Committee on the Future," October 18, 1962, pp. 1f. The consideration and evaluation of applicants for administrative office were transferred from the proposed Educational Policies Committee to special committees elected for the purpose, and a proposed "Reappointment, Promotion and Tenure Committee" was redesigned into a Faculty Status Committee.

48. *UCM* 2, no. 2:2, 3, 4.

49. *Ibid.*, p. 3. Dr. Green (B.S., M.A., Ed.D., New York University) became dean of the Samuel J. Silverman College of Business Administration in 1965. In 1972 he became Associate Vice-President for Academic Affairs.

50. *Ibid.*

51. *Ibid.*, p. 2 (November 10, 1962).

to maintain all-university cohesion while permitting a great deal of diversity and self-government in the colleges and campuses. This becomes apparent when the details of the plan are considered.

For each campus the Structure established an official body called "The Campus Faculty," to consist of all persons teaching full time at the campus, regardless of college affiliation.[52]

The campus dean was to preside, and could bring before the group matters of importance to the campus.[53] Committees and faculty members could do the same. A check upon its area of responsibility was the provision that proposals that were the responsibility of the University Council or that concerned more than one college would have to be presented to the University Council for consideration and review.[54]

The chief campus committee was to be the Campus Faculty Coordinating Committee, to consist of four faculty elected at large, the chairmen of all the other campus committees, and a representative of the department chairmen on the campus.[55] This group served essentially as a cabinet for the campus dean.

The other campus standing committees were those on student life; buildings, grounds, and services; and library. The campus committee on student life was composed of three faculty members, the Director of Student Activities, and three students.[56] It was quite unusual to have students serving on a committee with faculty members as early as 1962. This was one more established channel for faculty-student interrelationship that proved of great value in the later years of the nineteen sixties, when conditions tended to become critical and acute in this area.

The Structure also provided formal organization for the faculty of each of the four undergraduate colleges.[57]

The standing committees for each college were to consist of one on educational policies and another on faculty status. The committee on educational policy of each college was elected by the college faculty with representation from each campus. Working with the college dean, this committee was to be concerned with educational

---

52. *Campus and College Structure* (Fairleigh Dickinson University, 1963), paragraphs 2.1 and 2.2.
53. *Ibid.*, 2.5.
54. *Ibid.*, 2.7.
55. *Ibid.*, 2.12.
56. *Ibid.*, 2.13a.
57. The faculty of the Graduate School and of the School of Dentistry were not included under the Structure until some years later.

plans and policies, curricula and courses, and academic standards of each individual college.[58]

Each college's Committee on Faculty Status, to consist of six elected faculty members with tenure, was to consider and recommend to the college dean the granting of tenure and promotions and the termination of faculty membership.[59]

In order to link all of these new local campus and college committees on an all-University basis, the standing committees of the University Council were condensed from 14 to five: Planning (agenda and bylaws); Educational Policies; Faculty Research; Faculty Status; and Student Life and Welfare. Each of these (except for Planning) was to be composed of appropriate administrators, faculty members elected from among the Council's membership, and faculty delegates from the local equivalent campus or college committees.[60] Thus, for example, the University Council Educational Policies Committee was to consist of the academic administrators and college deans, of twelve members elected from and by the Council at large, and of three delegates from the educational policies committee of each of the four colleges.

In this way a criss-crossing membership linked each of the Council Committees with each of the various college and campus committees. Diversity of campus and college goals was stimulated by the local committees, yet the basic cohesion of all in one University was also preserved. At the four regular Council meetings during the academic year and at the many meetings of Council and local committees, a constant interchange of views, proposals, and action took place. All these committee deliberations resulted in a stream of proposals to the Council. Those which finally achieved Council approval were then funneled to the President and Trustees for ultimate decision.

In order to make certain that this final point of transmission would not lead to any difficulties or delays due to misunderstanding, a meeting was held once a year attended by the trustees, the president and the administrative council, and the officers and committee chairmen of the University Council. At these meetings there were periods for discussion of Council proposals that had been sent to the trustees but had not yet been acted upon, and for

---

58. *Ibid.*, 3.12.
59. *Ibid.*, 3.13.
60. *UCM* 3, no. 1:2. The part of the Council Bylaws amended was Art. VI, Sec. 11.

the ventilation of any problems or question any of the participants might wish to raise. This unusual meeting acted much like a conference committee between the two houses of a bicameral legislature and helped to maintain a cooperative relationship between the trustees, administration, and University Council.

A significant provision of The Campus and College Structure was the establishment of a University Faculty Review Committee.[61] This panel, to consist of tenured and elected senior faculty, would be available to hear the appeal of any full-time faculty member with at least two years service who felt that his termination constituted an infringement of academic freedom. During the years that followed, a number of faculty members sought to use this means of appeal to prevent such termination.

It soon became evident from these proceedings that violations of academic freedom at Fairleigh Dickinson University were practically nonexistent. The hearings did bring out, however, that there were certain grievances pertaining to promotions and other matters that ought to be considered by a body with suitable jurisdiction. Some thought was given by the Council Chairman working together with the Council's Planning Committee to broadening the Review Committee's jurisdiction to hear appeals on other matters besides termination of faculty members for reasons that might be considered violations of academic freedom. After some study of the matter, the Council Chairman and Planning Committee realized that the establishment of an entirely different body for this purpose would be the best way to deal with the problem.

As a result, the establishment of a University Faculty Grievance Committee was proposed to the Council, to consist of nine tenured faculty members without administrative responsibilities elected by the campus faculties, three from each campus.[62] This committee was empowered to hear any and all grievances except those involving academic freedom. These were, of course, reserved for the University Review Committee. The proposal was approved by the trustees and the new grievance committee quickly showed that it was needed and was also effective. A large number of faculty grievances, ranging from termination and nonpromotion to relatively minor complaints, were settled by this "court."

The Structure established a probationary period of seven years for the granting of tenure.[63]

61. Campus and College Structure, 3.14.
62. *UCM* 7:10.
63. *Campus and College Structure* (Rutherford, mimeographed MS, 1963), 3.16.

A final provision of the Structure established that administrative posts above the position of department chairmen should be filled with advice of an elected faculty committee.[64]

Thus, in the years from 1961 to 1963, by the creation of the University Council and of the Campus and College Structure, a system of interlocking parliamentary bodies of the university, college, and campus was established, which constituted in essence the legislative branch of the University's government.

The Faculty Review and the Faculty Grievance Committee constituted the beginning of a judicial branch.

THE ADMINISTRATIVE STRUCTURE

The elaboration and redefinition of the institution's executive branch was achieved through the Administrative Structure, which was approved by the trustees on May 20, 1964.

This document set forth the responsibilities of the trustees in connection with the University's finances; basic institutional policies in the areas of academic matters, personnel and public relations, and their legal responsibilities.[65]

The descriptions of the two chief administrative officers at the University were of great significance. The president was characterized as "the chief executive officer of the University through whom the Board of Trustees carries out its program and exercises its control."[66] He was to approve educational and faculty policies and to determine policies affecting business management and public relations. The responsibility for the final development of the overall budget, of plans for major building additions, for fundraising, and for the University's educational development was entrusted to him.[67]

The newly created position of Provost was described as being responsible to the president and as being "the administrative officer for the academic affairs of the University."[68] Broad responsibilities for formulating educational directions in consultation with faculty bodies and administrators for developing the academic budget, for recommending promotions, tenure, terminations and related matters, and for directing observance of bylaws, rules and regulations, were given to the Provost.[69] By contrast, the role of

---

64. *Ibid.*, 3.17.
65. *Ibid.*, p. 3.
66. *Ibid.*, pp. 5f.
67. *Ibid.*, p. 5.
68. *Ibid.*
69. *Ibid.*, pp. 5f.

the Vice-President was left rather limited and vague.[70] The roles of the Vice-President for Development, and of the various deans were set forth much as they had developed during the previous year. There was an effort to define the college dean in strongly academic terms, whereas the campus dean was given a more general mandate, reflecting responsibilities for physical arrangements, general operations, and student life and welfare on his campus.[71]

When all these organizational and structural developments are taken together, they actually constitute the establishment of a formal constitution for the University.

The development of such a massive, detailed constitution was probably needed. Half a decade later, as a result of unrest and demonstrations, similar constitutions were created at most other American colleges and universities. Yet, at times, individuals who had experienced the relative simplicity and directness of relationships and operations at the institution when it had been smaller felt that something had been lost due to the complex elaborations introduced at this time. There is something to be said for this point of view.

OTHER REPORTS OF THE COMMITTEE ON THE FUTURE

Under the chairmanship of Dean Clair Black, the Committee on the Future's Subcommittee on Educational Policy prepared a report including long-range future plans for curricula, students, faculty, admissions standards, and graduate studies.[72]

The report recommended that the core curriculum be included in all programs; that selected studies, honors courses, seminars and student research be encouraged.[73] In order to benefit from ever improving curricula

> a deliberate policy of actually seeking out talented and ambitious students is advocated. Our obligation is to select actively rather than admit passively.[74]

To this end the subcommittee called for evaluation of every prospective student on the basis of his intellectual ability, other

---

70. *Ibid.*, p. 7.
71. *Ibid.*, pp. 11f.
72. Loyd Haberly, ed., "III. The Subcommittee on Educational Policy," *Summary of the Committee on the Future* (mimeographed MS).
73. *Ibid.*, chap. 3, p. 9.
74. *Ibid.*, p. 13.

abilities (athletic, artistic), motivation and application, and personality structure.[75]

In order to encourage faculty competent to teach such a student body, the subcommittee recommended that criteria for promotion should be varied and should take into consideration such areas as excellence of instruction, research results, administrative duties, and contributions to curricula development, to student life and welfare, and "to the general atmosphere of the campus."[76] In order to encourage such outstanding faculty, the report further urged that "the University should make every effort to maintain a salary scale that will attract and retain a capable faculty."[77]

It was recommended that the graduate school should exist as a separate unit in the university structure, but that graduate and undergraduate faculties should be integrated under each college dean, to whom was entrusted the responsibility for graduate staffing, curricula, and standards. The position of "Director of Graduate Studies" was created to coordinate the work of the various colleges on the graduate level. He was further to preside over a Graduate Council, to consist of representatives from each of the colleges.[78] In this way it was hoped that central coordination of the burgeoning graduate curricula would be achieved.[79]

The Subcommittee on Research (Dr. Harold Weinberger, chairman), after two years of work, presented its report to the University Council in the spring of 1960.[80] The keynote was set forth in the words: "Basic research should predominate over applied research or routine testing and, of course, excellence of teaching should take precedence over all research."[81] Balance between scientific and technological research and between research in the humanities and in the social sciences was recommended. The report inextricably linked the "development of a sound research program at this University" with "the simultaneous development of sound graduate programs."[82] Each should be used to strengthen the other. The institution of faculty seminars and symposia for the consideration of research results and work in progress was

75. *Ibid.*, p. 14.
76. *Ibid.*, p. 17.
77. *Ibid.*
78. *Ibid.*, p. 20.
79. The report was approved by the University Council on December 13, 1963, after it had added a number of minor amendments proposed by the Council's Committee on Educational Policies (*UCM* 3, no. 2:5, 6, 7).
80. *UCM* 3, no. 3:6.
81. Haberly, ed., chap. 6, p. 6.
82. *Ibid.*

urged also involving, whenever possible, both the scientist and the humanist.[83]

Research grants to individual faculty members by the University had long been in practice. They consisted of a reduction in the teaching load, generally three classroom hours a week. The subcommittee recommended that this system be continued. University Research Grants should be viewed "as seed money for exploratory or pilot studies rather than as large-scale or long-term support."[84]

In the area of research funded from outside of the institution, warnings were presented against relying upon such support for the recruitment and retention of faculty, since termination of such support would impose a burden in carrying such staff. Moreover, each sponsored research should fit into the University's pattern of academic work. But if these caveats were observed, "such research can actually result in the creation of a stronger academic program, especially at the graduate level."[85]

A final caveat regarding support ran as follows:

> The Sub-Committee feels that it is not advisable to seek or to accept classified research contracts except in times of dire national emergency. The very nature of the work and the conditions under which it is conducted are considered to be inimical to the freedom of inquiry, discussion and expression so essential to higher education. Furthermore, the enforced isolation of the research personnel involved means that their contribution to the educational program of the University is, at best, minimal.[86]

In a separate section the rights and obligations of the University and of the faculty member to any patents and royalties that resulted from research were carefully spelled out. Any patentable ideas resulting from sponsored research were to become the property of the University, which might grant a license to the sponsoring agency. These limitations applied to research in the scientific and technological fields only.[87] Rules regarding outside consulting work were also established.

The various aspects and problems of the growing research activities at the University were in need of some control orienta-

---

83. *Ibid.,* p. 8.
84. *Ibid.,* p. 11.
85. *Ibid.,* p. 14.
86. *Ibid.,* p. 17.
87. *Ibid.,* p. 19.

tion and guidance. The report recommended the appointment of a University Research Coordinator for these purposes.[88]

An area that had moved into the forefront of the University's attention had been that of the medical arts. The early programs in nutrition, dental hygiene, and nursing had been crowned by the establishment of the School of Dentistry. By 1962, the time of the work of the Committee on the Future, the dental school had reached full four-year enrollment and was earning a considerable reputation. A Subcommittee on the Medical Arts, headed by Dean Walter A. Wilson of the School of Dentistry, presented a report that explored the existing situation and made pertinent proposals.[89]

The central proposal recommended that the various facilities for the medical arts be concentrated on the Hackensack property owned by the University immediately across the river from the Teaneck Campus. This was the general area in which Edward Williams College was later built. The whole development would be designated "University Park." The existing School of Dentistry, School of Nursing, and School of Dental Hygiene, as well as a Health Center and a Dental and Biological Research Center still to be formed, should all be housed in a building suitable for their needs to be constructed in University Park.[90]

The report also called for recognition of "a public need for a two-year medical school in the Bergen County and Northern New Jersey area and project plans for its establishment as soon as feasible," but this aim was not achieved.[91]

The Subcommittee on Business Affairs, Buildings, Grounds and Finance was headed by Marinus C. Galanti. In order to deal with these large areas smaller working groups had been formed under Dr. Frank Cannizzaro (Buildings and Grounds) and Professor George Geier (Business Affairs).[92]

The former group had visited each campus and had interviewed the campus deans as well as other administrators and faculty members.

---

88. *Ibid.*, p. 15. The report of the Subcommittee on Research was approved by the University Council on December 13, 1963, with one minor deletion (*UCM* 3, no. 3:6, 7).

89. Haberly, ed., "The Subcommittee on the Medical Arts," chap. 7, pp. 1–21.

90. *Ibid.*, pp. 1f. This project was carried out at the end of the nineteen sixties.

91. *Ibid.*, p. 2.

92. Haberly, ed., "The Subcommittee on Business Affairs, Buildings, Grounds and Finance," *Summary* . . . , chap. 8.

In view of the nature and heavily used condition of the class-rooms in the various temporary facilities at Rutherford, the construction of a new, modern classroom building on the southwestern corner of the campus was recommended.[93] The need for expanded dormitories, for a renovation of the Castle with a fire-proof interior, and increased off-the-street parking facilities was pointed out.[94]

The Madison Campus plan called for the addition of a dormitory for 500 students, an expansion of the library, and much other construction.[95] Most of this was not realized in later years.

For Teaneck a new classroom building (the later Becton Hall), greatly expanded new dormitories, a new student commons, and a field house were proposed.[96] These were all built in the following years.

After conducting an introductory survey of the institution's handling of its business affairs, the subcommittee recommended that an outside organization be called in to give the type of full-time study to this area that was required.[97]

The report on development and fund-raising was prepared by Trustee Samuel J. Silberman and Dr. John E. Vaughan.[98] The establishment of a University Development Committee to consist of the president, provost, and director of development, to serve as the mechanism for proposal, review, and approval of all projects that would need financial support, was proposed.

The Trustees should first determine the feasibility, priority, and timing of any fund-raising campaign. The proponent of the campaign would then, together with the director of development, have the responsibility for it. Campaigns involving the whole University would be the primary responsibility of the president.[99]

The report also pointed out that the imminent development of a system of public community colleges and the expansion of existing state colleges would require the more intensive and increased development by private institutions of financial contributions from private sources.[100]

---

93. *Ibid.*, pp. 4f. The Round Building was built to meet this need.
94. *Ibid.*, p. 7.
95. *Ibid.*, pp. 7–16.
96. *Ibid.*, pp. 17–22.
97. *Ibid.*, pp. 32–33.
98. *Ibid.*, pp. 23–29.
99. *Ibid.*, p. 29.
100. *Ibid.*, pp. 25–26. The report of the Subcommittee on Development was approved by the University Council on March 6, 1964 (*UCM* 3, no. 3:6). It was approved by the Trustees shortly thereafter.

The Subcommittee on Governmental Relations consisted of Trustee Silberman and Campus Deans Samuel Pratt and Marinus C. Galanti. In its report, the impact of expanded public higher education on private institutions was clearly, and as the event showed, accurately prophesied.[101] It was pointed out that Fairleigh Dickinson could participate on a larger scale in setting forth the role of private higher education amid increasing federal and state involvement.[102]

The report emphasized that the University

> accepts as one of its first obligations the task, with all the inherent difficulties of being a private university which respectfully fulfills its moral and legal responsibilities while vigorously upholding and exercising its freedom to determine its educational policies and programs, responsive to but independent of governmental or private pressure. The assumption in which this is rooted is that one of the essential ingredients of a democracy is a highly diversified system of higher education and that this needed diversification is possible only when there are strong public and private colleges and universities. It is thus our social obligation to remain private and to act both in cooperating with all agencies and levels of government. . . . The University must remain free to will its destiny, but it should so act as to encourage government officials to seek it out freely, just as the University will freely seek them out.[103]

In order to move in this direction, the report called for the creation of a University officer specifically charged with the responsibility for these tasks.[104] Ultimately this was done by establishment of the position of vice-president for governmental relations.[105]

The final report in the series prepared by the various subcommittees of the Committee on the Future was the one on community services and continuing education. This subcommittee under the chairmanship of Nasrollah S. Fatemi had formed three task forces. These had studied the existing structure and functions of the evening division (Dr. Heinz Mackensen, Chairman), the University's community relations (Dr. Ann Lucas, Chairman), and the structure and operations of other evening schools (Dr. John Vaughan, Chairman).[106]

---

101. Haberly, ed., "The Subcommittee on Governmental Relations," *Summary* . . . , chap. 10.

102. *Ibid.*, p. 4.

103. *Ibid.*, pp. 6f.

104. *Ibid.*, p. 5.

105. Dr. Clair W. Black held this position from 1965 until 1971. Dr. John Vaughan succeeded him in the post.

106. Haberly, ed., "The Subcommittee on Governmental Relations," *Summary* . . . , chap. 4, p. 1.

The subcommittee met with Dr. Ernest MacMahon, dean of University College and of the University Extension Division of Rutgers University, and with Dr. Louis Hacker, who had been dean of Columbia University's School of General Studies for many years. Dr. MacMahon and Dr. Hacker were nationally recognized leaders in the field of continuing education. High school principals, representatives of industry, and M. C. Galanti, the former dean, and Byron C. Lambert, the current dean of the Evening Division were all interviewed.

The subcommittee's report emphasized the size and variety of the evening student body. The Evening Division, it was felt, could not be simply a replica of the day session at night. Improved counseling and guidance were needed by the thousands who worked during the day and studied at night.[107] A separate admissions office was recommended for evening students. Since the part-time instructor teaching at night varied in attitudes and needs from the instructor teaching full time during the day, the possibility of developing a completely separate organization for the part-timers was suggested as worthy of study.[108] Separate evening student councils, newspapers, and catalogues were also recommended.[109]

With regard to meeting needs of the local community the report proposed establishment of a mental health unit, close working relationships with high school guidance directors, and the establishment of an elementary or secondary school at the University for use by the College of Education.[110] The first two of these proposals were ultimately realized but the third was never instituted.[111] The report on Community Services and Continuing Education was the last in the series prepared and presented by the Committee on the Future. The whole study had taken three years and had gone into every aspect of the University's operations. After its completion the institution as a whole was aware of its strengths and weaknesses. Concrete proposals for future developments were being implemented or were available for future reference.

The new position of provost at the University was clearly designed to relieve the president of much of the burden of administration as it affected the faculty and the specifically academic

---

107. *Ibid.*, p. 9.
108. *Ibid.*, p. 10.
109. *Ibid.*, pp. 13f.
110. *Ibid.*, pp. 22ff.
111. On October 10, 1964, the University Council adopted the report of the Subcommittee on Community Services and Continuing Education, Committee on the Future, (*UCM* 4, no. 1:5, 6). It was approved by the Board of Trustees on November 19, 1964.

aspects. To borrow a phrase from ecclesiastical terminology, the provost would be a sort of "vicar-general in matters academic" for the president. Some felt he would be a sort of "top sergeant."

In view of the problems that had arisen involving the faculty during the preceding several years, the filling of this important new position was clearly of crucial significance. A faculty committee for screening applicants was elected, consisting of one member from each campus.[112]

The result of their activity was the appointment of Dr. Richard M. Drake by the trustees as provost. Dr. Drake began his duties with the fall semester of 1962.[113]

Having been a university president himself, Dr. Drake had considerable personal experience of the opportunities and problems of such a position. He had also served as provost elsewhere, and thus had previous experience for the arduous position he was to hold at Fairleigh Dickinson for nine years. He introduced a new note into the University. Drs. Sammartino, Miller, and Decker, the institution's highest administrators so far, had all been characterized by personal, emotionally involved approaches to their work. Dr. Drake, a Bostonian, established a mood of calm, cool, and correct practice. His decisions were formulated after careful thought and were, in general, not subject to reconsideration. When he spoke at formal occasions he did so with clarity, dignity, and, on occasion, wry humor. He could be quite incisive and direct when dealing with the many difficult problems that arise involving faculty members, whether individually or in groups, at any college or university. Whereas Drs. Miller and Decker had assimilated themselves to the administrative style they found in existence at Fairleigh Dickinson, Dr. Drake brought with him and maintained something of the mood of the older, more traditional, universities at which he had served previously. Both in temperament and abilities Dr. Drake was probably just the sort of "vicar-general" who could best supplement and assist the University's president during the last decade of his administration.

The experience of the Committee on the Future had been all-inclusive. As the recommendations came forth and the trustees adopted them, Sammartino implemented them. At a meeting of the Board of Fellows, Dr. Drake, the provost, was to remark

112. They were as follows: Rutherford—Dr. Kenneth MacKenzie; Teaneck—Dr. Joseph Green; Madison—Dr. Bernard Budish.
113. Richard Masters Drake (B.S., A.M., Ph.D., University of Minnesota) was provost from 1962 until 1971. From 1967 until 1971 he also held the position of Acting Dean of the Maxwell Becton College of Liberal Arts.

wryly toward the end that the Committee of the Future had become a "committee of the past." On March 30, 1964, Sammartino issued a report to the trustees listing 109 specific recommendations. Of these, 52 had already been or were being implemented. Thirteen were to be implemented as soon as money became available. Sammartino was to make six a reality before he retired: dental research space incorporated in the new $9,000,000 dental building; new classroom buildings constructed in both Rutherford and Teaneck; an addition for the Madison Library; a dormitory in Teaneck; and a modest nursing building in Rutherford. Not realized were a $45,000,000 endowment fund; a $100,000-a-year research fund; dormitories for nursing students; a connecting building in Rutherford; the modernization of the Castle in Rutherford; a new gymnasium in Teaneck; and a research center in Hackensack. Twenty-three recommendations were considered but were not deemed feasible for the time being, although the Teaneck Commons was later constructed and an auditorium for the Health Center was included in the new dental building. A new residence hall for Madison was completed, but was not limited to graduate students. Others, such as a demonstration elementary school, a two-year medical school, a school of public health, a chapel in Rutherford, and an eight-building program for Madison estimated to cost about $40,000,000, never really got off the ground.

Twenty-one recommendations were left to future consideration because they needed further study and refinement. Eventually fourteen of these were implemented, although not in the original form.

10

The International University, 1963-1965

Historians have a hard time dividing the unbroken sequence of time hour by hour, day by day, into periods that reveal clearly the significant changes, distinguishing one stage from the next in series of events or in the growth of an individual or institution. Retrospective contemplation seems the best means when exercising the fine art of periodization. Looked at in this way, the direction of Fairleigh Dickinson's evolution into the structure of a federal university with quite elaborate constitutional forms of government in response to serious and urgent problems, dominated the years from 1960 to 1963. During the remaining four years until the completion of the institution's first quarter of a century, and of its first presidential administration, a significant emphasis was growth in stability. The new constitution proved a great success in practice. What was really remarkable was the manner in which all levels of the community accepted and adapted to the newly devised forms and methods of governance. It is this type of adaptability that keeps institutions and men young and healthy.

This stabilization did not mean the disappearance of the creative élan that had built the University. The events of the last years of the University's first administration reveal the continuity of creative energy and spirit.

ESTABLISHMENT OF ANOTHER JUNIOR COLLEGE — EDWARD WILLIAMS COLLEGE

The benefits of values inherent in a small college were the original motivation that had created Fairleigh Dickinson Junior College. Every effort had been made to preserve the benefits of a small institution even in the much larger one that ultimately appeared. The existence of several smaller campuses instead of one large campus for all 20,000 students helped to prevent impersonality.

Dr. Sammartino had in 1961 proposed the creation of an experimental two year college. On June 12, 1963, Fairleigh S. Dickinson, Jr., appeared before the University Council to seek, in behalf of the Board of Trustees, the Council's judgment on the advisability of establishing such a college, to be named in honor of Edward T. T. Williams and to be affiliated with Fairleigh Dickinson University.

Mr. Dickinson stated that the University had been a success because of its experimental pragmatic approach. This approach must be strengthened and continued. Edward Williams College would be wholly student oriented. It would stress appreciation of the human heritage, sensitivity to the contemporary environment, and the sense of responsibility.[1]

His mother, Mrs. Fairleigh S. Dickinson, Sr., and he would give three-quarters of a million dollars as an initial gift to launch the new college.

In a detailed question-and-answer period between Mr. Dickinson and the Council members, many points were brought out. The proposed new junior college would be located on the University's property in Hackensack, immediately across the Hackensack River from the Teaneck Campus. It would stress citizenship, would place special emphasis on preparing students for the upper college level, and would supplement the two-year public colleges that were being developed throughout the state. It would have a first-year student body limited to 100 and its eventual enrollment would be no more than 400 students. Its qualified graduates could be admitted directly to the University's third year.[2]

In a subsequent mail vote the University Council voted in favor of the proposed Edward Williams College.

Construction of a building to be called "Edward Williams Col-

---

1. *UCM* 2, no. 6 (June 12, 1963):1.
2. *Ibid.*, p. 2.

lege" and to serve as the home of the new junior institution was begun on the Hackensack side of the University's property in the river valley. This area was later developed into University Park by the addition of the new Dental School building and other structures. The facilities on the Teaneck side of the river were made available to the students of the new college by the construction of a bridge across the Hackensack River.

The Edward Williams College building was one of the finest ever built by the University. Its appointments included many works of art, paintings, and murals, and outdoors a replica of a statue of Ulysses bending his bow, which stands outside the Messler Library at the Rutherford Campus.

The building provided a compact, self-contained, beautiful home for the small learning and teaching community of faculty and freshmen who began their work there in September 1964. It was designed by Roland Wank in his contemporary, international idiom.

Edward Williams College was dedicated at a ceremony held in the auditorium of the new building on April 14, 1964. Sammartino set forth the aims of the new institution as experimental and dedicated to the development of intellectual and social leadership. It would be a student-oriented college with master teachers who would seek to meet the students' needs.[3] A central Seminar, to be attended by both the faculty and students, would hear speakers from both outside and inside the University on significant current problems that were not being considered in any existing course. Emphasis was also to be placed on the development of a sense of dynamic citizenship, effective writing and speech, and extensive reading, and the ample resources of the metropolitan area were to be used as a laboratory for educational development by the student. In short, much of the aims, methods, and spirit of Fairleigh Dickinson Junior College would be reincarnated in Edward Williams College.

The new junior college's first bulletin summed up its goals as follows:

> Edward Williams College represents a departure from the conventional pattern of a two-year college. It will endeavor to develop in each student, through close personal guidance and stimulation, a zest for learning and an appreciation of the significance of a thoughtfully planned liberal arts program for his future, whatever direction it may take.

3. From notes taken at the ceremony.

This educational goal can be accomplished only through associating a group of selected students with a carefully chosen faculty, dedicated to the central philosophy of the school, and in particular to its accent on the individual student.

John Henry Newman, in discussing this aspect of education, once said, "The general principles of any study you may learn by books at home; but the detail, the color, the tone, the air, the life which makes it live in us, you must catch all these from those in whom it really lives."

By regarding the student as a member of an intelligent cooperating group, made up of students and faculty, the college will create an atmosphere for learning.[4]

Since the dedication coincided with the Tercentenary Celebration of the founding of New Jersey, representatives of the state, of Bergen County, and of the City of Hackensack attended.[5]

In the fall Dr. Sammartino as Chairman of the University Council's Special Committee on Edward Williams College, reported to the Council on the progress made. A curriculum was proposed as follows:

First Year

1. Reading and Composition
2. Contemporary History
3. Ancient History
4. Psychology
5. Mathematics

Second Year

1. Literature
2. Economics
3. Human Growth and Development
4. Philosophy and Ethics
5. An elective course to be taken at the University.

Upon graduation from the new junior college, students would transfer into the University.[6] They would thus, by crossing the bridge over the Hackensack, move into the large University complex, whose facilities they had already been using for two years. Teaneck faculty were to note in later years that students who

---

4. *Edward Williams College* (Rutherford, N.J.: Fairleigh Dickinson University, 1963), p. 63. Published as vol. 21, no. 8 of *Bulletin of Fairleigh Dickinson University* (August 1963).

5. Earl E. Mosier, Assistant Commissioner of Higher Education represented the state; Arthur W. Vervaet, Director of the Bergen Board of Chosen Freeholders represented the county; and the mayor, the Honorable Kazmier Wysocki, represented Hackensack. Program, "Fairleigh Dickinson University Dedicates Edward Williams College."

6. *UCM* 3, no. 1 (Oct. 19, 1963) :4, 5, 6.

had been part of the Edward Williams community frequently had had a richer experience as freshmen and sophomores to sustain them when they got to the two upper years than did their counterparts who had spent their first two years in the much larger and somewhat more impersonal setting on the Teaneck side of the river.

The first dean of Edward Williams College was Waldro Kindig. An elderly, kindly man, with experience chiefly in high schools, he established a mood of concern and interest in the individual student. After several years he was succeeded by Ray Lewin, under whose energetic and imaginative leadership the college has continued to develop, not simply in numbers but also in stature.[7]

After Edward Williams College had been in operation for one year, a report on its development was presented to the University Council.[8] Only two of the original students who had begun their studies in the fall of 1964 had dropped out. There was a large number of applicants for the next academic year. Students were participating actively in the varied extracurricular activities, including trips to cultural centers in New York City. In order to give them some practical business experience, each student had been encouraged to buy one share of stock.

A FOURTH LOCATION IN NEW JERSEY — THE WAYNE EXTENSION

During the fall semester of 1964, the possibility of acquiring a fourth center for the University's work in New Jersey appeared. The United States Army had built and maintained a Nike missile base on very high ground located in Wayne, New Jersey. This area, in Passaic County, is dominated by the outlying foothills of the Catskill Mountains, located immediately to the north in New York State. On a property of about 27 acres, the army had constructed a missile base, several barracks buildings, and a high observation tower with a good view of the whole surrounding area. The town of Wayne was essentially a residential community located about fifteen miles northwest of Rutherford, twenty

---

7. Ray Lewin (A.B., M.A., Montclair State College; Ed.D., Teachers College, Columbia University) had varied experience in public school teaching and administration and as director of an educational department of the National Association of Manufacturers. Dr. Lewin became dean of Edward Williams College in 1965.

8. Dr. Sammartino and Dean Kindig of Edward Williams College. *UCM* 4, no. 4 (May 6, 1965):13, 14.

miles southwest of Teaneck, and fifteen miles east of Madison. Its location placed it almost in the center of the geographic triangle formed by the three Fairleigh Dickinson campus towns. The area was growing rapidly as a residential region. Some years later the vast Willow Brook Shopping Center was built in Wayne.

In the spring semester of 1965 Dr. Sammartino reported to the University Council that the Nike site had been acquired from the United States Army as "surplus government property."[9] A very favorable agreement had been worked out, which provided for acquisition of the property contingent upon the transformation of this military base to peaceful and educational purposes and its use by the University for at least ten years.

The property was renamed "The Wayne Extension," since it was decided not to develop it as a separate and complete campus, even though it was twice the size of the Rutherford Campus. It was considered a part of the Rutherford Campus for purposes of administration, in the manner of the small East Rutherford annex.

Two of the three existing one-story barracks buildings at Wayne were converted into classroom buildings, including one general science laboratory. The third building provided for a small library and offices. The observation tower, located on the hilly elevated area's highest point, was used as a platform for a small astronomical observatory.

During the day the Reading and Study Institute and the Guided Study Programs conducted classes at Wayne. In these daytime classes, students who had had difficulties at other institutions or who had difficulty in being admitted to college were given special remedial courses in small groups under tutorial guidance.

Each evening regular credit classes of the University's Evening Division were offered at the Wayne Extension, and Fairleigh Dickinson evening students in the Wayne area did not have to commute to Rutherford, Teaneck, or Madison until they reached the upper levels of their curricula, for these advanced courses were not available at Wayne. Ultimately the day students in the remedial programs at Wayne numbered about 200, while the evening students in the regular credit classes increased to a maximum of 600. The remedial students, if they showed promise, were permitted to take one of the regular evening credit courses at Wayne.

From the beginning there was no intention of developing the Wayne Extension into a complete campus. At the University

9. *UCM* 4, no. 3 (Mar. 5, 1965) :5, 6, 7.

Council meeting at which Dr. Sammartino presented his report on this matter, he stated:

> The people of Wayne would like nothing better than to have a new campus or branch of Fairleigh Dickinson University. This is out of the question since it is too small for any such purpose. There will probably be some sort of two year institution established in that area, which is one of the fastest growing areas in the United States.[10]

The establishment of many public community colleges in New Jersey, financed by the state and the individual counties in accordance with a state wide master plan, began to be implemented at this time. This development began to affect the potential of growth for Fairleigh Dickinson, particularly in its first two years. Both Edward Williams College and the Wayne Extension had been responses to the movement toward junior colleges. Both centers would ultimately be strongly affected by the growth of the public community colleges in New Jersey.

With Wayne, the University had added a location on a mountain side to its campuses in a town (Rutherford), in a river valley (Teaneck), and on an estate (Madison). Before our story is told, we shall see a rural village in a foreign country and an island added to this list.

THE UNIVERSITY BECOMES INTERNATIONAL — WROXTON COLLEGE

As has been frequently pointed out, the international note had been consciously emphasized at Fairleigh Dickinson since its foundation. Travel tours were encouraged, culminating in the world tours by ten faculty members during the summer of 1959. There was the relationship with the Instituto Edison in Havana, Cuba, which had lasted for six years until it ended due to the advent of the Castro regime. For many summers Dr. and Mrs. Bogdan Raditsa conducted small summer sessions at their villa near Florence, Italy, in the art and literature of the Renaissance. Mrs. Raditsa had inherited the villa from her father, the famous historian Guglielmo Ferrero.

Dr. George Nelson, director and then dean of libraries at Fairleigh Dickinson, conducted summer study sessions in his compound at Cuernavaca, Mexico, for a number of years.

All these developments were ultimately revealed to have been

---

10. *Ibid.*, p. 7.

unconscious preliminary steps toward the major advance into international education finally undertaken by the University.

On December 13, 1963, Edward T. T. Williams, following a special invitation by the Council Chairman, spoke to the University Council about this major step. Williams related how Wroxton Abbey, a Jacobean great house on a property near Banbury, England, after being owned by the Pope and North families, had eventually come into the hands of Trinity College of Oxford University. Trinity College had recently announced an auction of the property. Dr. Loyd Haberly had been sent over to England to discuss the possibility of having Wroxton Abbey sold to Fairleigh Dickinson University, since he knew the president of Trinity College, who had been one of his teachers when he was a Rhodes scholar at Oxford.[11] As a result of these negotiations, Williams added, the Abbey had been acquired. It was located near Oxford and Stratford. Oxford University had agreed to supply guest lecturers.[12]

Mr. Williams then answered questions by members of the Council regarding the curricula and courses that would be offered at this newest campus, overseas.[13] Essentially it was proposed that Wroxton serve as a center for American students who wished to pursue studies in the areas of British literature, history, government, and sociology. Instruction would be by Oxford dons, but the administration and direction of the new campus would be in American hands. There would be opportunities for Fairleigh Dickinson faculty members to participate in a variety of ways.

Thus the institution's international emphasis achieved a culmination that no one could have foreseen—a whole overseas campus of 56 acres in England.

The rural village of Wroxton, catalogued in Domesday Book, is about 26 miles from Oxford and 17 from Stratford on Avon. In this small village Augustinian friars had, during the reign of King John (1199–1216), established a priory. Wroxton Priory (always erroneously called "Abbey") served its original purposes, among which education was one for four centuries, until the suppression of the monasteries by King Henry VIII in 1535. At that time the priory passed into the hands of Sir Thomas Pope, a close friend of Sir Thomas More. Pope later founded Trinity College, Oxford, and endowed the new institution with the extensive

11. Interview with Loyd Haberly, March 31, 1971.
12. *UCM* 3, no. 2 (December 13, 1963) :3.
13. *Ibid.*

properties held by Wroxton Abbey. He retained the right to live in and lease the Abbey from Trinity College and, since he was childless, left the leasehold to his younger brother, John. The lease on the property was thereafter passed from generation to generation of the Popes and later, due to inheritance by the female line, to the North family. The eleventh and last Lord North died in 1932.[14]

During the Eighteenth Century the most significant member of the family occupied the Abbey—Frederick, Lord North of Kirtling, who was King George III's Prime Minister during the American Revolution. It was a strange destiny that brought his ancestral home into the hands of a university located in the "rebellious" American colonies. Lord North probably turned in his grave several times when the leasing agreement between Trinity College and Fairleigh Dickinson was signed.

The abbey building, consisting of 43 suites, a banqueting hall, a Regency dining room, nine reception rooms, and a chapel had been rebuilt as a Jacobean mansion in 1618 by Sir William Pope, the son of John Pope. There was also an entrance lodge and a stable block with several apartments. On the 56 acres of grounds surrounding the great house stands an obelisk, erected on the occasion of a visit by the father of George III to Wroxton Abbey in 1739; a columned white temple front inspired by the Greek revival; and several "Chinese" bridges over Wroxton brook, built when George IV made the "Chinese" style popular. A lake, lawns, gardens, and woodlands give the Abbey a majestic setting.

When he visited Wroxton Abbey, Sammartino was discouraged beyond words. Everything was in disrepair and the place looked like a great big, empty barn. Quickly he and Sally drew up plans with Loyd Haberly. A competent architect and general contractor were secured. Sammartino arranged for some $300,000 worth of paintings, tapestries, sculptures, and furniture to be taken from the three New Jersey campuses and shipped over to Wroxton. He donated his own armor collection and got friends, especially Mr. and Mrs. Thomas Kelley and Mr. and Mrs. Franco Scalamandré, to donate $150,000 more of valuable furnishings. He designed the chairs for the main study hall and had them manufactured, while Sally chose the furniture for the students' rooms

14. "Wroxton Abbey in History," *The Dedication of Wroxton College and An International Conference on Higher Education, Rhodes House, Oxford, June 29 to July 1, 1965* (Oxford: Oxford University Press, 1965).

at Minty's in Oxford. They worked harder than they had ever done before.

A library of about 6,000 volumes was quickly acquired and was especially strong in Shakespeariana and in bound collections of old British magazines. After the death of the last Lord North, the abbey had fallen on evil days. It was for a while a storehouse, used by the manufacturers of ladies' garments. After the Second World War the rooms were rented out by the leaseholders to individual roomers. A tea room operated on the first floor and guided tours were conducted through the public rooms.[15]

WROXTON DEDICATION AND THE INTERNATIONAL CONFERENCE ON HIGHER EDUCATION

The new, yet very old campus, as well as Oxford, provided the settings for two events held on the last weekend of June 1965. The dedication was combined with an International Conference on Higher Education conducted by Fairleigh Dickinson University at New College and Rhodes House in Oxford.

Institutions represented by delegates at the conference numbered 155. They ranged from Oxford University (founded c.1224 and represented by A. L. P. Norrington, M.A., Pro-Vice-Chancellor) and twelve Oxford colleges over such ancient institutions as Rostock, Louvain, Amsterdam, Harvard, Yale, to such distant institutions as Kyung Hee University in Korea and Alaska Methodist University, just eight years of age in 1965. A great many of the delegates were the presidents or rectors of their institutions. The ministries of education of Ceylon, India, The Sudan, and Thailand also sent delegates. A total of twenty learned societies and associations were represented. In accordance with Fairleigh Dickinson tradition, industry took part. Representatives of Barclay's Bank, Becton, Dickinson and Company, United States Lines, and other corporations were present. Ambassador Cornelius V. H. Engert was the honorary chairmanship of the Welcoming Committee.

---

15. Interview with Dr. Robert Neiman, August 25, 1972. Neiman was director of Wroxton College during the academic year 1968–1969. Dr. Neiman (B.A., Queens College; study at Zurich Univ.; Ph.D., New York Univ.) became a part-time faculty member in 1958 and full time in 1962. He was chairman of the department of history and political science on the Teaneck Campus from 1970 until 1972, becoming professor in the latter year.

There were also in attendance a considerable number of administrators and faculty members from the three campuses in New Jersey. Loyd Haberly took a leading part in the activities. The University Council Chairman, Dr. Heinz F. Mackensen, carried the Wroxton College Banner at the dedication ceremonies and gave a summary of the chief points made by the various speakers at the luncheon held for this purpose at the end of the conference.

On Monday evening, June 28, 1965, an opening reception was held in the Founders Library of New College. Almost 600 years before this event the founder of New College, the great medieval English bishop William of Wyckham, laid down his outlines for a new type of institution at Oxford University, which had been in existence for about a century and a half at that time. Bishop William wished to realize more effectively the concept of a commune in which living and learning were joined through more than mere study and were developed through personal encounter and active involvement of teacher and student in their daily lives. He therefore built his philosophy of education into the buildings of the first and oldest quadrangle of New College, Oxford. In his founding scheme, as completed around the year 1377, Bishop William placed a chapel for spiritual sustenance and a great hall for bodily sustenance and for the cultivation of intellectual life through informal social encounter on one side of the quadrangle. Two other sides he devoted to dormitories for the teachers and students who, as celibates, were to make the college their home. On the fourth side of his quadrangle Bishop William placed the library, within easy walking distance of the whole college community, and he gave and left it many books. He also supplied his new creation with a magnificent cloister for walking and meditation. This new arrangement for a living-learning commune, which actually grew out of older Benedictine models, has worked quite well for six centuries.

Did the good bishop's shade hover over the opening festivities held in his library on that warm June night in 1965? If so, he recognized a kindred mood and spirit. Here were persons who had been originally inspired by the ideal of a "New College" and who had created a whole series of such communities in a land overseas as yet undiscovered in his own time. The founder of New College, Oxford, would have approved.

On the next day Dr. Carpenter, The Lord Bishop of Oxford, conducted an opening service in William of Wyckham's magnificent All Saints Chapel of New College. In academic cap and gown or ecclesiastical vestments or in the costumes of their native countries (some came from Arabia), the participants filed into the high-vaulted Gothic structure. A service of song, prayer, and readings was held, beginning with "My Country 'Tis of Thee" and ending with "God Save the Queen." A huge, magnificent, white-marble reredos of late medieval origin served as a backdrop behind the altar. The scene was dimly yet warmly illuminated by the light that fell through the huge stained-glass windows facing the quadrangle side of the chapel.

From New College the procession passed through the ancient streets of Oxford to Rhodes House. In this solidly British, early twentieth-century structure, built by and named after the great empire builder, the participants went to work. The theme was: What should be the Common Elements of a University Education in all Countries of the World?

Peter Sammartino's opening remarks emphasized that

this is an exciting decade. By 1970, all over the world, there will probably be twice as many colleges and universities as are in existence today. The thirst for knowledge is sweeping through all countries, young and old. During the next five years, as many new buildings may be constructed as have been built in the last two hundred years. I have traveled in thirty-three countries. In every country there is this urge to build and to serve thousands of students. Dedicated teachers throughout the world are straining to provide education for masses of students hungry for education.

There is excitement, enthusiasm and a spirit of progress. As the nations of the world come closer, the universities may be the instrument to unify them. Perhaps we, as heads of these institutions, may be a force for peace and understanding throughout the world. While we serve the needs of our countries and our own cultures, we can serve the cause of brotherly love that can bring greater understanding among all peoples.

But I see dangers too! First, we cannot be too parochial, too inbred, or we lose the opportunity to understand all humanity, all civilization, if we give our students a limited point of view that is no longer a true university education.

Second, we must not take on the form and coloration of a university education that exists in an older country simply because it seems to be the pattern for achieving status. Each university must seek to develop its curriculum along five lines:

1. The acquisition of a set of moral values that will help the student to live a peaceful and useful life.
2. Training in intelligent and dynamic citizenship.
3. The appreciation of beauty in all its forms, whether created by nature or by man.
4. The understanding of cultures and philosophies in other countries so that the unity of many can be achieved.
5. Competence in some speciality or profession.

Now, when old institutions are expanding and new institutions are being created, is a splendid period to reappraise the true goals of our universities so that they may serve better our students, our country and the fellowship of man.

The first panelist on the formidable main theme was no other than Arnold J. Toynbee, the world-famous philosopher and historian of civilization. Toynbee's main emphases, as presented by him in a summary distributed at the session, were:

1. In our time, the World has become a physical unity, whether for salvation or for destruction, as a result of the astonishing progress of technology.
2. But the World is as far as ever from being a moral and social and political unity. We are all as nationalistic-minded as ever— and today there are about 125 sovereign independent states in the World.
3. Human beings in all these states have to learn that they are citizens of the World, besides being citizens of their respective local states. They have to give their paramount allegiance, not to their local states, but to the World, because today the whole human race is in danger of self-destruction—and no local state will survive if mankind destroys itself.
4. We have to learn to act as responsible citizens both of the World and of our respective states. We have to recognize that the individual citizen can influence the course of events, and that therefore he has a duty to be politically active.
5. In University education, the different branches of the human race have to learn about each other and about each other's history, in order to be able to cooperate with each other.

Lady Barbara Ward Jackson, the well-known economist, spoke next. She warned against overemphasizing the role of economics in history, yet pointed out the need to use it nevertheless in order to get a full understanding of any development. Lady Jackson also warned against the theory of the "two cultures"—science and the arts. She felt that this was an oversimplification and that there were not two but hundreds of cultures in our civilization. Yet every statistical and analytical approach, no matter how valid in the factual sense, suffers because it must inevitably disregard man as he is *within himself.*

There is another factor which has nothing to do with statistics, however, the fact that man is *himself.* He is one man, and there is nothing that the computer can tell you about him. Man is unique, and he makes his own single contribution and is always the exception. It is necessary to keep in mind the balance between the broad averages and the statistical on the one hand, and the absolute fact of life on the other.

In view of the eruption of a new romanticism through the hippie movement and its many consequences during the next ten years, Lady Jackson has been revealed as a foresighted prophetess indeed.

Kenneth Holland, President of the International Institute of Education, stressed that

> there is more than one common element for a university education, no matter where it is pursued. Without ideals, without effort, without intellectual curiosity and honesty, there is no such thing as education. A common element of higher education should be the sharpening of the mind, not the stuffing of it.
> Our times demand the recognition that education transcends human boundaries and that education is crucial to the conduct of human society.[16]

In the discussion Toynbee emphasized that the world was rapidly becoming one community. All human beings have a variety of relationships—family, town, country, and the world. He felt that the most universal relationship should be paramount.[17]

Representatives of developing countries stressed their need for technicians, engineers, and scientists. Yet often, after receiving a suitable education abroad they did not return to their original country, a fact pointed out by Toynbee.

On the following day, June 30, 1965, the conference traveled to Wroxton to participate in the official dedication of Wroxton College. After robing in the abbey, the procession moved out to the strains of the "Wroxton Ceremonial March," written for the occasion by Professor Stanley A. Purdy of the Rutherford Campus, and played by the band of the Third United States Air Force stationed in London, which had come to Wroxton for the ceremony.

The procession was led by Dean Haberly, bearing the University's ancient Sheffield mace that had been brought back to its country of origin for the occasion. Dr. Heinz F. Mackensen, carrying the new Wroxton College Banner, followed Haberly. Next came the Lord Bishop of Oxford in full pontificals. The bishop was in something of a dither since he was accustomed, according to ancient ecclesiastical usage based on "the first shall be last," to bring up the rear of any procession. However, Dr. Mackensen, who had some clerical experience himself, calmed the bishop and kept him in place at the head of the procession by pointing out that this was not an ecclesiastical but an academic procession, in which the first indeed came first.

Immediately behind the vanguard of mace, banner, and bishop,

---

16. One-page mimeographed abstract distributed at the session.
17. Based on notes taken by Dr. Heinz Mackensen at the time.

Dr. Sammartino speaking to the Class of 1965 at commencement at the Madison Campus. Edward T. T. Williams is at his right.

The Marine Biology Laboratory on St. Croix in the Virgin Islands.

The twenty-fifth anniversary celebration and the naming of the Peter Sammartino College of Education. Left to right, front row: Dean Donald L. Herdman, Dr. Peter Sammartino, Mrs. Sammartino.

came the main force led indeed by the University's first men—
Peter Sammartino and Edward T. T. Williams. These two gentle-
men were accompanied by no less than a king and a lord. King
Umberto II of Italy had accepted the invitation to be present.
Lord Harlech was to be the principal speaker.

Then followed the serried ranks of delegates, administrators,
faculty members, and guests. The whole procession slowly moved
onto the spacious lawn before the manor house and out into Wroxton Village. Turning right, the procession proceeded through the
streets of the ancient settlement with its beam-and-plaster, thatch-
roofed cottages toward the medieval Gothic pile of Wroxton
Church, situated on a slight hill overlooking both village and
manor.

As he proceeded onward, the banner-carrier was struck by the
healthy, intelligent appearance of the tow-headed village children,
who had turned out in great numbers to watch the procession.
The words of Gregory the Great, the pope who had sent the first
missionaries to England from Rome almost 1400 years earlier,
inevitably came to mind: *Non Angli sed angeli sunt,* "They are not
Angles, but angels."

In Wroxton Church the Oxford bishop blessed the banner and
dedicated the new college.

His Lordship did not fail to bring out in his brief address his
satisfaction that Wroxton Abbey was once again to be the seat
for a community of scholars and students. This had been the intention of its founders, the Augustinian friars who had established
a priory at Wroxton eight centuries before. After a lapse of 400
years as a family seat, the abbey was being returned to the educational purposes of a community of scholars and students, but in
new ways and to meet new needs.

Wherever they were, the souls of the ten Augustinian friars at
Wroxton whom Thomas Cromwell, acting in the service of Henry
VIII in suppressing the monasteries, had expelled must have been
edified by the bishop's words.

After the service the procession returned to a large striped tent
pitched upon the Abbey grounds. Here the ceremonies continued
with a brief welcoming address by Edward Williams and the conferring of the honorary degree of Doctor of Laws upon the Right
Honorable The Lord Harlech, K.C.M.G., who, as Sir David
Ormsby-Gore, had been British Ambassador to the United States
during President Kennedy's administration.

Lord Harlech responded to the honor with eloquence and intelligence, stressing the need to strengthen the special relationship between the United States and the United Kingdom also in the crucial area of higher education. He hailed the establishment of Wroxton College as an important step forward in this direction.

After the ceremonies the participants enjoyed an informal box dinner with champagne in the tent, on the lawns, and in the abbey itself. A festive yet relaxed and most pleasant mood prevailed, commented upon by many who were coming into contact with Fairleigh Dickinson University for the first time, yet quite familiar to those who had been associated with the institution for some time. It was reassuring to note that this creative spirit could be generated in regions overseas and far from New Jersey.

On the next day, July 1, 1965, the final session of the conference was held at Rhodes House. The speakers included the Pro-Vice-Chancellor of Oxford University, A. L. P. Norrington, M.A.; Carlos P. Romulo, the famous Philippine diplomat, in his capacity as chancellor of the University of the Philippines; and Jean P. Getty, the American oil magnate. It was an informative contrast to hear the restrained, traditional comments of a typical product and leader of Oxbridge; the ebullient, imaginative remarks of the Philippine statesman; and the practical, incisive observations of the American multi-millionaire on what higher education would need as a common core in the global village that was developing.

At a concluding luncheon at the Randolph Hotel in Oxford, an effort was made to sum up the discussions of the various sessions. This task fell to Dr. Heinz Mackensen, who tried to catch the essence of what had been said in the following brief statement:

> How can all the many points that have been made best be summarized? What is their general drift? What do they all have in common that could inspire universities everywhere?
>
> Perhaps we can best draw together the widely ranging points which have been made by the various distinguished speakers by citing the favorite motto of the Conciliarists of the Fifteenth Century. Like us they had to deal with a divided, torn world. They had the problem of polycentrism in their world organization,—the medieval, universal church. There were two, then three different popes. Everyone was divided, also here at this ancient institution.
>
> As the Conciliarists sought to solve these schisms out of their endless discussions their watchword became: "Freedom in non-essentials, unity in essentials, charity in all things."
>
> Through the practice of charity, of good-will, based on this watchword man can evolve higher. Thus he will, on a truly world or universal basis, find himself in harmony with nature, for all living things,— plants, animals and man himself have evolved from lower to higher forms, and this process still continues.
>
> Man will then also find himself in harmony with the universal world of the spirit, for this too, like the outward world of nature, works

towards an ever higher evolution of man—in knowledge, in under-standing, and finally in his own personality, in justification of his own existence. But we must never be glibly optimistic. Man can also will to remain where he is or to go lower. Education has its limits. The highly-educated Dr. Jekyll can use his education to become Mr. Hyde.

What then is the universal assignment for universities as the world becomes ever smaller and more tightly knit by ever quicker means of transportation and communication?

The world's universities should seek to be among the most important instruments and focal points for the continued higher evolution of man in nature and spirit, in both outward and inward terms.

Jacob Grimm said, "The universities are a nation's conscience." As the world becomes ever smaller and as the world's universities draw closer together may we paraphrase this word of Grimm to read "The universities must become the world's conscience."[18]

For all who experienced it, the dedication of Wroxton College and the international conference on higher education represented a high point in the growth of Fairleigh Dickinson as an institution aware of, and participating fully in the evolution of the world into one community closely knit in terms of contemporary communications and transportation, but still fragmented by a variety of civilizations and cultures separated in some cases by millennia of intellectual, cultural, and technical developments or the lack of them.

These affairs made Fairleigh Dickinson known to university and government leaders in many parts of the world. A film about the conference and dedication was shown on BBC-TV and, on the smaller stage of Britain, had a much greater impact than it would have had in the United States. As the owner and operator of a campus in Europe, the institution had become an international university.

In the years that followed, Wroxton College increased in activities and numbers. Self-contained semesters on the undergraduate level were conducted from September to December and again from February until May. During the summer two sessions of six weeks were held on the graduate level. Students came to Wroxton not only from the campuses in New Jersey but from all over the United States. The sessions at the college were interspersed with visits to famous Shakespeare festival performances at Stratford and with tours to Oxford and London for educational and cultural purposes. The enrollment finally attained 65 students, but here numbers bore very little relation to the impact and effect of the college.

---

18. Based upon the notes used by Dr. Mackensen at the occasion.

11

Culmination and Transition, 1965-1967

In twenty-five years of ceaseless activity at the head of the institution, Peter Sammartino showed little or no hesitation or exhaustion in pursuing his goal of building Fairleigh Dickinson *fortiter et suaviter*. He was ceaselessly active from morning to night, and often on weekends as well. He managed, step by step, to meet the challenges, and to solve the problems created by each stage of the institution's development from a single-building junior college to a multi-campus international university. He adjusted to and worked as enthusiastically with the complex constitutional structure that existed during his last decade in office as he had in the patriarchal framework of the small familylike community that had first flourished in the Castle. No hint of any change or slackening of pace had been given when, at the first University Council meeting of the academic year 1966–1967, held as usual at the Madison Campus, he asked permission to make an important statement to the Council at the end of the meeting. When Sammartino arose at that time to speak out, the members of the Administrative Council, who had been informed beforehand, knew what he was going to say. Just before the Council meeting, the president had read privately to his administrative cabinet, the declaration he was about to make. The following declaration by Sammartino therefore came as a bolt from the blue to the great majority of Council members:

A university presidency today encompasses many complex areas. The number of faculty and students has grown tremendously. Research and governmental contracts have multiplied. Fund-raising and public relations are more wide-reaching than ever. International relations, practically nonexistent twenty years ago, are now a continuing and time-consuming factor. As a university progresses arithmetically, its complexity rises geometrically. It is no longer possible for the president to clear his desk on Friday afternoon, and have a new person take over on Monday morning.

As a university president approaches the age of 65, there are three things he can do: try to linger on until he becomes senile, quit suddenly at 65, or provide for a comfortable period during which the new president can learn as much as possible from the person he is replacing.

In light of the complex character of Fairleigh Dickinson University, the third alternative seems the most reasonable.

I have been president of Fairleigh Dickinson University for twenty-five years. As the responsibilities have increased and the scope of the University has widened, I have been fortunate in having more and more assistants and deputies to participate in the carrying on of the work of our institution. But the force of habit is not easily broken, and I find upon examination that I am still doing many of the things I did twenty-five years ago. I also find that the minutiae of everyday administration keeps me working seventy, and in many cases, eighty hours a week. At the age of 62, I have decided that this is too much. I should like to cut it down to about fifty hours a week. The only way to break the force of habit is to find a different pattern.

My day starts early in the morning, and my telephone begins to ring at home even before breakfast. By ten o'clock, I have put in half a day's work. Until four years ago, there was not a single day when I was not involved in some form of university work. Two years ago, there were exactly five days when I was incommunicado and absolutely cut off from any work. This year, there were eleven such days.

Whatever friends I have, eventually, in some way or other, become involved with the University. The pleasant corollary is that outside people involved with the University soon become my personal friends.

We haven't minded the work because it motivated our lives and gave us what people crave most, a reason for living, an opportunity to serve, an absorbing pattern of living.

But now a more important change is coming upon the University. We started very humbly, with very limited objectives, in a purely local way, with 59 girls and 1 young man. Our area of service has been increasing throughout the years. Now we are a complex University with three campuses, an experimental two-year college, an extension in Wayne and a campus in England. We are, of course, known nationally, but it is now a matter of acquiring an outstanding national reputation so that we may attract an increasingly selective student body, so that an ever increasing number of gifts from individuals, companies and foundations may be attracted to us, and so that increasing grants from the various Federal agencies can flow to us. If we can make as much progress during the next twenty-five years as we have made during the past twenty-five, then we shall have cause to rejoice.

I have presented all of this to the Trustees. They see my point of view and have accepted my request that we seek a new president. They have also elected me Chancellor. As Chancellor, I shall devote more of my time to the Fairleigh Dickinson family which now comprises, in addition to the Board of Trustees, the Board of Fellows and the President's Council.

There are major areas of research that require special attention. Subsidiary institutions within the University require more extensive guidance. The overall educational building development necessitates integrated planning. Our international liaisons can be greatly strengthened. For the next decade there is plenty of work to keep both the president and the chancellor busy.

The founding and building of Fairleigh Dickinson University has been an exciting adventure. Freed from the pressures of day-to-day operation, I can look forward to an even more absorbing period when I can help the new president in strengthening the national character of our university.[1]

After Sammartino had read his statement, the Council sat for a moment in surprised silence. It then arose, and with acclamation and prolonged applause unanimously adopted the following resolution, which the Chairman of the University Council had prepared while Sammartino was speaking:

THAT the University Council of Fairleigh Dickinson University expresses its profound appreciation and recognition to Peter Sammartino for his unparalleled achievement as the founder and only president for the first quarter century of the University's existence. As was voted by the Senate of ancient Rome in praise of its great men so we unanimously resolve:

THAT Peter Sammartino has deserved well of Fairleigh Dickinson University.[2]

After passing the resolution, the Council adjourned. A major turning point in the history of the institution had been reached. Fairleigh Dickinson University had been so completely identified with, and so largely built by Peter Sammartino that his leaving the helm would inevitably mean a change of course.

No one realized better than Edward T. T. Williams what "dropping the pilot" might mean. Williams therefore emphasized strongly to the Chairman of the University Council the need to elect a competent search-and-screen committee to find the institution's second president. At their next meeting the trustees acted on this matter and the following memorandum was sent to the University Council:

At the October 25th meeting of the Board of Trustees, it was requested that the University Council choose three faculty members for a committee of five, which would be involved in the screening of can-

1. Fairleigh Dickinson University, *University Council Minutes* 6, no. 1 (October 22, 1966) :16, 17, 18.
2. *Ibid.*, p. 18.

didates for the presidency of Fairleigh Dickinson University.
The Trustees should like the faculty members of this committee to
be limited to persons with tenure.
Mr. Dickinson and Mr. Silberman are the two Trustee members of
this committee.[3]

As a result, a special meeting of the Council was held at the
Teaneck Campus on November 9, 1966. At this meeting the delegation of Council members from each campus met in separate
caucus and elected a representative to the Presidential Search and
Screen Committee. The following were elected: Teaneck—Dr.
Amedeo Sferra; Rutherford—Professor William G. Robinson;
Madison—Dr. Bernard Budish. Thereafter the Council convened
as a whole and elected Professor Charles Angoff of Rutherford
and Dr. Harold Weinberger of Teaneck as alternate members of
the committee.[4]

After the election of the search committee, the Council engaged
in discussion as to the qualities the new president would need.
Dr. Sferra, who had just been elected to the committee, felt that
the man should be a first-rate scholar, not over 45 or 50, and
should have had some administrative experience. Dr. Raditsa
emphasized that "imagination and creativity are more important
qualities than bureaucracy, and humanism is more important than
scholarship."[5]

Because the twenty-fifth anniversary of the founding of the
college was approaching, the trustees decided to celebrate it on
December 4, 1966, and to make it an outstanding event by naming
the education unit of the University the Peter Sammartino College
of Education.

The naming of the college in his honor had a good rationale.
He had been immersed in educational experiments all his life.
There was hardly a facet of education within the State that he
hadn't been involved in. That year he had pushed through the
old State Board of Education authorization to establish the
doctorate degree in education for the College of Education. He
had mapped out the curriculum and felt that, since the only
other such course in New Jersey was in New Brunswick, the
establishment of this program in northern New Jersey would
eventually create a phalanx of outstanding educational leaders
in the State.

A full-blown convocation in cap and gown was planned on

3. *Ibid.*, no. 2 (November 9, 1966):1.
4. *Ibid.*, p. 2.
5. *Ibid.*, p. 3.

the Rutherford campus with a marquee for 1500 people. It was a true community event with international overtones, for fourteen ambassadors attended, each with a color guard bearing his country's flag. The bagpipers were there in the colorful Macbeth tartans that incidentally, had been chosen years before by Dr. Sammartino himself. Even though the wind was howling and the cold fought with the artificial heaters within the large tent, nothing could diminish the warmth of the outpouring of sentiments. Fannie Hurst was there as the ever-present godmother and said, "I knew Fairleigh Dickinson University when it was only a gleam in Peter's eye." Townspeople were there, and high school principals, mayors, college presidents, legislators, corporation presidents, and, of course, the faculty and representatives of the student body. And then came a surprise: the trustees, in secret session behind Sammartino's back, had voted honorary degrees for him and for Sally. The citation for Sammartino read:

> In the world of higher education, you are a master builder. Under your inspired leadership, a small college started by you in the Castle building in 1942 has become, in a short quarter-century, the eighth largest private university in the United States. From its humble start in the wartime years, the institution has grown from sixty students to more than nineteen thousand.
>
> During the years of extensive physical growth, you have constantly reaffirmed your faith in the basic ideals of what education should offer, emphasizing the importance of appreciation of the cultural aspects of life. Your awareness, too, of the educational importance of international understanding has made possible, both for students and faculty, opportunities for valuable experiences in international relations.
>
> With zeal and dedication beyond measure, you have faced one challenge after another in the growth of this university, and you have met all of them in ways that contribute toward helping to cope effectively with the tremendous needs of higher education in the world today.
>
> As the years pass, not only are beautiful campuses an enduring monument to your leadership, but the lives of thousands of people are enriched because of the university education that would not have been possible for them if you had not been inspired with the dreams, and been endowed with the talent to make dreams come true.
>
> In the full realization that without you there could have been no Fairleigh Dickinson University, in appreciation of all that you have accomplished in the past and your dreams for the future, and with pride and affection, Fairleigh Dickinson University takes great joy in conferring upon you the honorary degree of Doctor of Laws.

For Sally, the citation read:

> Your dedication through the past twenty-five years to the ideals you have shared with your husband, has brought about one of the

most remarkable achievements in the educational history of our day—participation in what is virtually the founding of five colleges.

An economics and history major at Smith College, you later received a master's degree in history at Columbia University and did further graduate work at Middlebury Language School and New York University.

Following experience as a teacher in the New York City High Schools, you held executive positions with Scaramelli and Company, and with two publications, before you were given the many responsibilities that came with the planning and founding of a college in Rutherford. Serving as registrar for the first eight years of the new institution, your role was always, through the twenty-five years that have followed, far more important than any title could convey. You have made significant contributions in every phase of the expanding university.

Many of the special projects for which Fairleigh Dickinson University has become well known are the result of your energy and your ability to turn ideas into realities. You have given of your talents not only to the educational profession, but also to your community.

In the future that lies before Fairleigh Dickinson, the University will continue to benefit from the complete dedication with which you have worked through these many years. In appreciation of all that you have done for young people, and for this university, Fairleigh Dickinson takes great pride in conferring upon you the honorary degree of Doctor of Laws.

Dr. Ulrich May, in charge of dining services, outdid himself in providing the most delectable buffet in the history of the institution. Telegrams poured in from President Johnson, from the heads of eight countries—Dahomey, Sikkim, France, Ivory Coast, Korea, Liberia, Philippines, Thailand, from Senators and Cabinet members, from other university presidents not only in the United States but in many lands in four continents, and from many friends. It was a night to be remembered. Afterwards, the trustees and members of the Board of Fellows had arranged a more private party at a nearby country club to round out the evening. It was truly an apotheosis, a fitting climax to an extraordinary career.

ESTABLISHMENT OF THE HONORS PROGRAM

With the administration of Peter Sammartino drawing to a close, it will be instructive to follow the formulation, presentation, approval, and establishment of an important new program through the various steps that were now established constitutionally and functioning for this purpose. On October 5, 1966, the university president appeared before the Educational Policies Committee of the University Council in order to present a proposal for an "Honors College." In essence he proposed that a small number of academically outstanding students from each campus be selected to carry on individual study. Each student would be assigned to a faculty member who would help the student arrange a program consisting of courses, seminars, and other activities in the area of the student's interests. Each student who showed financial need would receive a $500 scholarship. The mentor was to receive a similar amount for his work with the student, for one academic year.[6]

The Educational Policies Committee, after carefully studying the proposal, questioned the president about it. It then passed the following recommendation, which it presented to the University Council on October 22, 1966, at the Madison Campus, at the meeting at which Sammartino announced his impending retirement as president:

> THAT this honors program be adopted in principle and that the implementation of the program be left to the Educational Policy Committees of the individual colleges.[7]

On the floor of the University Council, Dr. Sammartino began the discussion of the proposal by pointing out that ten years before, such a program would not have been possible because the university had neither the faculty nor the students to carry on such an honors program. Now we had grown further and we should try the program, perhaps for a few years to start. After having two years of class work, outstanding students could be approached with this program, perhaps only ten students on each campus. There should be no time limit as to when a student's mentor felt that the student was mature enough to graduate. Possibly he might even go right on to qualify for his master's degree. Now was the time to do something for the superior student. An added advantage was that recruiters could go into the high schools when seeking new students for the University, and could present the honors program to a selected group of students.[8]

After a discussion centering on the practical problems involved in implementing the program, the University Council unanimously approved the recommendation of its Educational Policy Committee.[9] As with all Council recommendations, this proposal was

---

6. *Ibid.*, 6, no. 1 (October 22, 1966) :8, 9, 10.
7. *Ibid.*, p. 9.
8. *Ibid.*
9. *Ibid.*, p. 10.

thereupon sent in writing to the Board of Trustees for consideration at its next meeting. In a letter dated November 28, 1966, the Board replied that it had accepted the Council's recommendation for the establishment of an Honors College as presented.[10] With this step the proposal went into effect.

One problem that arose at once in the practical implementation of the Honors program was caused by the proviso that "the implementation of the program be left to the Educational Policy Committees of the individual colleges."[11] There were four of these, yet the program would only make sense if it were conducted as one academic program. In order to bring this about, a coordinating committee was formed consisting of the chairman of the University Council Educational Policies Committee, the chairmen of the three subcommittees of that committee, and of the chairmen of the educational policies committees of each of the four colleges. In this way an *ad hoc* working group was established for correlating the work of the Honors Program with that of the various colleges and their curricula. Leonard J. Saunders was appointed as coordinator of the new program.

The admissions criteria required that an honor student have completed the first two years along with the requirements of his curriculum for these years; that he have a general average of B in his marks; that he be recommended for the program by a faculty member; and that he have demonstrated the ability and motivation to do independent study.[12]

After a student had been nominated for selection, he had to obtain written recommendations from two faculty members and from the chairman of his major department. These, along with his records and files, were then studied by the coordinator of the honors program and a special selection committee, which made the final decision.[13]

The honors scholars were permitted to carry from 16 to 20 credits of independent study each semester. They attended weekly tutorial sessions with their mentor, weekly seminars with other students and faculty members, and colloquia held at various times throughout the year.[14]

The scholar could also follow a program that combined inde-

---

10. *Ibid.*, 6, no. 3 (December 9, 1966) :7.
11. *Ibid.*, no. 1 (October 22, 1966) :9.
12. Fairleigh Dickinson University, *The House College* (mimeographed document of 15 pages, dated "May 3, 1967"), p. 4.
13. *Ibid.*, p. 5.
14. *Ibid.*, p. 6.

pendent study, graduate or undergraduate courses taken for credit or audited, and courses taken at other universities.[15]

The mentors were chosen by the scholars themselves, and were appointed by the program coordinator with the advice and consent of the appropriate department chairman and college dean and of the provost.[16] The mentors were to work closely with their scholars and not to be merely academic guides, but to play something of the role of the don in the British tutorial system. On May 12, 1967, the program was inaugurated at a ceremony at which Dr. Sammartino delivered the charge to the 32 scholars and their 32 mentors present.

In practice, a great deal depended on how knowledgeable the student was and how much he was able to contribute. Some mentors took their scholars to New York City museums and had them write papers on their visits. Others took their scholars to faculty social events in order to expose them to a cultural and intellectual environment in an informal social setting.[17]

CRISIS IN THE COLLEGE OF LIBERAL ARTS AND ITS RESOLUTION

At the beginning of the academic year 1965–1966, Dr. Loyd Haberly announced that he intended to retire as dean of the College of Liberal Arts in June. A special meeting of the college faculty was held and a search-and-screen committee elected, which proceeded to interview candidates. The position of liberal arts dean was a most significant one, since the faculty of that college were by far the most numerous on all campuses and the scope of liberal arts courses was extremely wide and varied. Traditionally the liberal arts dean ranks almost as a *primus inter pares* among his fellow deans.

There were many candidates from both inside and outside the University. After eight months the committee's search bore fruit and the appointment of Dr. Mark Peisch as liberal arts dean was announced. Dean Peisch was youthful and energetic. He had spent a number of years at Columbia University in a variety of administrative positions.

That institution had been ruled in a monarchial style by Nicholas Murray Butler for 40 years. Butler's successors did nothing to

---

15. *Ibid.*, p. 7.
16. *Ibid.*, p. 10.
17. Interview with Dr. Robert Neiman, August 3, 1972.

develop faculty participation in university government. In 1968 the long-standing frustrations of students and many faculty members erupted in the sit-ins, led by Mark Rudd, that were ended only by massive use of the New York City Police Department.

Peisch therefore came, in 1966, from an institution in which little or no faculty participation in governance existed, to one in which it had existed in various forms since the beginning and in which such organs as the University Council and the College and Campus Structure had been developed and had become active and vital during the six years just before his arrival.

Moreover, Columbia was a bastion of "traditional" standards of "faculty excellence." No faculty member had much of a chance there or at any Ivy League school without the magical letters *Ph.D.* after his name. At Fairleigh Dickinson, on the other hand, there was a wide variety of faculty background and preparation. A large percentage of faculty held the Ph.D. degree, but many others did not. As the institution had passed through the various stages from a small junior college to a large university in only a quarter of a century, a great variety of faculty members had become associated with the institution. Those that had had good formal credentials for a junior college might not have them for a large university. Yet they had participated in good faith, had made important contributions for years, and in many cases were excellent or good teachers.

Dean Peisch tried to impose retroactively the requirement of the Ph.D. degree for the granting of tenure at Fairleigh Dickinson University. Moreover, his administrative style stood in great contrast with that of his predecessor. Dean Haberly knew the institution inside out. He appreciated the strong pressures among the faculty for greater campus autonomy. Haberly had not opposed the separation of all-University departments into campus departments under their own chairmen. Whenever sufficient demand had grown for such a move, Haberly had concurred. Thus, he had presided in a benign, patriarchal style as the College of Liberal Arts had in fact become three separate campus organisms still held together by one dean and by tri-campus committees on faculty status and educational policies. He was the feudal overlord of a congeries of separate academic fiefs at three different locations.

Dean Peisch sought to pull in the reins of this loosely driven troika much more firmly. One of his steps was to appoint at each campus an assistant who would help him in these efforts at central control. This had a negative effect on the department chairmen at each campus, who had been accustomed to operate with considerable latitude on their own and, in many areas, with the various campus deans. In his efforts to draw the reins more tightly, Peisch appeared to strain the pace beyond the scope of a new school.

An interesting problem now presented itself, and speculation about its possible repercussions began to be bruited about among Fairleigh Dickinson *cognoscenti* months before the March days of 1967. Could an outsider with a background in administration and principles about faculty standards quite alien to an institution like Fairleigh Dickinson succeed, by energetic administrative action and fiats *à la* Nicholas Murray Butler, in reorienting the most important tri-campus college at the University to a quite different direction? Could he use the techniques and methods of old-style autocratic college administration in dealing with the organically grown academic community of the Maxwell Becton College of Liberal Arts, especially since the organs and practice of faculty participation, in its own governance, had been greatly intensified by the College and Campus Structure put into effect five years before his arrival?

The efforts of Dean Peisch were well meant, and a man of great intelligence, vision, and industriousness, he gave his best. This became one of those situations in which large organizations sometimes become embroiled.

For those who experienced it, in some cases through deep personal involvement, the Peisch affair, as it was called, was a trying experience indeed.

The college began the new academic year under its new dean with a faculty meeting in September 1966. On this occasion the liberal arts faculty still formed a self-governing tri-campus community held together by established bonds of tradition, affection, and cooperation, and the new smoothly working links of the Structure. Six months later the same college had been torn apart by strife and disturbances of various kinds. Trust had been replaced by fear, confidence by antagonism, and gratitude by resentment. Colleagues of many years' standing had been turned against each other.

The first public action in this crisis was taken at the University Council meeting of March 2, 1967, held at Teaneck. The meeting began with another matter of faculty concern, thus setting the stage. The faculty of the Dental School had never been included under the College and Campus Structure. There had been nothing invidious about this omission but it had been decided originally to apply the Structure at first only to the undergraduate colleges on the three campuses. After four years the Structure was an obvious success, both as an instrument of faculty self-government and as a means to safeguard orderly and fair practice in matters of faculty status. The faculty of the School of Dentistry had become eager to come under the Structure and their dean, Dr. Walter A. Wilson, concurred with their wish. When the matter was presented at the Council meeting, Dean Wilson supported the proposal and personally moved an amendment to it that provided the following:

> AND THAT a faculty member who teaches six (6) hours or more in the School of Dentistry shall be considered a full time faculty member as concerns membership in the University Council and shall be eligible for membership in the University Council and any committee established under the Campus and College Structure.[18]

In the discussion Dean Wilson explained that if the normal teaching load, as prevalent in the University's other schools and colleges (12 hours), were used as the criteria for "full-time" status then only 15 percent of his faculty would come under the Structure. Dean Wilson in a heartwarming statement in favor of greater faculty participation in the governance of his school, said on the floor of the Council:

> I feel that the School of Dentistry's functions can best be served with more of its faculty represented rather than fewer.[19]

After adoption of Dean Wilson's amendment, and very brief further discussion, the Council unanimously voted to admit the dental faculty into the Structure. The proposal regarding the dental faculty had been introduced by Professor Irving Halevy, Chairman of the Council's Committee on Faculty Status, as part of his committee's regular report. He now moved a resolution that was not part of the Faculty Status Committee's report.

The Chair asked whether the resolution had been approved by the Faculty Status Committee and Professor Halevy answered no. The Chair thereupon ruled the resolution out of order, since it was not part of the committee's report, but it could be intro-

---

18. *University Council Minutes* 6, no. 4 (March 2, 1967) :8.
19. *Ibid.*

duced later in the meeting under new business. But concern about the crisis that lay behind this resolution was broad and deep among the Council's members. The Council voted to overrule the Chair and to consider the resolution at once. It was the only time a ruling of the Chair was overturned by the University Council.[20] The resolution ran as follows:

> RESOLVED: That no directives, standards or policies new to the University be imposed retroactively upon faculty members so that their achievements as measured by the standards in effect during their period of service to the University be either nullified or devalued, and that all such persons when recommended for tenure and/or promotion by the Department be accepted by the Deans.[21]

Everyone realized that the efforts of Dean Peisch to introduce the Ph.D. as a *sine qua non* in the College of Liberal Arts for the granting of tenure had produced this resolution. A brief, intense discussion now ensued on the floor of the Council, all in support of the resolution. Dean Peisch was present but said nothing. The resolution was carried unanimously.[22]

During the two weeks that followed this Council meeting, temperatures and the intensity of reaction continued to rise, as various groups maneuvered and fought. Feeling was so high at the Teaneck Campus that a local chapter of the United Federation of College Teachers (AFL-CIO) was formed. A Committee on Anti-Union Action was also formed, which stated that "the high standards of Fairleigh Dickinson University have been stained by the introduction of an organized labor movement."[23] Yet, the union and the anti-union forces both agreed in calling for the resignation of Dean Peisch.[24] A petition expressing no confidence in the dean and calling for his resignation or removal was ultimately signed by almost 100 liberal arts faculty members, chiefly at the Teaneck Campus. At a meeting on that campus presided over by Dr. Drake, a strong clash took place between Dean Peisch and many of the liberal arts department chairmen and faculty leaders. The meeting had been arranged to smooth the issues, but it only succeeded in intensifying them, since Peisch did not withdraw from his decision to terminate a number of the untenured faculty who did not have the Ph.D.

20. *Ibid.*, p. 16.
21. *Ibid.*, p. 15.
22. *Ibid.*, p. 17.
23. Teaneck, N.J., *Tarrevir* (student newspaper), March 14, 1967, p. 1.
24. *Ibid.*, pp. 1, 2, 6.

The Teaneck faculty thereupon held a meeting at which it elected a committee of eight to present the matters at issue to the Chairman of the Board of Trustees, the University President, and the Provost. The results of this meeting were that the position of dean of the College of Liberal Arts was put into commission, as the British say. Dean Peisch would retain his title and office for one year, but its responsibilities and authority would be exercised by three associate deans, one on each campus. A year later Dr. Drake assumed the position of acting dean of the College of Liberal Arts. The three acting associate deans appointed at the time were: Rutherford—Clair W. Black; Teaneck—Marinus C. Galanti; and Madison—John Fritz. In September, Black and Fritz were appointed permanently and Amedeo Sferra became associate dean of liberal arts for the Teaneck Campus.

In this manner a crisis was solved that had threatened to disrupt the whole University and had caused considerable wounds among the faculty. What it revealed was that the faculty of Fairleigh Dickinson would not permit arbitrary administrative action. The effort to introduce policies and attitudes foreign and unacceptable to the experience of the organic community that Fairleigh Dickinson had become had failed decisively.

Another important result of this affair was the strong impetus it gave to greater campus autonomy. Now the liberal arts department chairmen on each campus were led by an associate dean who was on their campus and was thus closely associated with them. The official division of this important college into three entirely separate units could not be far distant. With this division, much of the University's cohesion in terms of faculty and curricula would come to an end and individual campus autonomy was given a decisive boost.

A SECOND OVERSEAS LOCATION — ST. CROIX

Wroxton remained the University's only overseas campus for two years. From June 20 to June 22, 1967, a marine biology laboratory was dedicated on St. Croix, Virgin Islands, with appropriate ceremonies. In connection with the dedication, a conference on oceanography was also held. Such well-known authorities as Robert Abel, chief of Sea Grant Programs of the National Science Foundation; Dr. Milner B. Schaefer, Director of the Institute of Marine Resources of the University of California at San Diego;

Mr. Robert D. Gerard of the Lamont Geological Observatory at Columbia University; and Dr. Arthur E. Maxwell, Associate Director of the Woods Hole Oceanographic Institute led in the presentations and discussions at the conference. Dorothy Gordon was present to produce two shows, which were ultimately shown on television and broadcast over the radio in the United States.[25]

Senator Fairleigh Dickinson had given the University eight acres of land on the northeastern part of the island.[26] It is a beautiful spot, right on the sea, with Buck Island looming just a short distance to the north. The lovely blue of the Caribbean contrasts harmoniously with the white of the beaches, the gray of the rocks, and the green of the shrubbery on land. This lovely tropical spot became the University's center for oceanographic study and research. A laboratory, library, dining hall, dormitories, staff residences, dock, and a floating dock, as well as auxiliary buildings, were erected on the property in later years. Curricular development led to the establishment of a bachelor of science degree in Marine Biology at each of the three New Jersey campuses. The student taking this degree spent the entire last (spring) semester of his senior year in residence at the laboratory in St. Croix. The College of Science and Engineering established an installation at the site to study corrosion in the framework of materials-environment interaction.[27]

The conference theme was "Man returns to the sea for knowledge and abundance." This subject was examined from many points of view by the assembled scientists and experts. One government scientist presented plans for a city to be built underground beneath the sea. Small submarines and diving equipment would permit the denizens of this subterranean underwater community to travel about whenever they left their watertight, air-filled residences. The speaker suggested that such a center could carry on mining and oil drilling. Another scientist spoke of the food potential of the sea and how man could learn to harvest square miles of ocean the way he had long harvested acres of land.[28]

That the sea could indeed provide food in new ways was illustrated at a dinner at the Grape Tree Bay Hotel overlooking the

25. See Peter Sammartino, "Underseas Capers," *Of Castles and Colleges* (South Brunswick and New York: A. S. Barnes and Company, 1972), pp. 122–28, for a detailed account of the dedication and conference at St. Croix.
26. *Ibid.*, p. 122.
27. *West Indies Laboratory* (St. Croix, V.I.: Fairleigh Dickinson University, 1972), p. 10.
28. Based upon notes taken by Dr. Heinz Mackensen at the occasion.

sea not far from the laboratory site. Most of the sessions were held at the hotel. Representatives from 51 colleges and 27 professional and learned societies took part.[29] The writer of these lines[30] well remembers marveling at the variety and good taste of the many different dishes served at the dinner. He particularly enjoyed some cupcakes. His amazement was shared by most of the dinner guests when Dr. Sammartino announced after dessert that everything in the meal except for such items as coffee, sugar, and the like had been derived from sea products. The cupcakes had been made from fish meal, although they had not tasted "fishy" at all. It was a vivid lesson in the still undeveloped possibilities that are contained in the sea.

Another high point was the dedication and submersion in the sea nearby of a sculpture by Chaim Gross, showing a bird catching a fish. A plaque with the conference theme and an informative inscription was bolted onto the statue's base, which was then sunk into the sea for scuba divers to encounter on their rounds in the area. The Governor of the Virgin Islands, Mr. Ralph Paiewonsky, attended the ceremony and spoke briefly. Others participating, besides Dr. Sammartino, were Leonard Dreyfus and Martin Weiner of the Board of Trustees, and Adolf Robison, chairman of the Board of Fellows.

Edward T. T. Williams, who attended the conference, was also scheduled to take part in the dedication of the statue, but did not appear, to everyone's mystification, since he never missed such an occasion if he could help it. Word came later that he had been involved in an automobile accident, but had not been hurt.

THE CHANGING OF THE GUARD

In a way this incident was an omen. Edward T. T. Williams died in January 1968, half a year later, at his home in Rutherford, of a heart ailment. He was succeeded by Senator Fairleigh S. Dickinson, Jr., as Chairman of the Board of Trustees. By that time the University also had a new president, and a real change of the guard in the highest leadership of the University had occurred.

Williams's role and contribution in the building of Fairleigh Dickinson should have become quite obvious in the preceding pages, and any additional emphasis upon them seems hardly

29. Sammartino, p. 126.
30. Dr. Mackensen.

necessary. He would not have wanted long panegyrics. Yet it is hard to close the subject of Edward T. T. Williams without re-emphasizing once again that his high intelligence, his great skill in dealing effectively with all sorts and conditions of men, and his energetic work for and devotion to the University and its goals were among the most important factors in building the institution. Seldom have a chairman of the board and a university president worked together as a team so effectively and so successfully and with such supplementation of each other's skills and aptitudes as did Edward Williams and Peter Sammartino. Williams's death was a very great loss to the whole University and particularly to the Board of Trustees, which he had led so effectively as its chairman for twenty-five years.

The Presidential Search and Screen Committee, which had been elected at the University Council meeting of November 9, 1966, had in the meanwhile been proceeding with its work. Of the two trustees on the committee (Dickinson and Silverman), Dickinson acted as co-chairman. Of the five faculty members (Angoff, Budish, Robinson, Sferra and Weinberger), Sferra acted as co-chairman. A first decision taken by the committee was that the two faculty alternates elected by the Council (Angoff and Weinberger) should participate fully and have a vote.[31] In this way the faculty had five votes and the trustees two votes on the committee. Three basic requirements were established. The candidate must have a rich and strong human personality, which could relate to others and "read between the lines." He must have a certain amount of successful administrative experience. And, finally, he must have a sense of humor.

Letters were sent out to about sixty individuals, professional organizations, and other sources of possible nomination. The faculty were consulted on nominations. During the spring and summer of 1967, the committee interviewed about twenty candidates face to face. The roster included many academicians of high repute and attainments, and also several significant political figures.

Toward the beginning of the summer, Edward T. T. Williams had suggested to Sferra the names of several possibilities on the West Coast whom he might usefully go to see. Sferra did so, and interviewed one possible candidate in Colorado and two in California.[32] Yet, none of these men were willing to consider leaving their current positions. Shortly before he was to return from

31. Interview with Dr. Amedeo Sferra on August 23, 1972.
32. *Ibid.*

California, Sferra received a telephone call from Fairleigh Dickinson, Jr., who said that Dr. Sammartino had suggested the name of an administrator at the University of Hawaii for Sferra to see.

Sferra flew on to Hawaii and spent a delightful and instructive evening with the man and his family at his lovely home. However, at the close of the evening, the Hawaiian academician explained that he was deeply committed to his present university and to its president. He then suggested the name of a dean in Ohio whom he knew and with whom he had worked for years.

In this circuitous way, Sferra and the committee were led to interview and consider J. Osborn Fuller, at the time dean of the College of Arts and Sciences at Ohio State University. Passing through the ranks of the academic profession at the University of West Virginia and Ohio State University, Dr. Fuller served as a dean at the latter before coming to Fairleigh Dickinson University.

As a consulting geologist of oil, gas, and nonmetallic minerals, he was active in geologic services of a large variety, especially in Newfoundland, a region of great interest to scientists because nearly all the great ancient rock systems situated between the Lower Laurentian and the Long Range are represented on the island, occupying a commanding position off the east coast of North America.

The committee was impressed by Dr. Fuller and recommended his appointment as the second president of Fairleigh Dickinson University to the Board of Trustees. The board acted affirmatively to this recommendation and Edward T. T. Williams publicly announced the appointment and that it would take effect on October 1, 1967.

On September 12, 1967, exactly twenty-five years had passed since the Day of Dedication of the new little junior college had been celebrated on the lawn outside the Castle on a beautiful Sunday afternoon. On that same day, a quarter of a century later, Peter Sammartino had only eighteen more days left him as president of Fairleigh Dickinson. On that same day, a quarter of a century later, Edward T. T. Williams had less than four months left to live. With the departure of these two leading personalities from the direction of the institution's course, and with the many changes in structure and goals that were soon to be introduced, not only the first quarter of a century, but the first period of development for Fairleigh Dickinson had come to an end. The second quarter of a century was to begin under new leadership and to chart new directions.

This is then the appropriate place at which to bring our story of Fairleigh Dickinson University to a close. The institution's first quarter of a century was brief in time as the lives of universities go, but it was long indeed in accomplishments. Probably, if all the various campuses with all the buildings of Fairleigh Dickinson University both in the United States and abroad had to be recreated, the cost would run to $150,000,000 or $200,000,000. All of this creative educational enterprise had to be done in a period of minimal federal help, of relatively low tuition, and of need to increase faculty salary schedules to compare with others in the same league. That it was done successfully was a *tour de force,* to say the least.

Since the establishment of Fairleigh Dickinson University, the number of American colleges of all varieties has grown more than threefold, with a corresponding expansion of student enrollment. During the same period, the United States has become the Mecca of students from the developing world, in search of higher learning. The case history of the college presented in this book is a microcosm, reflecting the vast macrocosm. Its record calls for notice because it expresses the spirit of our times. It also deserves notice because of the boldness of its conception, a multi-campus suburban university complex within the shadow of the greatest concentration of institutes of higher learning. This is an illustrative model of the fabulous growth of higher education, pacemaker of our extension of learning. This is a record of gestation, travail, great efforts, successes, setbacks, and the inevitable errors; *errare humanum est* and on that ground alone colleges must rate as exceptionally human institutions. But as a counterpoise, one should recall the words of Terence: *Humani nihil a me alienum puto.* "Nothing human, indeed, should ever remain alien to us." And if it does not, higher education is bound to raise not only the standards of perception and knowledge, but also a greater capacity to understand ourselves, and, above all, others—the entire human race. Perhaps as a result of a genuine effort in understanding, the human race will one day become really human in the best sense of the word. And when that is so, it will never again drop back into the savage habits of destruction. This, in turn, may lead to the greatest human achievement, the serenity of lasting peace. "By nature, men are pretty much alike. It is learning and practice that set them apart." Thus spake Confucius, the Oriental Sage.

Index